TM

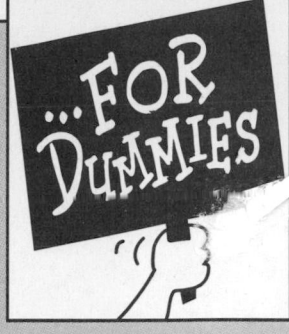

...FOR DUMMIES

BESTSELLING BOOK SERIES

References for the Rest of Us!

Are you intimidated and confused by computers? Do you find that traditional manuals are overloaded with technical details you'll never use? Do your friends and family always call you to fix simple problems on their PCs? Then the For Dummies® computer book series from Hungry Minds, Inc. is for you.

For Dummies books are written for those frustrated computer users who know they aren't really dumb but find that PC hardware, software, and indeed the unique vocabulary of computing make them feel helpless. For Dummies books use a lighthearted approach, a down-to-earth style, and even cartoons and humorous icons to dispel computer novices' fears and build their confidence. Lighthearted but not lightweight, these books are a perfect survival guide for anyone forced to use a computer.

> "I like my copy so much I told friends; now they bought copies."
> — Irene C., Orwell, Ohio

> "Quick, concise, nontechnical, and humorous."
> — Jay A., Elburn, Illinois

> "Thanks, I needed this book. Now I can sleep at night."
> — Robin F., British Columbia, Canada

Already, millions of satisfied readers agree. They have made For Dummies books the #1 introductory level computer book series and have written asking for more. So, if you're looking for the most fun and easy way to learn about computers, look to For Dummies books to give you a helping hand.

Hungry Minds™

1/01

Creating Web Pages

FOR

DUMMIES®

6TH EDITION

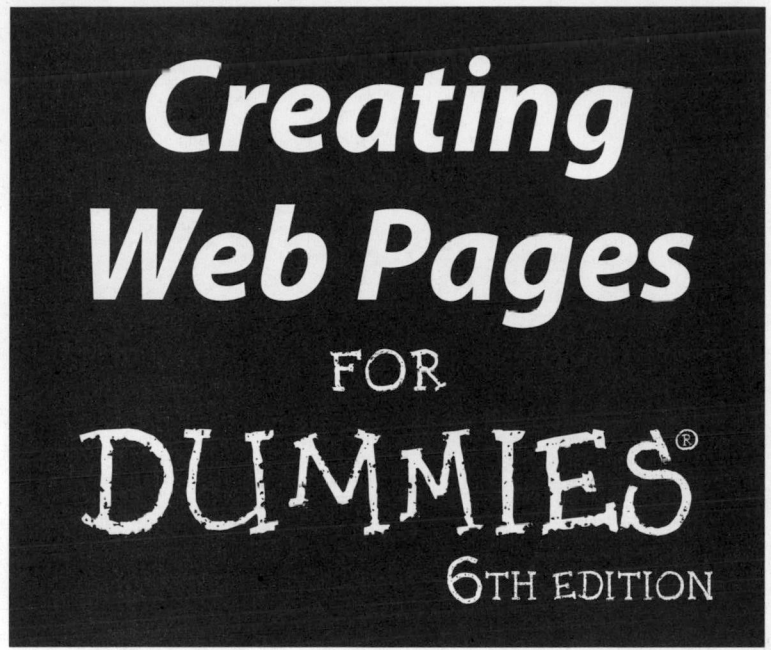

Creating Web Pages FOR DUMMIES® 6TH EDITION

by Bud Smith and Arthur Bebak

Hungry Minds™

Best-Selling Books • Digital Downloads • e-Books • Answer Networks • e-Newsletters • Branded Web Sites • e-Learning

New York, NY ◆ Cleveland, OH ◆ Indianapolis, IN

Creating Web Pages For Dummies®, 6th Edition

Published by
Hungry Minds, Inc.
909 Third Avenue
New York, NY 10022
www.hungryminds.com
www.dummies.com

Library of Congress Control Number: 2001099741

ISBN: 0-7645-1643-4

Printed in the United States of America

10 9 8 7 6 5 4 3 2 1

6B/QU/QT/QY/IN

Distributed in the United States by Hungry Minds, Inc.

Distributed by CDG Books Canada Inc. for Canada; by Transworld Publishers Limited in the United Kingdom; by IDG Norge Books for Norway; by IDG Sweden Books for Sweden; by IDG Books Australia Publishing Corporation Pty. Ltd. for Australia and New Zealand; by TransQuest Publishers Pte Ltd. for Singapore, Malaysia, Thailand, Indonesia, and Hong Kong; by Gotop Information Inc. for Taiwan; by ICG Muse, Inc. for Japan; by Intersoft for South Africa; by Eyrolles for France; by International Thomson Publishing for Germany, Austria and Switzerland; by Distribuidora Cuspide for Argentina; by LR International for Brazil; by Galileo Libros for Chile; by Ediciones ZETA S.C.R. Ltda. for Peru; by WS Computer Publishing Corporation, Inc., for the Philippines; by Contemporanea de Ediciones for Venezuela; by Express Computer Distributors for the Caribbean and West Indies; by Micronesia Media Distributor, Inc. for Micronesia; by Chips Computadoras S.A. de C.V. for Mexico; by Editorial Norma de Panama S.A. for Panama; by American Bookshops for Finland.

For general information on Hungry Minds' products and services please contact our Customer Care Department within the U.S. at 800-762-2974, outside the U.S. at 317-572-3993 or fax 317-572-4002.

For sales inquiries and reseller information, including discounts, premium and bulk quantity sales, and foreign-language translations, please contact our Customer Care Department at 800-434-3422, fax 317-572-4002, or write to Hungry Minds, Inc., Attn: Customer Care Department, 10475 Crosspoint Boulevard, Indianapolis, IN 46256.

For information on licensing foreign or domestic rights, please contact our Sub-Rights Customer Care Department at 212-884-5000.

For information on using Hungry Minds' products and services in the classroom or for ordering examination copies, please contact our Educational Sales Department at 800-434-2086 or fax 317-572-4005.

For press review copies, author interviews, or other publicity information, please contact our Public Relations Department at 317-572-3168 or fax 317-572-4168.

For authorization to photocopy items for corporate, personal, or educational use, please contact Copyright Clearance Center, 222 Rosewood Drive, Danvers, MA 01923, or fax 978-750-4470.

About the Authors

Bud Smith is a computer book author with over ten years of publishing experience. *Creating Web Pages For Dummies,* 6th Edition, is one of a dozen books Bud has written; his Hungry Minds titles include *Internet Marketing For Dummies* and the recently published *Web Usability For Dummies*. In addition to writing books, Bud has been a computer magazine editor and a product marketing manager.

Bud got his start with computers in 1983 when he left a promising career as a welder for a stint as a data-entry clerk. Bud then moved to Silicon Valley to join a startup company, followed by work for Intel, IBM, Apple, and AOL. His work and interests led him to acquire a degree from the University of San Francisco in Information Systems Management.

Arthur Bebak received a degree in Computer Engineering at the University of Illinois, where he attended on a fencing scholarship. He has designed mainframes, managed large engineering projects, and studied business administration. Arthur is founder of Netsurfer Communications, Inc., a highly successful electronic publishing company. Arthur has done a lot of writing, which has led to his current "surprising" (though only to him) role as coauthor of this book.

At Netsurfer, Arthur oversees a large staff of people who create Web sites for numerous clients. They also write, edit, and publish several Web-based electronic magazines, popularly known as "e-zines."

Authors' Acknowledgments

The authors thank Steve Hayes, acquisitions editor, and the staff that helped produce this book: Project Editor Colleen Esterline, Technical Editor Mike Lerch, as well as the many people responsible for page layout, proofreading, indexing, and graphic art.

The Web was built more for love than money, and that tradition was continued by the many people who generously gave their time and support for this book. We especially thank the providers of Web tools who supplied us with an excellent set of programs for the CD-ROM and the Web authors who agreed to let us use their sites for the figures in this book.

Publisher's Acknowledgments

We're proud of this book; please send us your comments through our Hungry Minds Online Registration Form located at www.dummies.com.

Some of the people who helped bring this book to market include the following:

Acquisitions, Editorial, and Media Development

Project Editor: Colleen Williams Esterline

(Previous Editions: Kathy Cox, Jeanne S. Criswell)

Acquisitions Editor: Steven H. Hayes

Technical Editor: Michael Lerch

Editorial Manager: Constance Carlisle

Senior Permissions Editor: Carmen Krikorian

Permissions Editor: Laura Moss

Media Development Specialist: Marisa Pearman

Media Development Manager: Laura Carpenter VanWinkle

Media Development Supervisor: Richard Graves

Editorial Assistant: Amanda Foxworth

Production

Project Coordinator: Regina Snyder

Layout and Graphics: Jackie Nicholas, Jacque Schneider, Mary J. Virgin, Erin Zeltner

Proofreaders: John Greenough, Andy Hollandbeck, Susan Moritz, Charles Spencer, TECHBOOKS Production Services

Indexer: TECHBOOKS Production Services

General and Administrative

Hungry Minds Technology Publishing Group: Richard Swadley, Senior Vice President and Publisher; Mary Bednarek, Vice President and Publisher, Networking; Joseph Wikert, Vice President and Publisher, Web Development Group; Mary C. Corder, Editorial Director, Dummies Technology; Andy Cummings, Publishing Director, Dummies Technology; Barry Pruett, Publishing Director, Visual/Graphic Design

Hungry Minds Manufacturing: Ivor Parker, Vice President, Manufacturing

Hungry Minds Marketing: John Helmus, Assistant Vice President, Director of Marketing

Hungry Minds Production for Branded Press: Debbie Stailey, Production Director

Hungry Minds Sales: Michael Violano, Vice President, International Sales and Sub Rights

Contents at a Glance

Cartoons at a Glance

By Rich Tennant

page 227

page 163

page 91

page 285

page 7

page 273

Cartoon Information:
Fax: 978-546-7747
E-Mail: richtennant@the5thwave.com
World Wide Web: www.the5thwave.com

Table of Contents

Introduction

● ●

*1*t may be hard to remember, or it may seem like only yesterday, but some years ago, the personal computer was introduced. The rise and rise *and rise* of the personal computer — with maybe an occasional stumble but never a real fall — seemed certain to be the most important social and technological event at the end of the twentieth century. From Wozniak and Jobs's Apple II to Bill Gates's Windows 98, it may have seemed as though nothing could ever be bigger, or more life- changing and important, than PCs.

But, people do talk. In fact, talking is one of the main things that people are all about, and in the beginning, the personal computer didn't let you interact with others. However, first with modems, and then with networks, and finally through their combination and culmination in the Internet, personal computers became the tools that opened up a new medium of communication. The most visible, graphical, and fastest-growing part of the Internet is the World Wide Web. Now communication, not computation, is the story. Computers are still important, but mostly as the means to an end; the end result is further enabling people to interact.

If the most exciting channel of communication is the Web, the means of communication is the Web page. Ordinary people demonstrate amazing energy and imagination in creating and publishing diverse Web home pages. And although ordinary people have a *desire* to create Web pages, businesses have a *need* to set up shop on the Web. So the rush to the Web continues, often with the same people expressing themselves personally on one Web page and commercially on another.

So you want to be there, too. "But," you ask, "isn't it difficult, expensive, and complicated?" Not any more. As the Web has grown, easy ways to get on the Web have appeared. And we discuss the best of these ways in the pages of this book.

About This Book

It's *about* 380 pages.

Seriously, what do you find here? Easy ways to get published on the Web for any kind of Internet user we could think of. Ways to make your first Web page rich with carefully arranged text, graphics, and multimedia. Plus the information you need to go beyond your first Web page and create a multi-page personal or business Web site. And tools — which we describe in the book or provide as demos or in full versions on the CD-ROM — to help you go as far as you want to go in creating a Web site.

Foolish Assumptions

Lots of good information is in this book, but almost no one is going to read every word of it — except our long-suffering editor. That's because we cover Web page topics from beginning through intermediate levels, including how to publish a Web page via Web-based services and the major online services, how to use several different tools, and some Mac-specific and Windows-specific stuff. No one needs to know all of that! But anyone who wants to get a Web page up on the Web does need to know some of it.

But what do *you* need? We assume, for purposes of this book, that you have probably used the Web before and that you want to create a Web page. We further assume that you are not yet a Web author, or that you're fairly new to the process. To use the information in this book, you need access to a personal computer running Mac OS or Windows, and you need access to the Web — either through an online service or a direct Internet service provider (ISP). You should be running a Web browser such as Microsoft Internet Explorer, Netscape Navigator, or a browser provided by an online service. If you have a UNIX system and an Internet connection, much of this book will work for you, but you won't have access to the online service or Web page creation tools that we describe, except those available directly on the Web.

If you don't have Web access from your personal computer, see Appendix B for a list of service providers who can help you get it. You should already have spent some time surfing the Web, or be willing to do so as you gather information and examples for your Web page. In other words, if you're wired, or willing to get wired, you're in. With that, the door to this book is open to you, whether you want to create your first Web page or add new features to one you already have.

The figures in this book show up-to-date Windows screen shots for a consistent appearance. We wrote the instructions and steps in this book to work equally well for the Macintosh and Windows.

Jump around in the book and go straight to information that you need. Later, you can back up and read something that interests you, page through the how-to sections, try using one of the tools on the CD-ROM, and then go look at something on the *Creating Web Pages For Dummies* home page (created by one of the authors) at the following address:

```
www.netsurf.com/cwpfd
```

CD (-ROM) for Me, See?

The CD-ROM that comes with this book is a rich source of software for creating World Wide Web pages. You can find plenty of software for either Macintosh or Windows. For details about what's on the CD-ROM, see Appendix E. For details about how to use specific programs, see the chapters and sections of this book. For information on how to install the software on the CD-ROM, see the instructions in Appendix E.

Conventions Used in This Book

When our publisher first told us that this book was going to have *conventions,* we got out our silly hats and our Republican and Democratic paraphernalia, but apparently she just meant that we had to be consistent. The conventions in this book are standard ways of communicating specific types of information, such as instructions and steps. (One example of a convention is the use of italics for newly introduced words, as with the word "conventions" in the first sentence of this paragraph.)

Here are the conventions for this book:

- Things that you, the reader, are asked to type are shown in **bold.**
- New terms are printed in *italics.*
- Information used in specific ways is formatted in a specific typeface. In this book, one of the most common kind of information displayed this way is HTML tags; that is, formatting information used to create Web pages (see Appendix A for a more complete definition). An example of a tag is <TITLE>.

  We also use a special typeface for URLs (Uniform Resource Locators), which are the addresses used to specify the location of Web pages. For example, the URL for Hungry Minds' Dummies Press is as follows:

  ```
  www.dummies.com
  ```

- The Web is fast-paced and evolving. Some of the URLs listed throughout this book may have changed, may have become inaccessible, or may not be supported through your local Internet service provider.
- Representative browser versions appear among the figures.
- Menu selections look like this: File⇨Save. This particular example means that you choose the File menu and then choose the Save option.
- Related, brief pieces of information are displayed in bulleted lists, such as the bulleted list that you're reading right now.

 ✔ Numbered lists are used for instructions that must be followed in a particular sequence. This book has many sequential steps that tell you just how to perform the different tasks that, when taken together, can make you a successful Web author.

 To make the steps brief and easy to follow, we use a specific way of telling you what to do. Here's an example of a set of steps:

 1. Start your Web browser.

 2. Go to the Web site:

 `www.tryfreestuff.com`

 Note: This is not a real site, just an example.

 3. Click the link that matches the type of computer you have: Macintosh, PC, or UNIX.

Part-y Time: How This Book Is Organized

We wrote this book to a carefully plotted, precise, *unvarying* plan, with the predictable and predicted result: the book you're holding in your hands now. And the CD-ROM? Same thing.

Wait a second. Isn't it true that the Web is changing every day, that Web sites appear and disappear like so many jacks-in-the-box — or whack-a-moles, if that's a more familiar example to you — and that Web companies go from opening their doors to public stock offerings — and sometimes back to closing their doors — in weeks? So, what was that about a plan?

Well, okay, we did change things a little along the way. Maybe a lot. But we *did* have a plan behind the book, even if it was finalized in a conference call at 5:00 this morning. The following sections explain the parts that make up the book.

Part 1: Create a Web Page Today

You probably want to dive right into becoming a Web publisher. So we start the book with some ideas about what to do in your Web site, then give some basics of HTML, the underlying language of Web pages, and specific instructions on how to get your first, simple Web page up. You can start with Yahoo! GeoCities, a free service accessible to everyone, or built-in AOL or CompuServe features, if you use one of those as your ISP.

Part II: Building Pages

The free, easy-to-use services in Part I are great for your first few days as a Web publisher. But soon you'll want to use some "real" tools for managing and editing your Web pages. You'll also want to make your page richer with formatted text and links. You may even want to add META tags to make it easier for someone using a search engine to find your pages. We tell you how to do all that and more in this Part.

Part III: Better, Stronger, Faster Pages

Huge books have been written about Web graphics. Cool — but definitely more information than most people need. In this Part we show you not only how to create Web-friendly graphics, but how to place graphics in your Web page. Then we show you how to publish your customized Web page where everyone can get to it.

Part IV: Getting Interactive

Most Web pages just sit there. But the fun ones interact with the user. We show you how to add animation, multimedia, and more interactivity to your Web page. And we show you how to expand your "simple" Web page, which by this point might be quite large, into a multi-page Web site. Have fun!

Part V: The Part of Tens

A Top Ten list is a great way to make complex information fun and easy to remember. Our Top Ten lists show you key DO's and DON'Ts of Web publishing.

Part VI: Appendixes

Appendixes in books are usually like appendixes in people: funny little things that get taken out of the patient in a hurry if they act up. But for this book, we pack in great information that can really help you. In Appendix A, a complete glossary defines the Web and Web publishing terms that may be confusing to you. In other appendixes, you see information about Internet service providers and Web page developer resources, including a guide to the CD-ROM that comes with this book.

Icons Used in This Book

 Tells what is on the accompanying CD-ROM.

 Marks information that you need to keep in mind as you work.

 Warns you of effects that may make your page take a long time to appear.

 Points to things you may want to know but don't necessarily need to know. You can skip these and read the text, skip the text and read these, or both.

 Flags specific information that may not fit in a step or description but that helps you create better Web pages.

 Points out things (in addition to slow downloads) that may cause problems.

Part I
Create a Web Page Today

The 5th Wave   By Rich Tennant

"Before the Internet, we were only bustin' chops locally. But now, with our Web site, we're bustin' chops all over the world."

In this part . . .

*J*ump right in with HTML and simple Web page publishing. Use Web-based services or your ISP to get a page online today. Your reward: telling your friends and colleagues your Web address tomorrow!

Chapter 1

Web Page Publishing Basics

The Web is an incredibly easy way to get your message — any message — out to anyone in the world who's interested in it. By putting up a Web page, you can stay in touch with friends and family, entertain people, help yourself get a job, or help yourself do your job. You can start a business, grow a business, or just have fun expressing yourself.

Over half a million people have purchased this book since its first edition several years ago, and as far as we can tell, they've used every technique we describe in this book, and more, to get their first Web pages up. By reading this book you're starting on a path that many, many people before you have followed to Web page success.

Web Basics 101

You may have begun using the Internet and Web without really getting a chance to learn how they work. Knowing how they work will help you become a better Web publisher. Here's a brief, pointed description. For more information, you can search on the Web; the World Wide Web consortium site at w3.org is a great place to start.

Understanding how the Web works

The Web is formally called the *World Wide Web,* and it's a collection of a bunch of text and graphics files that make up *Web pages.* The base of the Web is the Internet. The Web depends on the Internet to connect its many files together and to allow people to get to the Web. E-mail is a separate function that also depends on the Internet.

The Web is defined by two specifications: Hypertext Transfer Protocol (HTTP) and Hypertext Markup Language (HTML). The underlying idea behind the Web is *hypertext* — text that can contain links to other pieces of text stored anywhere on the Internet. The Web got its name from the way all the links connect the pieces of text together like a huge spider's web.

You look at Web pages using a program called a *Web browser*. A Web browser uses HTTP to request a Web page from a Web server. The Web page, in turn, uses HTTP to request any other files, such as graphics images or ads, that are part of the Web page. After you request a Web page, your Web browser pulls the files that make up the Web page from one or more Web servers and assembles those files into one page on your machine.

The most popular Web browsers are Microsoft Internet Explorer, which you can use separately or as a built-in part of America Online software; Netscape Navigator, part of Netscape Communicator, a set of related software programs; and Opera, a lesser-known but increasingly popular Web browser from a much smaller company.

At this point, HTML steps in. Each Web page includes a text file written in a format called *HTML* (for Hypertext Markup Language) and usually one or more graphics files. HTML defines a Web page's appearance and functionality. Actually, HTML doesn't precisely specify the Web page's appearance: Different Web browsers display various HTML commands differently. Also, users can specify how they want things to look as well. So what one user sees when she looks at a Web page may be very different from what another user sees. (Chapter 4 goes into detail about HTML.)

It's surprisingly easy to get a Web page up on the Internet. In fact, if you're in a hurry, you might want to go straight to Chapter 2 (for AOL or CompuServe) or Chapter 3 (for everyone else) and follow the instructions there to get your first Web page up in a few hours.

Getting webbed

This book talks a lot about the Web but doesn't discuss how to get on it. And even if you're on the Web already, perhaps through a connection at work, you may also want to get on the Web from home. How do you do that?

The most popular online service is America Online (AOL). AOL has robust Web publishing features, robust coverage around most of the world, and many other good features. Also popular are MSN (Internet access from Microsoft),

Earthlink, and CompuServe (owned by AOL), each of which have their advantages. Because AOL has both robust Web publishing features and by far the most customers, we describe in detail how to publish your first Web page using AOL's publishing features in Chapter 2. If you have another Internet service provider, use the information on quickly publishing your first Web page using Web-based services in Chapter 3.

Getting up URLy

The *Internet* is the giant computer network that connects other computer networks around the world. At its base, the Internet is just a giant mechanism for moving files from one computer to another. It finds files using a kind of address called a *URL (Uniform Resource Locator* — which sounds like something the Armed Forces invented to track down clothes!). The acronym URL is usually pronounced "you are ell," though some pronounce it "earl." "You are ell" is more understandable to people, and that's what we use.

The address that you type to get to a Web page is a URL. For example, `www.netsurf.com` is the URL for Arthur's Netsurfer Communications Web site. A URL consists of three parts (see Figure 1-1):

- **Protocol:** The *protocol* is the name of the communications language that the URL uses: HTTP (used on the Web), FTP, Gopher, and so on.

- **Domain name:** The *domain name* is the logical name of the server that the file is on.

- **Pathname:** The *pathname* tells the server how to find the file you want to retrieve.

REMEMBER

Web terms to know

We want to clear up how we define and use some Web terms:

- **Web page:** A text document that is published on a Web server, has HTML tags in it, almost always includes hypertext links, and usually includes graphics. When you click the Forward and Back buttons in your Web browser, you move chronologically through the Web pages that you already visited.

- **Web site:** A collection of Web pages that share a common theme and purpose and that users generally access through the site's home page. Some Web sites have only a home page; others have many pages.

- **Home page:** The Web page that people generally access first within a Web site. You let people know the URL (address) of your home page and try to get other Web page creators to provide links to it. Your home page is your Web site's starting page and contains links to any other pages that you put in your site.

- **HTML tags:** Brief formatting or linking commands placed within brackets in the text of an HTML file. For instance, the `<bold>` tag tells the Web browser to display text after the command in bold type; the `</bold>` tag tells the Web browser to turn bolding off. See Chapter 4 for more on HTML.

Figure 1-1:
URLy to
Web, URLy
to rise.

←— Protocol —→   ←—— Domain name ——→   ←— Pathname —→
http://   www.server.com/   folder/filename.ext

The For Dummies Way to Web Publishing

Reading this book is going to make you a Web publisher — anyone who places even a single, simple home page is a publisher on the World Wide Web. Congratulations in advance!

Putting up a Web page involves a few steps that are the same no matter which tools or techniques you use. The steps may have different names, or be intermingled with each other, but they're still basically the same. Here they are:

1. **Create the HTML text file that's the basis for your Web page (see Chapter 5).**

2. **Create or obtain the graphic images you'll use to spice up the appearance of your page (see Chapter 9).**

3. **Link the graphics into your HTML text file so they appear where you want them to (covered in Chapter 10).**

4. **Preview your Web page on your own machine (see Chapter 5).**

5. **Find Web server space (see Chapter 12).**

6. **Transfer the HTML text file and the graphics files to the Web server (also in Chapter 12).**

7. **Check that your new Web page works the way you want it to work (again, see Chapter 12).**

These steps are usually simple if you're creating a basic Web page. However, they do get more complicated sometimes, especially if you're trying to create a multi-page Web site. This book tells you several different, easy ways to create a Web page, and gets you started on expanding your Web page into a multi-page Web site.

Once you create a Web page that has complex formatting, or that mixes text and graphics, you'll want to test it in all the popular Web browsers. See Appendix B for the Web addresses from which you can download Microsoft Internet Explorer, the America Online client, Netscape Communicator, the Opera browser, or other tools.

For an example of a good-looking Web page, check out the For Dummies Web page, shown in Figure 1-2. It has an attractive layout, interesting information, and links to a great deal more information on the For Dummies site and other sites. The For Dummies Web site is very well done, but you, too, can achieve results like this with a reasonable amount of planning and hard work. In this book we'll concentrate on helping you create a simple, individual Web page and combine several Web pages into a closely linked group of pages called a *Web site.*

Note: The Hungry Minds home page is shown in Microsoft Internet Explorer, the most popular Web browser. For consistency, we use Internet Explorer for most of the Web page images in this book.

Making simple things simple

If all you want to do is create a simple "I exist" Web page, either for yourself or for your business, you shouldn't have to go through the rigmarole of figuring out HTML or learning a tool, finding server space, and so on. Chapters 2 and 3 show you two ways to get your first Web page up quickly and easily, using existing templates or simple HTML. Chapter 2 is for those who want to use AOL's built-in Web page publishing tools; Chapter 3 is for those who don't use AOL.

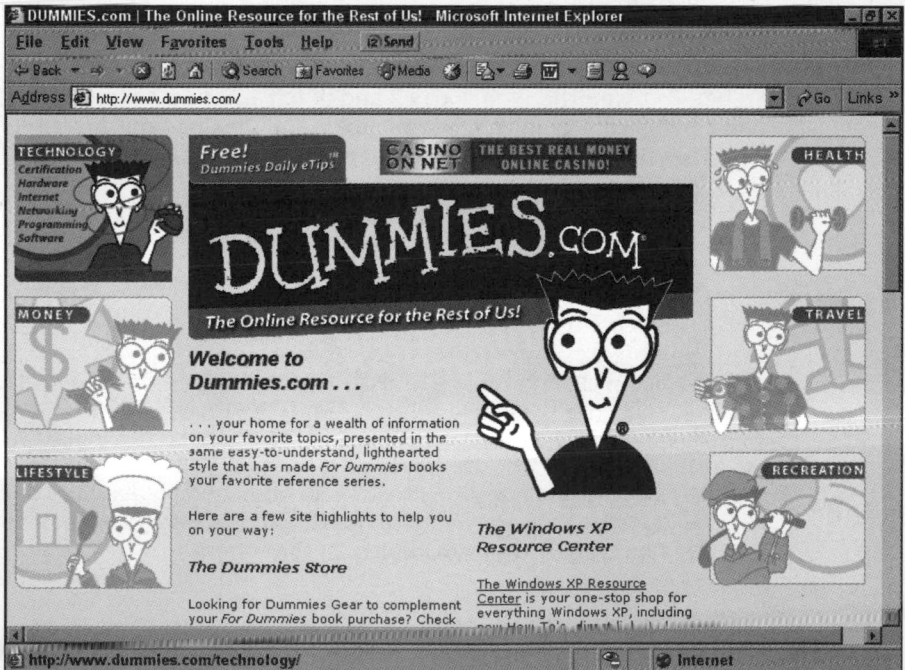

Figure 1-2:
The For Dummies home page shows Web publishing skill.

Seeing HTML

When Tim Berners-Lee invented HTML at CERN (the European particle physics research facility) a few years ago, he probably never imagined that so many people would be interested in seeing it. Today, most browsers include a command that enables you to see the actual HTML source that makes the page look and work the way it does.

For example, in Internet Explorer, choose View⇨Source to view the underlying HTML file. You see all the HTML tags that make the Web page look and act the way it does.

Once you open the HTML file, you can edit the text and the HTML tags, save the file, and then open the file again in your browser to see how it looks with the HTML changes.

To see how easy it is to publish on the Web, just turn to Chapter 2 or 3 and get started. You'll be a Web publisher with just an hour or two of effort.

Making difficult things possible

The free services and online services we describe in this book differ in how far they allow you to go without outgrowing what you can get for free. If your site gets too large or gets too much traffic, or if you want to use your site for business, at some point these services will ask you to start paying for the site.

The rest of Part I describes what you need to know to get an initial, simple Web page up on the Web. Parts II and III tell you how to improve your Web page, by placing graphics, adding links, and making your layout look attractive. Part IV tells you how to add animation and interactivity, plus expand your Web page into a Web site.

Types of Web Sites

The Web offers examples of nearly every communications strategy known to humanity, successful or not. But not every example of a Web page that you find online will apply to your situation. For one thing, the resources of different Web publishers vary tremendously, from an individual putting up family photos to a large corporation creating an online commerce site. For another, several different types of Web sites exist, and not every lesson learned in creating one type of Web site applies to the others.

The major types of Web pages are personal, topical, commercial, and entertainment sites. In the next sections, we describe some of the specific considerations that apply to each type of Web page and not to the others. Decide in advance what type of Web page you want to create, and look for pages like it online.

Personal sites

Personal Web sites can have many goals. Often, your goal is simply to share something about yourself with coworkers, friends, family, and others. Personal Web pages are a great way for people to find out about others with similar interests and for people in one culture to find out about other cultures. You can also use a personal Web site to share family photos and events — kind of like a holiday letter that's always up to date. Figure 1-3 shows part of the personal site of Jeff Lowe, who's piloting a remote-controlled blimp in the pictures. You can find the site at

```
www.jefflowe.com/site/pictures/index.php.
```

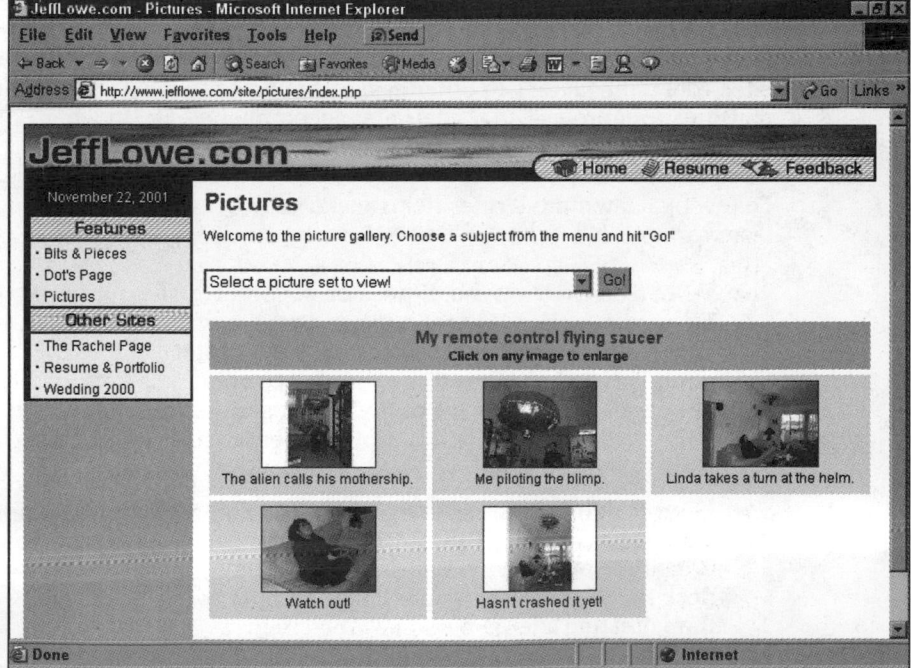

Figure 1-3: Jeff Lowe pilots the blimp (and posts his résumé too).

Are personal Web sites still relevant?

Most of the activity you hear about on the Web these days relates to large, commercial sites, political sites, and so on. Personal Web sites have gotten somewhat lost in the shuffle as better-funded sites belonging to organizations get all the attention. Never fear; personal Web sites are still fun and easy to create. And did we mention that they're fun?

Part of what's driving the continuing interest in personal Web pages is that more and more people all over the world have access to the Web. The chances are better than ever that a high percentage of your friends, family, and colleagues can visit and appreciate your site. So don't be put off by the tremendous growth of business on the Web. The personal and fun side is growing, too; it's just getting less media attention than the commercial side.

Creating a personal Web site is a great deal of fun and great practice for other work. But personal Web sites are often left unchanged after the initial thrill of creating and publishing them fades. Be different — keep your Web site updated!

As personal Web sites evolve, their creators tend to add more information about a single key interest, in which case the pages may become topical Web sites (described later). In other cases, the Web site creator adds more information about professional goals and accomplishments, in which case the Web page becomes more like a business Web site.

Following a few simple rules helps make your personal Web site more fun and less work:

- **What's on first?** No, no. What's on second . . . The upper part of your Web page — the part that appears first when you bring the page up onscreen — should make the main point of the site clear. If the main point is "you," the first thing people see should be your name, your photo, and links to some of the things about "you" that are in your site. If the point of your site is a topical interest, business interest, or professional self-promotion, you should make that clear, too.

- **Keep it simple.** Start with modest goals and get something up on the Web; then create a "To Do" list of ways in which to extend your site. Consider spinning off commercial and topical pages that reflect your desires and interests — each page with its own access point — rather than creating a large personal Web site.

- **Provide lots of links.** One of the best ways to share your interests is to share information about Web sites that you like, as well as books and other resources. You can put this list on your one and only Web page or make it a separate page that's part of a personal Web site. If you develop a thorough, carefully updated list of links for a specific interest area, you create a very valuable resource for others.

✔ **Consider your privacy.** A Web page is just like a billboard — except that 100 million or more people can see it, not just a few thousand. Don't put anything up on your Web page that you wouldn't want on a billboard. And think twice before putting up information about your kids and other family members; you might be willing to compromise your own privacy, but you shouldn't make that decision for other people.

Topical sites

That's "topical," not "tropical." (See the Kaua'i Exotix home page later in this chapter for an example of the latter.) A *topical home page* is a resource on a specific topic. A topic can be an interest or volunteer group to which the author belongs, in which case the page may grow over time into something much like a commercial Web site. (Creating a Web site for a group is a tremendous contribution that you can make, but it can be a lot of work; watch what you may be getting yourself into!) Or your topical Web page can be about any interest, cause, concern, obsession, or flight of fancy that you have. In this sense, the Web is like an out-of-control vanity press, allowing anyone to go on and on about anything — sometimes offering something of great value, oftentimes not.

The best-supported topical interest area on the Web is on Web publishing itself. One such topical site is the Useless Pages page, shown in Figure 1-4, which started as a pet project of one of the talented employees of Primus Consulting, Inc. (The fun part is to guess which of the Useless Pages were intentionally designed badly just to get on the Useless Pages list!) Check out this site at www.go2net.com/useless.

Making a second career out of maintaining and extending a topical Web site is easy, but the pay is usually nil. Here are some things to consider when you create a topical Web site:

✔ **What's on first?** As with a personal Web page, the title of a topical Web page and the first screen that users see need to make unmistakably clear the topic that the page covers. And, to the extent possible, they must describe what resources the Web site offers about the topic.

✔ **Keep focused.** A topical Web site loses value if it goes beyond a single topic. How many of the people who share your love for Thai cooking also share your abiding interest in rotifers? (Which are too small to use in most recipes, Thai or not.) If you have two interests that you want to share on the Web, consider creating separate Web pages.

✔ **Create a succession plan.** If your Web site grows beyond your capacity to maintain and extend it properly, find someone to help out or to take it over. The first person you should ask about taking over is anyone who's complaining that you're not extending the site fast enough! Decide what role you can handle and then ask for help in doing the rest.

Figure 1-4:
A unique take on Web publishing.

Business sites

Business Web sites, also known as commercial sites, constitute the 50,000-pound gorilla of the Web, with a tremendous amount of time, energy, and money devoted to them. Business Web sites cover a wide range of styles because their goals and the expertise and resources behind them vary so much. This book provides enough information for you to create a competent "Web presence" site with several pages of contact and company information. But even these kinds of sites vary quite a bit, and you need to be sure that your company's page is well executed.

Figure 1-5 shows the Netsurfer home page created by Arthur Bebak, one of the authors. (So now you can call him "Author" Bebak!) Go surf around the Netsurfer site to see what a site designed and implemented by one of us looks like: www.netsurf.com/nsd.

The first question to ask about a business Web site is "Who can access it?" Some sites are intended for the World Wide Web and everyone on it; others are on the World Wide Web but are password-protected or otherwise restricted in access; still others are on private networks and inaccessible to outsiders. These inaccessible networks are described as being "behind the firewall." Any Web page that isn't accessible to everyone is considered to be on an *intranet*, if access is limited to one company, or an *extranet*, if access is limited to a group of companies that are business partners.

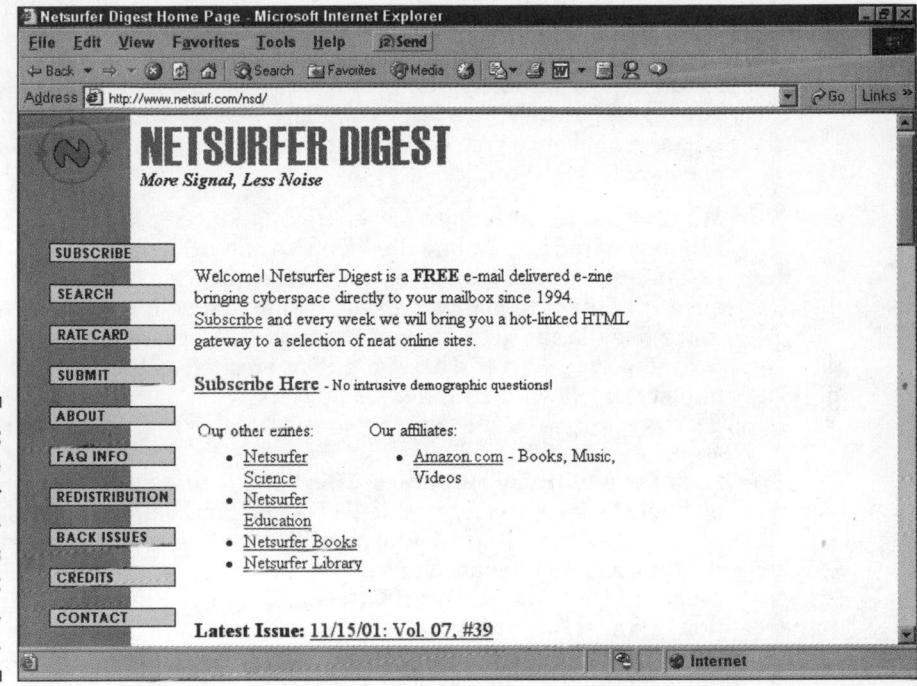

Figure 1-5:
The
Netsurfer
Communi-
cations
motto:
More signal,
less noise.

Despite the wide variety of business Web sites, following just a few rules can help you create a page that meets your goals:

- ✔ **What's on first?** A business Web page should make the name and purpose(s) of your business immediately clear. Also, the site should provide easy-to-find information on how to contact your business and what products and services the business offers.

- ✔ **Get the right look.** Telling someone you don't like their Web site is like telling them you don't like their haircut — they're likely to take it personally. But an ugly Web site, like an ugly haircut, can make a permanently bad impression. Make sure that the look of your Web site is up to the professional standards set by other parts of your business.

- ✔ **Get permission.** Unless you own the business, you should ask for permission before putting a company page on the open Web. You also need to make absolutely sure you have the permissions you need for any images or documents that you use before you publish your Web page.

- ✔ **Inside or outside the firewall?** Deciding who gets access is tricky. For example, a small amount of otherwise confidential information can make a site more valuable, but the presence of confidential information also prevents you from opening up the entire site to the broader public — including people who may benefit from it. Implementing access controls can also be difficult. Investigate how to password-protect a site, or ask a network administrator at your company whether you can physically control access. For instance, you may be able to prevent access based on what network the user connects from.

✔ **Find experts.** It's likely that businesses similar to yours — or even coworkers, if you're in a large company — have Web sites that have a purpose similar to yours. Look to the creators of those sites for guidance and inspiration.

✔ **Monitor usage.** Investing time, energy, and money in a business Web site requires a trade-off among the Web site and other things that those resources could go to. One of the crucial questions you may need to answer in order to justify Web site maintenance or expansion is how much use the site gets. Investigate ways to measure the use of your site. A good way to start is a basic hit counter, such as the free one you can find at the following URL:

```
www.bcentral.com/services/fc/.
```

✔ **Seek out additional resources.** This book focuses on hands-on creation of single Web pages and simple Web sites. For a larger business site, you need access to additional information to help you with the planning, hosting, and maintenance of the site. Consider purchasing *HTML 4 For Dummies,* 2nd Edition, by Ed Tittel and Natanya Pitts, for more information on the HTML specification, and *Internet Marketing For Dummies,* by Frank Catalano and Bud Smith (both books from Hungry Minds, Inc.), for more information on planning and creating a business Web site with a marketing bent.

Having a Web site that's too obviously "handmade," rather than professionally created, can be embarrassing for a business. However, many sites are going "back to the future" with a simple, clean look that's light on graphics. So how do you decide whether to make your look fancy or simple? The best way to get a quick reality check is to look at some competitors' Web sites and make sure that your initial site looks about as good as theirs. And remember that oftentimes the most embarrassing thing is having no site at all.

Entertainment sites

Entertainment is one of the top few reasons why people use the Web, and the number of entertainment sites is growing. Humorous pages and services such as multiuser dungeons (MUDs) and shared games on online services are now expanding onto the Web.

The high expectations that people have of entertainment sites can make these sites some of the most demanding ones to create. Here are a few suggestions for creating entertainment sites:

- ✔ **Don't start here.** Don't try to figure out Web publishing by creating an entertainment site. It's a very demanding task. Try another type first and edge your way into entertainment.

- ✔ **Keep it fresh.** How funny is a joke the second time you hear it? You have to either rapidly update the content or allow participants to provide the content through their interaction with one another — neither option is easy.

- ✔ **Push the technology.** Interactivity is also key to entertainment, which means going beyond HTML and static graphics. You need to figure out and use at least one advanced Web technology to make a fresh and interesting entertainment Web site.

- ✔ **Let the technology push you.** The technology can give you ideas that are in themselves pretty funny. Try using Java to create a Three Stooges-type animated routine, or use ActiveX to create a virtual reality environment that includes fun-house mirrors. (We describe both Java and ActiveX in Chapter 14.)

Is your page cybersmut?

For most Web page publishers, the best policy with respect to putting anything potentially offensive in your Web pages is to keep your site clean. The use of gratuitous sex and violence in your Web pages will simply put off many people and put the Web site itself in a bad light.

But what if the sex or violence is not gratuitous and is actually central to your point? Then send the authors your URL so that we can see it for ourselves. No, seriously: Be sure to make the first page a home page that warns readers that they may find your content offensive. That lets them gracefully opt out before they view whatever you show.

Even that enlightened approach may not be enough, however. Some Web server owners will drop your page if it violates their rules, and several countries have laws that may directly or indirectly specify what can and can't be on a Web page. Be sure to find out about the rules and laws that apply to you before you put anything questionable on your Web page.

Web Page Guidelines

A Web page or Web site is basically a publication, though an interactive one. Thinking through a few simple principles now, before you start, will help make your Web page much more interesting and useful to the people who see it. You can also revisit this section after you put up your initial Web home page; use these guidelines to revise your page and make it even more interesting and useful!

Ask "Why am I doing this?"

Ask yourself, as you're starting, "Why am I doing this?" (As you do more and more work on your page, your answer to this question may come to have some degree of profanity in it!) That is, why are you creating the page, and not having someone else create it for you? The answer helps you determine some important things about the page. The following list details the most common reasons for people to get involved in creating a Web page:

- **For work:** More and more people are being asked to create Web pages and Web sites as part of their jobs; for example, they use the Web to communicate with people inside or outside their companies. But unless you plan to be a full-time Webmaster, you need to balance the time you spend developing your pages with the time you spend on the other demands of your job. Be modest in your initial goals, and keep track of each step in creating and modifying your Web pages so that you — or the person who takes over for you — can refer to the records later.

- **For fun:** Fun sites are a good thing, and they are a lot of what makes the Web worthwhile. But if you create your site for fun, you may find time to work on it only after you spend time on other things, such as work, school, or time with friends and family. So don't be too ambitious in your initial plans, or you may take quite awhile to finish and publish your page.

- **As a career move:** So you want to be a full-time, or nearly full-time, Webmaster; or you want, in some other way, to make the Internet or Web part of your career. In this kind of situation, you can afford to plan an ambitious Web site that uses advanced tools, tracks usage, and otherwise gets closer to the cutting edge of the Web. To gain experience, create your initial Web page by using the accessible and broad-based tools and approaches we describe in this book. Then take your page closer to the cutting edge by using the more advanced techniques described and taught elsewhere, such as the JavaScript programs described in *JavaScript For Dummies,* 3rd Edition, by Emily A. Vander Veer (Hungry Minds, Inc.).

✔ **Who knows?** As famous baseball manager Yogi Berra once said, "When you come to a fork in the road, take it." You may not have a specific reason for publishing on the Web, but that shouldn't stop you. You may figure out a good reason after you have a little Web experience under your belt. Start simple, so you can score an early success in getting a basic Web page up, and then go from there.

Don't spend too much time on design

Designing a Web page is unlike designing any other kind of publication, because you don't have as much control over the look and feel of Web pages as you do with other types of publications. Modem and network connection speeds, browsers, screen sizes, and font and other settings within a browser vary so much that users can have very different experiences with your Web page.

With the latest versions of HTML, it's possible to control more aspects of your Web page's appearance. Advanced sites, such as amazon.com, use many different aspects of HTML as well as programming languages such as JavaScript to create dense, rich layouts more like a magazine than a typical Web page. However, many aspects of the newest versions of HTML are not yet standard across different Web browsers. In this book we stick with HTML 4.0, which works the same way for nearly all Web users.

Keep your design simple and don't spend too much time on it initially. Then improve it as you find out more about Web publishing generally and more about how people use your page specifically.

Put the good stuff first

Imagine the Web as a giant magazine rack and the person surfing the Web as someone scanning the front covers of all those magazines. People who see your Web page decide whether to stay at your site or go elsewhere based largely on what they see when your page first comes up.

If your purpose is to provide information or links, put that information first or, at most, one click away. For example, to create a site that provides information about a company, make getting the contact information — your company name, address, phone number, and fax number — very easy to find. To create a personal site that is attractive to potential employers, make clear what employment field you're in right at the top of your Web page and make your résumé easy to access.

Big issues for big sites

This book focuses on the needs of people who create a single Web page or a small Web site, and who do so on their own. Larger sites, or sites that need to be put up quickly or changed rapidly, need to have additional people working on them.

If you want to create a larger site down the road, start thinking now about what resources may be available to put into it. How many people in your company or other organization work on advertising, public relations, and marketing? How many people question whether those jobs are real work? (Just kidding — the lead author, who's a marketer, wrote that!)

You may reasonably expect your company to re-target some fraction of its advertising, marketing, and PR resources to support a presence on the Web. And what about sales? As Web-based business transactions take off, some portion of a company's sales effort becomes Web-based, necessitating a suitable up-front commitment to bring returns down the road.

Or your company may already suffer from Web burnout. Classic symptoms of Web burnout include massive early investment to create a beautiful site, months of failure to update or maintain the site, followed by finger-pointing about who wasted all that money. Usually the problem is that no one set goals for the site, so no one managed the site's design and construction with those specific goals in mind. Companies often designate too few financial and human resources for maintenance and improvement of the site. If this has happened in your company, you know the problems that result, so be sure to establish clear goals for your own Web efforts.

The most important element in adopting any new technology for business is a successful pilot project. As someone creating a smallish Web site, you're developing important skills and knowledge about the all-important convergence of your business's needs with the Web's opportunities. Set specific goals, strive to meet them, and record both your problems and your successes. By doing so, you position yourself to justify further investment of resources as the Web grows in importance for your company.

If your purpose is to draw people into your site to entertain them, educate them, or expose them to messages from advertisers — or to do all of these things at once — then the first part of the page should make a strong impression and invite the user to go further into your site. Figure 1-6 shows the Kaua'i Exotix Web page, certainly one that catches your attention, located at the following URL:

```
www.besttropicals.com.
```

But, like the Kaua'i Exotix Web page, your home page also should help people who seek a quick "hit" of information; they're more likely to come back later if you don't waste their time during their first quick visit.

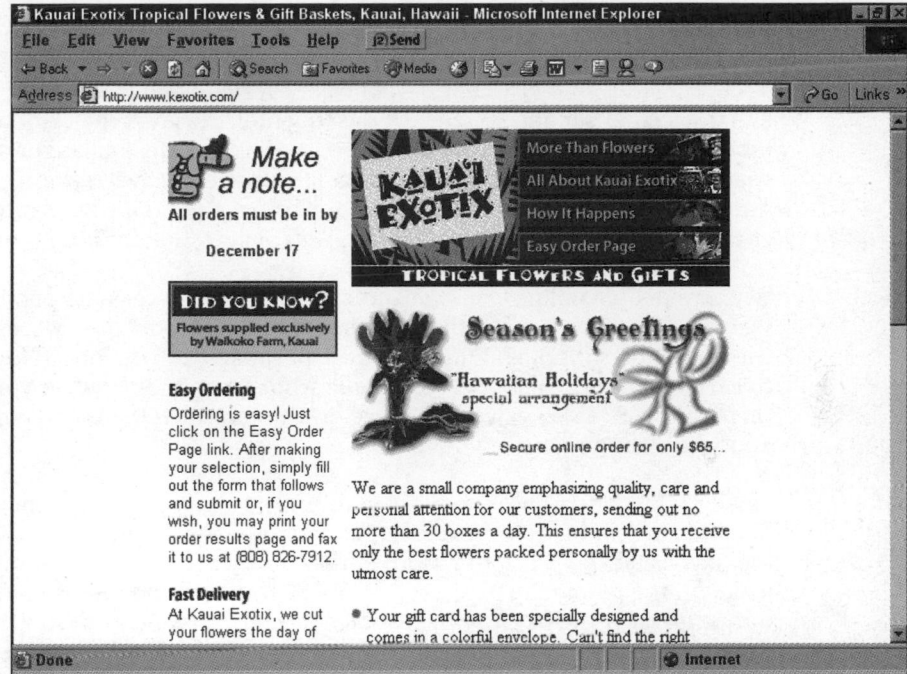

Figure 1-6:
Buds for
your buds.

Think twice about download times

Putting lots of graphics in your pages is time-intensive for you because creating or finding good graphics and placing them appropriately in your Web page can take a great deal of time and effort. Graphics are also time-intensive for those who surf your site because they can take a long time to download. So plan to use spot graphics (small images that download quickly) at first. Think twice before creating large clickable image maps or attractive opening graphics like those you find on the sites of large companies, such as General Motors or Apple. If you do use an opening graphic, keep it under 20K or so (see Chapter 9 for details).

You may find a good deal of coverage in the computer press, and even in mainstream newspapers and newsmagazines, about ongoing efforts to make faster access available to ordinary users. But for all the talk about cable modems, Digital Subscriber Line (DSL), and other advanced techniques, most home users are still on 56 Kbps or slower modems. (Business users are typically on faster connections.) So ignore the hype — the speed at which the average person accesses the Web is creeping upward slowly, not leaping ahead. For now, be conservative in how much data you put in each page, and test the download times of your pages over a modem-based connection before you publish them.

Know your audience

According to Web researchers, Web users overwhelmingly speak English as either a first or second language. Consequently, the great majority of Web content, Web creation tools, and Web browsers use the English language. Even ten years after the birth of the Web — which happened in Switzerland — North America is still the "center of gravity" for Web access. This will gradually change as other countries catch up to Web penetration in the United States.

Why are people online? Surveys indicate that the top reasons people use the Web are for information-gathering, entertainment, education, work, "time-wasting," and shopping. Which of these purposes do you intend for your site to serve? How do you appeal to people who are online? How do you help them find you? The answers to these questions will help you enhance the appeal and usefulness of your site.

Finally, what kind of browsers are your users running? Surveys indicate that over 80 percent of Web users run Microsoft Internet Explorer; most of the rest use Netscape Navigator. Both of these browsers, and most others that make up the remaining user base, support graphics and tables, and nearly all users run their browsers with graphics turned on (which doesn't mean that they appreciate waiting for complex images to load — unless those images are pretty cool!).

For more details about who's online, what they do there, and what it means to you if you're creating a business Web site, see *Internet Marketing For Dummies,* by Frank Catalano and Bud Smith (Hungry Minds, Inc.).

Use text bites

As we mention earlier in this chapter, when preparing a Web site, less is more. Saying something with less text makes users more likely to read and remember it. A *text bite* is like a sound bite — it's a short, clearly written piece of text that makes a single point.

Although you can overuse text bites, they are very important in Web page design. Text bites help you convey as much information as possible in the limited amount of time users spend looking at each Web page. And they help you balance the basic elements of Web page design: text, links, and graphics.

If you want to put long documents on the Web, consider rewriting them as a series of text bites. If rewriting them is too much work to be practical, at least create short, punchy text for navigation and for introductory paragraphs to the long documents. Within a long document, add headers to break up the flow of text and provide pointers on your Web site to key areas within the document. Without such guidance, users may well give up in frustration without reaching the information they're looking for.

Look at sites you like

Look at sites you like and at sites whose purposes are similar to your own. What's good about them? What's not? Imitate successful elements — without copying, which would be a violation of ethics as well as copyright laws — and avoid unsuccessful ones. As the development of your site progresses, keep checking it against the sites you previously identified and widen your search to get additional ideas — on what not to do as well as on what to do.

Very few original ideas exist on the Web, and your initial site is likely to contain one or two new ideas at best. The rest of your site may echo things readers have already seen, and you're better off if your site brings to mind other good sites, rather than bad ones. (But be careful. If you start yelling "Bad site! Bad site!" at your computer screen and swatting it with a rolled-up newspaper, you may not be allowed to have a working Internet connection much longer.)

Plan for ongoing improvements

As you plan and implement your initial Web page, you will, no doubt, find yourself creating a "To Do" list of things that you can't fit into the original site but want to add later, when time allows. (Creating this list for later use is great protection against trying to create a supersite right off the bat, getting stuck in the creation process, and never getting to a point where you can actually publish your first Web page.) This list is the start of a plan for ongoing improvements.

Some things that you put in a Web site need to be kept current. For example, if your business Web page shows your company's quarterly results, be ready to update it quickly when the next quarter's results come out. If it lists company officers, update it as soon as a change takes place. (Unless you're one of the people changed — then it's your successor's problem!)

Web site information that is obviously out of date is one of the best ways to leave a bad impression of you or your organization/company and to steer visitors away from your Web site.

Not only do you want to update the Web site, you want to avoid using "Under Construction" signs and otherwise apologizing for things that aren't there yet. Everything on the Web is under construction, which is half the fun of using the Web and creating pages for it in the first place. You get only one chance to make a first impression, and an "Under Construction" sign doesn't count in your favor.

Decide how you define success

Before you design and create your Web page, define what you believe will make it a success. For an initial effort, simply putting up something on the Web that clearly conveys basic information is probably enough. For follow-up work, get more specific. Are you trying to reach a certain number of people or type of people? Will measuring *page views* — the number of times that people look at one page from your site — be enough, or do you need some other measure of response, such as having people send e-mail or call an 800 number? Do you want to create a cutting-edge site in terms of bell-and-whistle features like fancy graphics and animation — and if so, are you willing to invest the time and money to make this happen? Talk to people who do advertising and marketing in the real world, as well as to people who work on the Web, and get a sense of what goals they set and how they measure success in meeting their goals.

Chapter 2

Web Publishing with AOL and Other ISPs

In This Chapter

▶ Finding the best ISP

▶ Finding the best Web publishing support

▶ Getting your page up with AOL or Compuserve

▶ Starting out with 1-2-3 Publish

▶ Publishing your first home page

Although the easy-to-use, open, ungovernable World Wide Web may seem as though it is going to wipe out traditional, closed, monitored online services such as America Online (AOL), circumstances are not really working out that way. The online services are adapting quickly. They have become gateways to the Web, and in some cases offer easy-to-use Web publishing services that include hosting your Web page for free.

If you already use AOL, it's probably the best place for you to start experimenting with Web publishing. You already know the interface, you can find online forums and discussion boards for Web publishing, and you can take advantage of the easy-to-use Web publishing features that AOL has scrambled to provide.

If you aren't an America Online or a CompuServe user, the quickest and cheapest way to get your first page up on the Web is to use GeoCities, the Web-based service we describe in Chapter 3. But if you are, you may well be better off for Web publishing. America Online, in particular, has strong features for intermediate Web publishing, including support for both Windows and Macintosh, several megabytes of free server space, and (at the time of this writing) no restrictions on using free Web pages for business.

Note: Just like the Web, online services are always evolving. The information in this chapter is accurate at the time of this writing, but you need to check online for the latest info. See the updates page for this book at www.dummies.com for more information.

The Best Internet Service Provider

You certainly have freedom of choice when it comes to the best way to get online. You used to have to choose between an online service such as AOL or CompuServe, which offered limited Internet access, or an Internet service provider, which had little online community or other online service features. Now you can get a range of online service-type and ISP-type features from a range of providers, all referred to as ISPs. And your choice truly is free, at least for awhile — most ISPs offer free sign up and a free trial period. You can try two or three different services before making a long-term choice. Just remember to resign from any service that you stop using, or the $20 or so a month charge to your credit card will go on forever!

You also have the option of using a traditional Internet service provider (ISP) like Earthlink. Earthlink has more and more built-in content and services, like America Online or CompuServe, but is really focused on open Internet and Web content and tools. Other ISPs vary in the amount of built-in content and services they offer.

In many areas you also have the ability to use a free ISP service like Netzero. A free ISP service will give you a fast, free connection to the Internet and a few additional frills. But who needs frills? If you like using the Internet and the Web for your information, chat, and so on, and a free ISP service is available in your area, you should seriously consider it.

With any ISP, you can use GeoCities (described in Chapter 3) or other free Web page publishing services to create your first Web page. With AOL or CompuServe, you also get the option of using built-in Web publishing services.

America Online is the biggest and best traditional online service. Because it's far bigger than any other online service — over 30 million users, about five times the number of the next competitor — it has more people to chat with online, more areas with existing content, and more people to support you. Many Gateway computers also include America Online service; Gateway had to give AOL part of the company to get this deal.

America Online owns CompuServe; CompuServe has been positioned as the "value" service — a little less content, a little less service, for a little less money. You can get basic service using CompuServe 2000, the latest version of CompuServe, for $9.95 a month. Or you can buy a bundle that includes CompuServe 2000 service for so many dollars per month with a big discount on the computer — even a free computer. But if you want the most-used online service, America Online, it will cost you extra.

MSN Internet Access is a Microsoft offering that's positioned as a value alternative to AOL. For $21.95 a month you get Internet access and use of Microsoft services such as Hotmail and the Microsoft Network (MSN). This may not seem like too good a deal because much of what you get as part of MSN Internet Access is free to any Web user, but MSN Internet Access is popular, with millions of users and growing steadily.

As for more general concerns, all three interfaces have a modern, relatively attractive GUI *(graphical user interface);* CompuServe 2000, the latest version, incorporates many features of America Online. The experience of using America Online also is increasingly marred by pop-up ads that you have to click to get rid of; these ad deals are worth tens of millions of dollars to America Online, Inc., but they are just as annoying as TV ads. (You can get rid of them if you take the time to change a couple of settings.) Figure 2-1 shows the clean and attractive interface of America Online, but watch out for those pop-up ads. Figure 2-2 shows the improved interface of CompuServe 2000; Figure 2-3 shows the revamped interface of MSN, which is simply a Web page available to any Internet user.

The examples show the versions for Windows. The Macintosh offerings on the Big Three tend to lag behind the versions for Windows, and MSN Internet Access doesn't work with the Macintosh or even with Windows 3.1. Many Macintosh owners choose America Online, which got an early start with Macintosh users. (America Online's software is based on work Apple did for its own defunct online service.)

Figure 2-1: America Online is easy for everyone to use.

Figure 2-2:
Compu-
Serve gets
more GUI
with time.

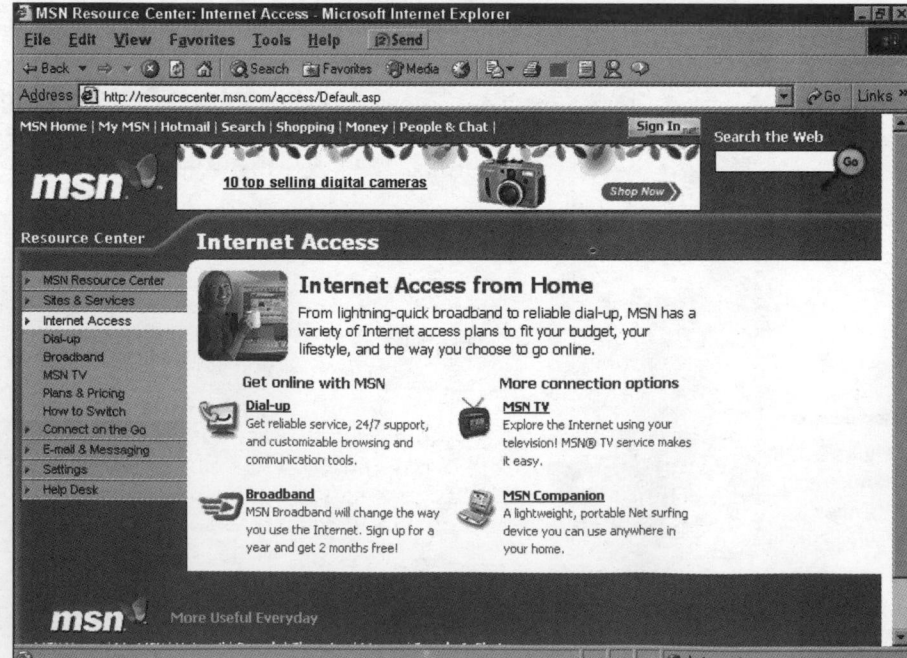

Figure 2-3:
MSN
Internet
Access —
Microsoft's
ISP.

If you have not yet chosen an online service, or have been considering switching, here are the high points — and low points, where applicable — of each service:

- ✔ **America Online:** So far, the market consistently votes most strongly for America Online, making it the largest and fastest growing of the services now with over 30 million users. It has recently launched Version 7.0, which adds locally focused content and other features to its familiar mix of Internet access, chat, e-mail, and Web publishing. America Online also has the most Macintosh users and Mac-related content of the major services. You can find current information about the services and download client software from www.aol.com.

- ✔ **CompuServe:** For business, CompuServe may still be a good choice. It has a vast array of business-oriented services and millions of business-oriented users, who help each other with both general and industry-specific questions, as well as robust offerings in other areas. However, more and more such support is moving to the open Web. With CompuServe being repositioned as a value service, price may be the main attraction for CompuServe. You can find current information about the services and download client software from www.compuserve.com.

- ✔ **The Microsoft Network/MSN Internet Access:** Microsoft basically gave up on the full-featured online service market and relaunched The Microsoft Network as MSN Internet Access. MSN Internet Access only works on Windows 95 or later versions of Windows. It uses the Internet Explorer browser — renamed MSN Explorer, and offers extra buttons and links to content — and the msn.com Web site as its entire user interface. It also limits extra services to free Hotmail accounts (which are also free to anyone else!) and a few special offers. See www.msn.com for details.

- ✔ **Prodigy:** Prodigy, once a leader, didn't maintain its momentum and growth while going through a change of ownership and a change of focus. Prodigy relaunched itself as Prodigy Internet and has introduced Web page creation services. Although in this book we don't cover Prodigy Internet, you may find it worth checking out.

- ✔ **Earthlink:** Earthlink is the winner of the wars among "pure" ISPs, having acquired the second-place contender, MindSpring, some years ago. Earthlink offers dial-up, broadband, and wireless Internet access, with your choice of browser software.

- ✔ **Netzero:** Netzero got into the online services game late, with free Internet access as its claim to fame. The company now gives away up to 10 hours a month of access — about enough to receive and upload e-mail — and charges $9.95 a month for unlimited use.

So what's the best online service for budding Web publishers? AOL is the most expensive, has the most users, and sports the most Web publishing features. If you already use one of the services, you should probably stick with it when pursuing your Web publishing efforts. Figuring out a new service is a big hassle, and CompuServe and AOL both have decent Web publishing support. You always have the option of using GeoCities or a competing Web-based publishing site (see Chapter 3), no matter who your ISP is.

The Web sites of America Online, CompuServe, and MSN are among the most popular sites on the World Wide Web. You can even use these sites to check your AOL, CompuServe, or MSN e-mail using a Web browser. You can also find many smaller national services and dozens of local online services around the world, though the number is gradually dropping through mergers, acquisitions, and bankruptcies. Each online service has its pluses and minuses, its fans, and its specific appeal. You may even discover a worthwhile local ISP by cruising one of the big services.

Some services offer language-specific support. If you want to work in a language other than English, ask users who have experience using your preferred language about available services.

Traditional online services: Pros and cons

The ISPs that started out as traditional online services, before the Web was created — AOL, CompuServe, and Prodigy — all offer Web access, but what's offered varies dramatically. In general, if all you want is Web access, you may be better off with an Internet service provider (ISP), a company that provides direct access to the Internet and that may well be cheaper, inflict less advertising on you, have better browser support, or offer more reliable access than the major online services.

The best news for a new Web publisher about these services is that you can find plenty of Web publishing support. Given the difficulties you may encounter in figuring out how to use the Web and publish on it, who wouldn't want a few million friends online to help out? All the online services offer support for Web use and Web publishing. Online forums can tell you what to do, point you to good sites, and more. Online technical support helps you get beyond Web problems and problems with the online service itself.

However, the online services also share some Web access problems. The default browser is usually an older version of Microsoft Internet Explorer. If you want to use Netscape Navigator, or the latest version of Internet Explorer, you may be able to, but only by doing extra setup work — and then you have a harder time getting questions about how to use your browser answered by your fellow online service users, who will tend to be users of the built-in version of Internet Explorer.

Using one of the online services can be a bit like using training wheels. Remember how free you felt when your parents finally took the training wheels off of your first bike? Having the interface of your online service take screen space away from your Web browser, having to fight off unwanted pop-up ads, having access to online newsgroups restricted by the online service, and switching back and forth between the "look and feel" of your online service and your accustomed browser may irritate you when compared to feeling the open air of the unregulated Internet.

Checking newsgroups for the real deal

For user feedback on online services, you may want to check Usenet newsgroups, which you may have access to at school or at work. Newsgroups are discussion groups, hosted on the Internet, that allow people to discuss shared interests. Web browsers often include the capability to read Usenet newsgroups, and the online services offer Usenet access along with Web access. Try the following newsgroups:

- `alt.online-service.america-online`
- `alt.online-service.compuserve`
- `alt.online-service.microsoft`

The Best Web Publishing Support

Online services are a good place to start your initial Web publishing efforts: low prices, good tools, lots of support — kind of like running downhill with a tailwind. Now that America Online, CompuServe, and The Microsoft Network are increasingly integrated with the Web, Web publishing is the cutting edge of Web-related functionality for the services to offer. America Online and CompuServe offer the following:

- **No extra charge for Web page authoring:** America Online and CompuServe both offer free support for Web page authoring; you pay only the normal access charges for creating and viewing your page and other Web pages.

- **Easy Web page authoring tools:** America Online and CompuServe offer easy-to-use, fill-in-the-blank tools that help you quickly create an initial Web page. AOL has several levels of Web page tools and support for additional features; CompuServe offers some, but not all, of the same features as AOL.

- **Free Web server space:** One of the biggest problems in creating an initial Web page is getting space on a Web server. America Online and CompuServe both offer free Web server space for personal and business home pages.

- **No file transfer hassle:** Getting your files onto a Web server is often a pain; the online services' easy-to-use Web page authoring tools can make getting your information online easy.

- **Upgrading to HTML tools:** The online services enable you to use separate HTML tools to create your own custom Web page and then to transfer your files to their server for free hosting.

The online services are rapidly developing their Web support in general and their Web publishing support in particular, so check updates on Web services before making a final decision about which online service to use.

Each online service has different specific features and restrictions on your Web pages. At this writing, the policies and offerings of the top online services are as follows:

- ✔ **America Online:** Several megabytes of free Web server space. More good news: AOL has a very easy-to-use tool called 1-2-3 Publish, and a more capable tool called Easy Designer, both integrated into the service. America Online also offers step-by-step instructions for using HTML and free add-ins to your Web pages, and allows you to use your free server space to put up business Web pages.

- ✔ **CompuServe:** CompuServe gives you free access to 1-2-3 Publish, the same built-in Web publishing tool offered by AOL. CompuServe offers free templates and the ability to upload your own HTML files and graphics to a free, 20MB space. You can also add counters and other cool features, and you can use your Web page for your business. (No business transaction capability is supported, though, and you aren't allowed to add your own.)

- ✔ **MSN:** MSN doesn't really do anything special for you when it comes to Web publishing — and if you look around the Web, you'll find that many Web pages on free, Web-based services such as GeoCities (see Chapter 3) are created by MSN members. Basically, as an MSN user, you're on your own.

All the publishing services we describe in this book enable you to include HTML commands in your text. For a description of key HTML commands, see the Cheat Sheet and Appendix C. (Feeling restless? Tear out the Cheat Sheet and tape it to the wall in front of you, where you can see it!)

What's a Mac user to do?

Two words: Get AOL. America Online has robust Macintosh support, including full cross-platform support for easy Web publishing. CompuServe doesn't support an easy-to-use Web publishing tool on the Macintosh, only on Windows. (Mac users have access to free Web server space, but no easy-to-use publishing tool.) The Microsoft Network doesn't support the Macintosh at all! So if you are a Mac user who wants an online service that supports your Web publishing efforts, get America Online.

Get Your Web Page Up with AOL or CompuServe

America Online is an amazing success story — and by far the leading Internet service provider in the world. It also offers solid Web publishing services, backed by a strong online community that can help you publish your first Web page and then steadily improve it.

America Online is such an amazing success story that it acquired its biggest rival, CompuServe. (This was a couple of years before it acquired something even larger, the media company Time Warner.) The 1-2-3 Publish tool, which we describe in this chapter, works in both AOL and CompuServe.

If you're not an America Online or a CompuServe user, GeoCities (described in Chapter 3) is an excellent choice. Anyone with Web access can use GeoCities. But if you're an America Online or CompuServe user, you have a choice between America Online's built-in services — available in CompuServe as well — and GeoCities. We suggest that you start with AOL's tools if you have that choice.

Why? The answer isn't really that AOL's tools are better; they're roughly equivalent to the GeoCities tools. The difference is community. Most AOL users spend more time in AOL's online forums than on the open Web. And in those open forums you can quickly get answers to your questions about using AOL's tools to get your initial Web page up, then improve it from there. The same goes for CompuServe.

If you're already an America Online user and are still on Version 3.0 or 4.0 of the service, do upgrade to the latest version before proceeding. All it will cost you is a little time, and you'll get access to the Web publishing capabilities described in this chapter.

Use this chapter to get started with the America Online tools and create your first Web page. Then use the more advanced information later in this book and the online forums in America Online to push your page to the next level.

Looking into What AOL Offers

America Online has several parts to their Web publishing service:

- **1-2-3 Publish:** 1-2-3 Publish lets you use a template to quickly create your first Web page. It removes most of the initial barriers of getting a Web page up quickly and easily. However, it doesn't let you create your own custom Web page design or work in HTML. 1-2-3 Publish is also available on CompuServe.

✔ **Easy Designer:** Easy Designer is the next step up from 1-2-3 Publish. It lets you drag and drop text and images and use HTML to extend the capabilities of your page. (Easy Designer replaces the Personal Publisher and Personal Publisher 3 services from previous versions of the AOL software.)

✔ **Verio services:** For a really big site, AOL has integrated Web hosting services from Verio, a major Web hosting provider, into its offering. The good news for you is that you get some Verio services free, and others at a discount, by accessing them through AOL.

We recommend that you use 1-2-3 Publish to get that all-important first Web page up, then continue editing your Web page with Easy Designer. The next section tells you how to create your first Web page with 1-2-3 Publish; it should take 30 minutes or less. You can follow the instructions for 1-2-3 Publish in CompuServe as well. If you already know something about Web page creation and want to go straight to a more challenging environment, try Easy Designer first. (At this writing, you don't have access to Easy Designer from CompuServe.)

Planning Before You Start

Putting up your first home page using AOL's 1-2-3 Publish tool takes only a few minutes, because you skip so many hassles that normally come with Web publishing. But, as with the GeoCities process in Chapter 3, you can help yourself by doing a few things in preparation:

✔ **Visit AOL Hometown Web pages.** To see other users' Hometown Web pages, click the Keyword button at the top of the AOL screen. Type Hometown in the Keyword window that appears, and then click Go. You'll see the AOL Hometown main page, which allows you to search for Web pages by keyword, or to visit Web pages in various communities.

✔ **Find out more about AOL Hometown by looking at Hometown-related Web pages.** You can learn more about Hometown by looking at the instructions for beginners; clicking on the Create, Edit, and similar links at the bottom of the Web page; or examining all the templates. Return to the Hometown main page to get started.

✔ **Look for the URLs of your favorite Web sites.** Many AOL Hometown templates let you list links to several of your favorite Web sites — but to link to them, you need the URLs. Surf around the Web and find the URLs of several sites that reflect your interests, or of sites of friends or family members. (The more obscure your favorites are, the better!)

✔ **Plan your page.** Use a word processing program or a few pieces of notebook paper to plan your initial Web page. (Use the paper for drawing only — neither origami nor paper airplanes translate well to the Web.)

Rough out what text you want to put in and what URLs to include. Then you can be ready to focus on the mechanics of getting the Web page right.

✔ **Scan a picture.** Many personal Web pages look much better with a picture — of you, or of something relating to the topic you're interested in. Scan in a picture of yourself and use an image editing program such as Photoshop to save it in a Web-ready format such as GIF or JPEG. (For more on graphics for the Web, see Chapter 9.) If you lack appropriate software, go to a copy shop, such as Kinko's, that rents scanners and time on personal computers with appropriate software. You can also ask your photo developer to put your pictures on disk; several nationwide chains do this.

For users' convenience, try to reduce the file size of the picture to 30K or less before adding it to your Web page. (A 30K image takes about 10 seconds to download when a user is viewing your page with a 56K modem.)

Getting a Start with 1-2-3 Publish

Beginning Web publishers can choose 1-2-3 Publish, the very easy-to-use tool that helps you put a Web page up fast, or Easy Designer, a more flexible tool that helps you do more with your Web page. Easy Designer can work with Web pages that you create initially in 1-2-3 Publish.

You can get to 1-2-3 Publish in CompuServe by typing **ourworld** in the Web address bar at the top of the CompuServe application window and then pressing Return. Then click the 1-2-3 Publish link in the upper-right corner. (The text link says "3 Steps to Happiness.") This takes you to roughly Step 5 in the following steps.

1-2-3 Publish offers the best of both worlds: an easy-to-use tool that isn't limiting, because you can use Easy Designer, add-ons that AOL makes available, or HTML to improve your initial page. Follow these steps to create your first Web page with 1-2-3 Publish:

1. **Start America Online.**

   The Welcome screen will appear.

2. **Click on the Computer Center channel.**

   The AOL Computer Center channel, consisting largely of C|NET content, appears. (C|NET is a major Web site for computing content and a partner of AOL.)

3. **Click on Web Building, Search underneath the Internet heading in the lower-left area of the screen.**

   The AOL Computer Center Build Your Web Page area appears, as shown in Figure 2-4

Figure 2-4:
AOL gives
you
a toolbox
full of ways
to start.

4. **From the Build Your Web Page screen in AOL, click on the Easy Web Pages tab.**

   The Easy Web Pages tab lets you get started with 1-2-3 Publish or Easy Designer.

5. **Click on Build Your 1-2-3 Publish Page.**

   The 1-2-3 Publish starting screen appears, as shown in Figure 2-5.

6. **Scroll down and examine all the different templates to see what options are available.**

   You can use one of the top-level templates or one of the more specific templates farther down for your first Web page. However, for the purposes of this exercise, we're going to avoid the other templates and use the "first home page" template.

7. **Click on the link, Your First Home Page.**

   A page with a series of steps will appear, as shown in Figure 2-6. The next section describes how to follow these steps.

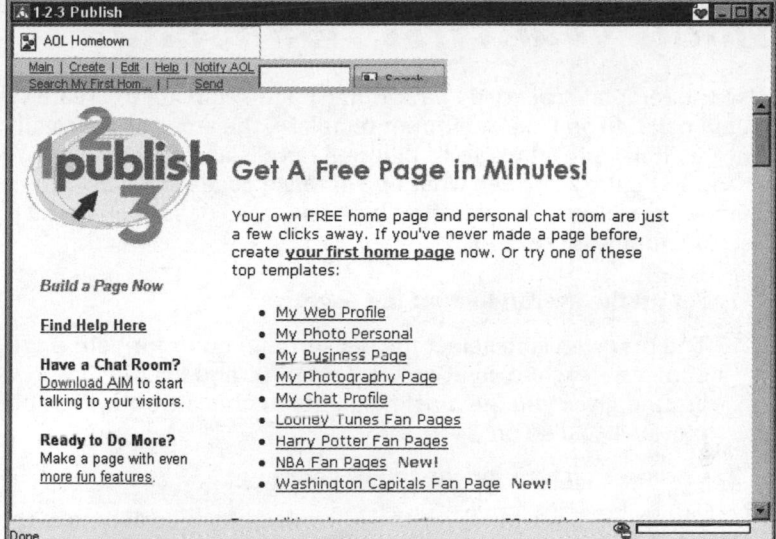

Figure 2-5:
1-2-3
Publish
gives you
scores of
choices.

Figure 2-6:
You're just a
few steps
away from
your Web
page.

Publishing Your First Home Page

Use the template called My First Home Page Template to create your first home page. (If you use a different template, the steps are basically the same, but you'll have to adjust to fit different details as you go along.) You can look ahead to Figure 2-8 to see what one of these pages looks like. Once you've reached the screen for your first home page, as described in the previous section, follow these steps:

1. **Set up the overall look of the page.**

   The first step is to select the background color for your page. The choices are white, light green, light pink, and light yellow. A white background gives you the most flexibility in choosing other graphics, adding pictures, and so on.

2. **Choose a picture for the top of your page.**

   The choices are My favorites, My quick bio, blue asterisks (no words), Welcome to my page, I recommend, and blank. Pick the picture that best fits the content you plan to put on your Web page.

3. **Add a title and a picture to your page.**

   Enter a title that describes your page. Include a keyword that people can search with — if your page includes information about your interest in horses, put "horses" in the title. Or put your name in the title to make it easy for your friends to search for your site.

   You can also upload a picture for your site. Click the Browse button to search your hard drive for a picture. To learn more about Web graphics, see Chapter 9.

4. **Choose a divider style.**

   Choose one of the six divider styles. This is a very important choice, because the divider between sections has a surprisingly strong effect on the overall look of your Web page. The first style, greenish dots, has a color scheme that matches the first picture, My favorites, which appears at the top of your page. The second style, orange and blue dots, goes with the second choice, My quick bio, or the fourth choice, Welcome to my page. The third choice, a bar of pastel colors, the fourth choice, a blue and white leaf design, and the fifth choice, a set of purple curlicues, don't really go with any of the top-of-page images. The final choice, no divider, goes with anything — but doesn't help break up your page.

5. **Enter one to three sections of text.**

   Here's the beef of your page. Enter a title and text for up to three sections describing you, your interests, hobbies, and so on. Enter a title and basic facts about you, your interests, your hobbies, your friends, or more specific topics such as your work history. Take some time with this; this is really where your Web page will stand or fall in terms of being interesting to other people.

Unlike in other entry-level Web services, HTML tags do not work within 1-2-3 Publish. You can't use HTML tags to format your Web page.

6. **Add links to your page.**

Enter the name and URL of three links that you want to put in your Web page. Your favorite links are like your gift to the Web community, giving people who share your interests quick access to the most valuable resources you've found. Enter Web pages that you like and use a lot and that other people might not already be familiar with. Also, choose links that relate to the text you entered above. (You can add to this list later, using other tools.)

7. **Decide whether to add special features to your page.**

Choose whether to allow AOL to run ads on your page — you're more likely to irritate people than to make big bucks — and whether to let your Web page visitors reach you via Instant Messenger (IM for short). If you like IM, this might be a fun addition.

8. **Click the Preview My Page button.**

Your Web page will appear! It has a special box at the top that allows you to go back and change the page (by clicking Modify) or save it to the Web (by clicking Save). Figure 2-7 shows the very simple Web page one of the authors created as an example.

9. **Continue to modify and preview your page until it's ready, and then choose Save.**

Your Web page now will be published on the Web! You'll see a Congratulations page, as shown in Figure 2-8, and the Web address of your new page. Write it down or save it in a safe place, and tell your friends!

All about the Benjamins?

AOL offers you the opportunity to make money for including an AOL ad banner in your page. The idea is that, whenever someone visits your Web page, they'll see an ad banner inviting them to join AOL. If they do so, and stay 90 days or more, AOL will pay you "up to" $15. (That's almost a "Benjamin," a U.S. $20 bill which has Benjamin Franklin's picture on it.) Don't do it! Don't add to the clutter and annoy the friends and family who will probably be your first Web page visitors by including an ad with your first Web page.

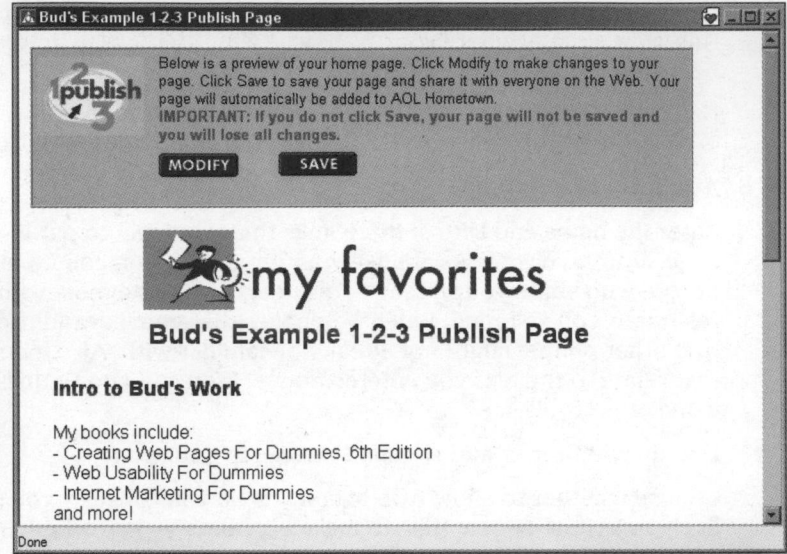

Figure 2-7:
Bud's
sample
1-2-3
Publish
Web page.

You can also make other changes, such as moving your Web page to a different area within AOL's home page categories. Click around on the Congratulations page and investigate the different options.

Use the link, "Send this page to friends and family," to get the word out. When you click on this link, you can enter e-mail addresses of several people, who will receive a link back to your home page.

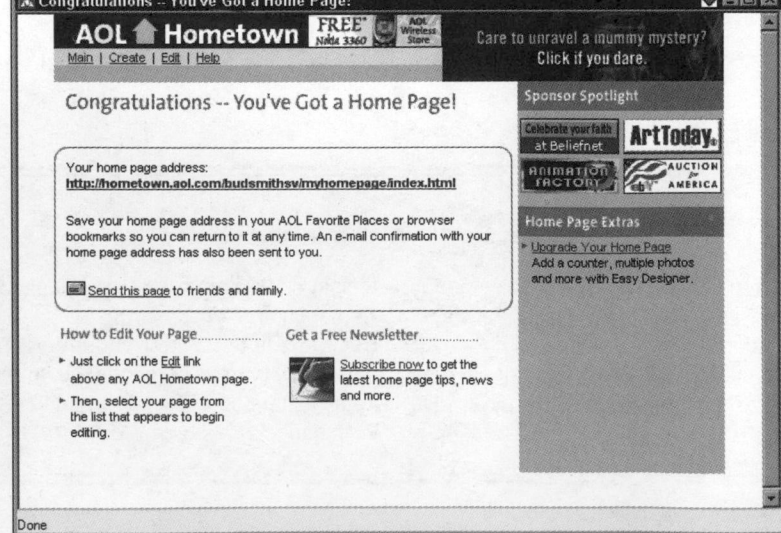

Figure 2-8:
AOL gives
you your
URL and
offers ways
to change
your page.

10. **To modify your page in the future, return to the Build Your Own Web Page screen in AOL. Then click the 1-2-3 Publish link at the bottom.**

    You'll be returned to 1-2-3 Publish and be able to modify your page.

To be able to see your Web page quickly, click on the link for your home page to make it appear in a Web browser window. Then click the Favorites icon at the top of the AOL screen. Choose Add Top Window to Favorite Places, and you'll always be able to return to your Web page again.

After you take your page as far as you can with 1-2-3 Publish — which may take awhile because the tool is pretty capable — you can move up to Easy Designer. Easy Designer allows you much more flexibility in the content and layout of your Web page, with drag-and-drop editing and placement of text and graphics.

Just use the steps at the beginning of this chapter to choose a tool, but choose Easy Designer instead of 1-2-3 Publish. You can choose the Web page you developed with 1-2-3 Publish as your starting point for work in Easy Designer.

Once you edit a page in Easy Designer, you can no longer edit it further in 1-2-3 Publish. So be sure you've taken your Web page as far as you want to in 1-2-3 Publish before editing it with Easy Designer.

Chapter 3

Going Worldwide with GeoCities

Getting your first page up on the Web seems like a tall order. So it may be hard to believe just how easy it is to get started. With the free Web-based publishing services we describe in this chapter, you can have your first Web page up within a couple of hours — at no cost. You don't have to figure out everything about HTML, you don't have to deal with typical publishing complexities, and did we mention that you don't have to pay anything?

If you're a member of America Online (AOL), you can use free AOL Web publishing tools to get a Web page up quickly and easily, as we describe in Chapter 2. AOL has the advantage of built-in support for your Web page efforts from the same help resources — including your fellow online service members — that you're already familiar with. So if you're a member of America Online, consider starting your Web page creation effort with Chapter 2.

If not, though, you have an alternative that's just as good: Yahoo!'s GeoCities site. GeoCities is the most popular site for free personal Web page publishing and has offered this service for more than six years. Since its inception, GeoCities has hosted the creation of more than 5,000,000 — yes, that's 5 *million* — personal Web page sites, with thousands of new sites added each day. And now that GeoCities has been acquired by Yahoo!, it has the resources to keep on growing for quite awhile to come.

GeoCities' high level of popularity means that their service is extremely popular with visitors as well as publishers. It also means that their advertising-supported, self-publishing model is so successful that it's likely to be around for a long time to come. (Other services featured in earlier editions of this book have since disappeared, a testament to the rapid rate of change on the Web.)

Follow the instructions in this chapter to become a Web page publisher on GeoCities. You can be a Web publisher in less time than most people take to start thinking hard about how to get their first home page published on the Web.

Start with a GeoCities Web Page

Putting up a personal Web page accomplishes a lot of things. For one, it's fun. Millions of people have gotten a real kick out of sharing information about themselves and their interests with their fellow Web users by putting up a Web page. Many personal Web pages that initially start out quite simple evolve into large and popular Web sites focused on topics of every imaginable sort. As the number of Web users increases, more and more of your colleagues, family, and friends can see your Web page, as can (of course) tens of millions of complete strangers.

Creating a personal Web page is also very valuable in helping you find out how to publish on the Web. Until you publish something on the Web, you may find the notion that you can actually do it hard to believe. After you put up your first Web page, you may find the notion that anything can stop you from doing it again hard to believe! The initial success of getting up your personal Web page will spill over into all your future Web efforts.

Now, you may feel that you should start out with a business Web site, a home page for a nonprofit organization, or something similarly serious. But the business or serious approach has a couple of problems:

- The "barriers to entry" — if we may use a marketing term — for a site that represents an organization are much higher because you're taking on a more complex task, and many people need to be involved.

- For a more serious site, the quality of your work has much more impact because you're representing a larger cause than just your personal interests. So your fear of failure is greater. And you're undertaking this important task with no background and no experience, which will make it hard to get anything worthwhile done.

- Finally, Web space for business sites almost always costs money. So you have a buying decision to make before you can even get started — yet another barrier.

So get on the Web first with a simple, personal Web page. Discover something new, have some fun, and prepare now for more ambitious endeavors later. And GeoCities is just the place to do it.

Check out Yahoo! GeoCities

To see what other people have done with their personal Web sites, visit GeoCities right now at

```
http://geocities.yahoo.com
```

Figure 3-1 shows the initial home page for GeoCities. Yahoo!, after buying GeoCities, put their name on the pages too. Don't be alarmed if you see something slightly different for the home page; GeoCities, like any popular Web site, often updates its home page. Even if the GeoCities home page has changed, the instructions in this chapter are likely to still be valid.

You can check the Web site for this book at www.dummies.com for any updates needed to keep up with changes in the site.

GeoCities initially organized the Web pages that users created into *neighborhoods,* with each neighborhood hosting home pages from people with a specific set of shared interests. However, Yahoo! has stopped supporting the neighborhoods idea; only people who created Web pages on GeoCities in the 1990s can still use them. As a new GeoCities user, you'll get a Web address based on the Yahoo! user ID that you get when you first visit GeoCities.

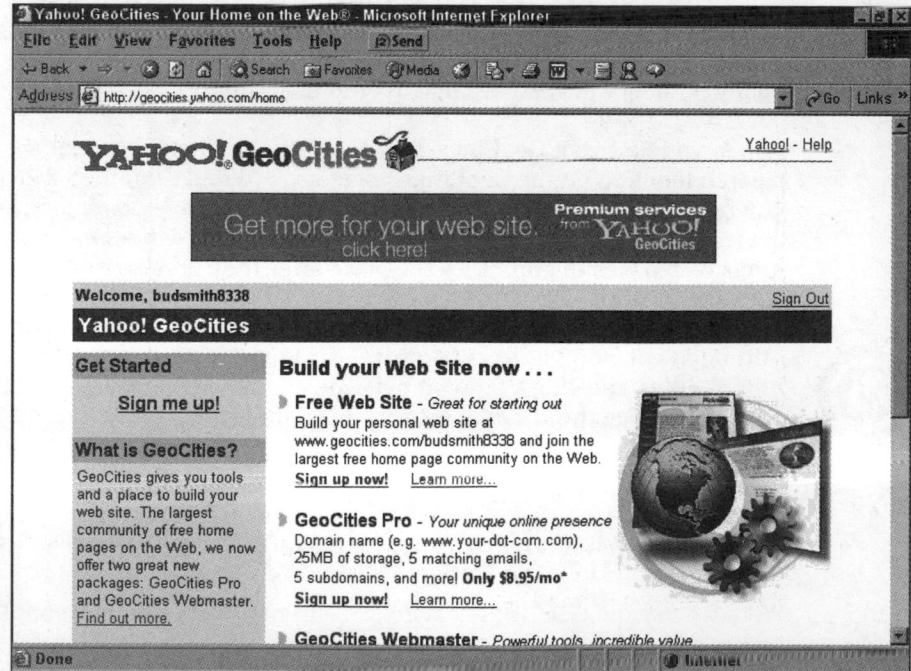

Figure 3-1: GeoCities is the home of more than 5 million personal Web pages.

GeoCities or online service?

If you are a user of an online service such as America Online, you have the option of creating a free personal Web page on GeoCities, on your online service, or on both. We recommend that online service users put their first Web page on their online service. Why?

The first and foremost reason is support. Online services are great sources of help for all kinds of online concerns, not least of which is getting your first Web page up and running. You can easily get a lot of help from your fellow members and from the support personnel of your online service.

Second is familiarity. You're already familiar with your online service. You're more able to take advantage of its free services than the services in any other kind of setup, even one as friendly and open as GeoCities.

Third is community. Online services try to foster a sense of community, as does Yahoo! with GeoCities. If you're a person who values this feeling, you probably have already developed it within your online service; you may as well take advantage of the community that you're already paying for!

So if you're an AOL user, go back to Chapter 2 and follow the instructions for creating and hosting a free Web page. If not, you don't need to join an online service just to get free Web hosting service; GeoCities is fast, easy, and fun.

Your Web page's Web address will be in the following form: www.geocities.com/*youruserid*. This is simpler than the Web addresses that GeoCities used to give people, which included the name of the neighborhood the user chose as well as a specific site number. If you look at existing GeoCities Web pages, many of them will still have neighborhood addresses.

When you first visit GeoCities, tour the GeoCities neighborhoods, and use the Search function on the GeoCities home page to find GeoCities Web pages that are not in neighborhoods. See what other people have done; look at some pages that are still initial efforts, and then see what others have done with their Web pages to spruce up the place after they first arrived!

Tear out the Cheat Sheet at the front of this book and tape it to the wall! Although you don't need to know HTML to use the services we describe in this chapter, knowing a little bit of HTML can help you make your initial page look better. See the Cheat Sheet for a list of tags that can spruce up your initial Web page.

Follow the city ordinances

You can use the GeoCities easy-to-use editing tool to create a simple home page quickly and easily. You can then use HTML, FTP (see Chapter 12), and other tools to create and transfer more sophisticated pages to build almost any kind of Web site you want, up to 15MB in size. But you have to keep in mind the restrictions listed in Yahoo!'s Terms of Service:

✔ **Not for your business:** You can't use this free Web page service for a business home page, although you can mention your business on your free personal home page. (Some people use their free personal Web pages to "mention" their businesses an awful lot.) That means you can't sell products or services, advertise, conduct raffles, or display advertising or sponsorship banners. You can, however, use Yahoo!-supported partnership programs that allow you to get paid for books, music, and other goods sold on your site. For details on what you can't do, check the Terms of Service at

```
docs.yahoo.com/info/terms/geoterms.html
```

If you do want a business Web site, try Yahoo!'s premium Web site programs. You can access them from the GeoCities home page at

```
geocities.yahoo.com
```

✔ **No monkey business:** Yahoo! imposes restrictions on what you can publish; obscenity, harmful or abusive content, libel, and invasion of privacy are prohibited, among other things. Check the Terms of Service at the URL given just above for details.

✔ **No more than 15MB:** All your Web files together must occupy no more than 15MB of disk space, which is about 15,000 pages of text or about 100 large, quarter-screen graphics. This restriction is not a problem for single Web pages, because only one Web page is almost certainly well below the limit. If you expand your Web page into a multi-page site and the limit becomes a problem for you, you can get more disk space and other goodies from Yahoo!'s premium Web site programs, which are mentioned on the GeoCities home page.

✔ **No guarantees:** Yahoo! doesn't guarantee that it will continue to provide free Web page service in the future. (The company has to include this disclaimer to protect itself from unanticipated events, but all indications are that it does indeed plan to continue this free service for quite awhile.) If Yahoo! does stop offering GeoCities, or even if you just find another hosting site you like better, you can always set up shop there instead. For now, the point is to take advantage of a valuable opportunity.

Web tools versus Web services

A *Web publishing tool,* such as Netscape Composer, is a program that helps you prepare content for the Web. A *Web publishing service* is a support function that handles part of the process of Web publishing for you, such as hosting your Web page(s) on a server. The Web publishing services we describe in this chapter and Chapter 2 also include online tools for preparing your Web page(s), but the free Web page hosting service they provide is most notable, so we refer to them as services rather than tools.

Plan Before You Begin

Putting up your home page on GeoCities takes only an hour or so — not bad for getting a free Web page set up, hosted, and published! Even so, doing a few things before you begin makes the process easier, more pleasant, and more productive:

- ✔ **Visit GeoCities Web pages.** GeoCities does a good job of helping you get your initial Web page up, but don't you want to see what others have done before you get started? Use the Search function and the categories of Web sites to find Web pages related to your interests.

- ✔ **Find out more about GeoCities in general by clicking and navigating around GeoCities-related Web pages in the Yahoo! Web site.** You can discover a lot about GeoCities by clicking around and reading press releases, the Terms of Service, and so on. One thing you may not discover is how Yahoo! can afford to give away free Web space through GeoCities. The answer is that free Web pages are a powerful way for sites like Yahoo! to attract and retain users for their other services. Also, Yahoo! places advertising on Web pages built in GeoCities; this means that Yahoo! makes a few cents every time someone (including you) looks at your home page.

- ✔ **Look for the URLs of your favorite Web sites.** Many GeoCities templates let you list links to several of your favorite Web sites — but to link to them, you need the URLs. Recall some of your favorite sites — they may be listed in you Web bookmarks — and write down the site names and URLs for use in creating your Web page. (It's much easier to do this research in advance than at the time you're creating your Web page.)

- ✔ **Look for the URLs of Web sites of friends and family members.** The Personal Page template that is used in the example later in this chapter gives you space to list the descriptions and URLs for one to four Web sites of friends and family members. Get the URLs before you start.

- ✔ **Plan your initial Web page.** In a word processing program or on paper, rough out the text and Web links for your initial Web page. This way you're ready to go when it comes time to actually get your page up.

- ✔ **Scan a picture.** Get a picture or other image onto your hard disk, in GIF or JPEG format, so you can easily upload it as part of your Web page. The picture should either be of you, or related to the topic you're interested in. Kinko's and other copy shops have hardware and software you can rent for this purpose if you don't have everything you need at home. Chapter 9 tells you a great deal about Web graphics.

Get Registered

The steps you need to follow to sign up for a GeoCities Web page may change after we complete this book. If so, go to www.dummies.com and look up the update page for this book to get the latest instructions.

If you don't live in one of the 50 states in the United States, click on the link Non-US Sign up form. You will be given a slightly different page than the one for U.S. residents. We wrote the following instructions so as to apply to either form.

The first step in setting up your GeoCities Web page is to apply for a Yahoo! user ID number. This user ID will enable you to use a variety of services on Yahoo! and, if you're not careful, to receive e-mail solicitations you don't really want. If you don't already have a Yahoo! user ID, follow these steps to set up your Yahoo! user ID and start using GeoCities:

1. **Open your Web browser.**

   The GeoCities Web site works with any browser.

2. **Go to** geocities.yahoo.com.

   The screen shown in Figure 3-1, or something very much like it, appears.

3. **If you are currently signed in as a member of Yahoo!, your user name will appear on the Web page you see. Skip the rest of the steps in this section.**

   If you are a member of Yahoo! but are not currently signed in, sign in by entering your Yahoo! ID and Password under the header, Sign In to Yahoo!, and then clicking Sign In. Then skip the rest of the steps in this section.

   If you are not yet a member of Yahoo!, click on the Get Started! link in the lower-left corner of the browser window.

   If you click on the Get Started! link, the screen named Sign up for your Yahoo ID! appears, as shown in Figure 3-2.

4. **Enter your desired Yahoo! ID and password. Retype your password.**

It's pretty unlikely that any Yahoo! ID that you would find desirable, like your first name and last name ("budsmith" for one of the authors), or your favorite sports team ("sfgiants," for instance), is available — one of Yahoo!'s existing tens of millions of users probably already got it. To save yourself a bunch of retries, pick a user name that makes sense, but is likely to be unique, such as your first and last name followed by the name of your state or hometown. Try to make it memorable, too — your home page's URL will be in the form `www.geocities.com/`, followed by your Yahoo! ID.

For your password, use three or more characters.

5. **Enter information in case you forget your password.**

Use the pull-down menu to select a question that Yahoo! will prompt you with if you forget your password. Enter your answer, your birthday (with a four-digit year, such as 1978), and your current e-mail address. (Enter your real birthday — "Always tell the truth, so you don't have to try to remember what you told people.")

"He tried, but he couldn't do it" — despite our best efforts, we were unable to get GeoCities to accept a Yahoo! e-mail address as the contact e-mail address for a GeoCities Web page. You will have to use a different e-mail account, not a Yahoo.com account. You can use an existing personal or work e-mail address or a friend's e-mail address. Or you can get a new, free e-mail account at `www.hotmail.com` (the most popular source for free e-mail), or any of several other sites on the Web.

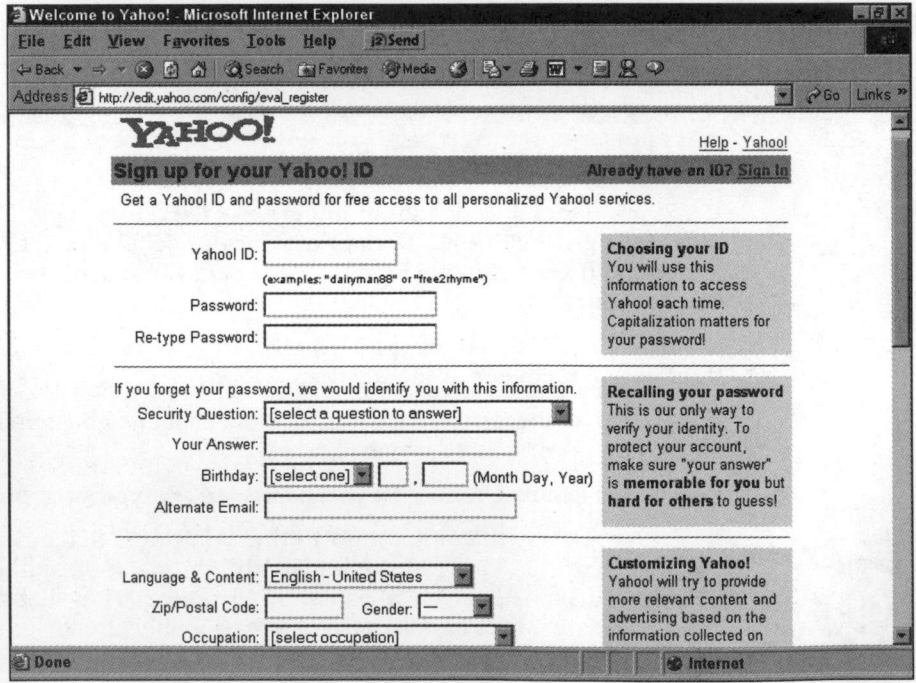

Figure 3-2:
Sign me up
for Yahoo!
GeoCities.

Yahoo! for privacy?

Yahoo! follows certain policies relating to your privacy. Some of the highlights:

✔ **No opt-in guarantee:** Some Web sites now promise not to put you on e-mail lists unless you opt in — take some affirmative action, such as checking a checkbox, to put yourself in spam's way. As of this writing, Yahoo! doesn't do this. So it's easy, when signing up for a Yahoo! service, to accidentally put yourself on an e-mail list that will then be used to send you advertising.

✔ **TRUSTe-certified:** Yahoo! is TRUSTe-certified. This means that Yahoo! has submitted a privacy statement to TRUSTe, an industry privacy organization. TRUSTe is not a strong organization at this point, but at least Yahoo!, through TRUSTe, has committed itself to putting its policy statement in writing and letting you see it.

✔ **Use of information:** Yahoo! uses the information you give it, and the information it gathers from the choices you make in using Yahoo!, to customize your Web-surfing experience to your interests and to send you customized e-mail.

✔ **Sharing with partners:** Yahoo! doesn't actually transfer data about you to partners without your permission. However, partners' agreements with Yahoo! may include access to you through Yahoo!.

✔ **Changing your information:** To change your account information, log into Yahoo! with your user ID and password, then go to `edit.my.yahoo.com/config/eval_profile`. There, you can change your account preferences to stop receiving e-mail offers or update your personal information and preferences.

6. **Enter your personal account information. Clear the "Contact me occasionally" checkbox if you don't want advertising from Yahoo! in your e-mail.**

   Choose your language-country combination, such as English - United States. Enter your ZIP code or postal code, your gender, your occupation, and the industry you work in. If you don't want Yahoo! to send you advertising to your e-mail account, clear the checkbox that says "Contact me occasionally about special offers, promotions, and Yahoo! features."

   Be sure to uncheck the checkbox unless you want to receive advertising e-mail from Yahoo! and its partners. Many Web sites have agreed to present boxes such as this one with the option unchecked, so only people who make the effort to click on the checkbox get signed up, but Yahoo! makes you do the unchecking yourself. See the sidebar, "Yahoo! for privacy?," for more.

7. **If you want to, indicate areas of interest to you.**

   You have the option of clicking on areas of interest to you by putting a check in each relevant checkbox. Like the pull-down menus for customizing Yahoo!, the Interests checkboxes help Yahoo! customize news and information for you on the Yahoo! site. The information also helps Yahoo! and its partners target e-mail they send you (if you don't uncheck the checkbox), ads they put on Web pages that you view, and otherwise personalize their marketing efforts to you.

8. **Type in the word shown onscreen.**

   Type the word shown onscreen. This is for Yahoo!'s benefit, a step to make sure a real person is filling out the registration.

9. **If you want to read the GeoCities Terms of Service, the Yahoo! Privacy Policy, or Yahoo Privacy Information, right-click on the link to open them in a separate window. Otherwise, or after you're finished, click the Submit This Form button.**

   If you click on this link with a regular mouse click, the GeoCities' Terms of Service replaces your current browser window contents. If you click the Back button in the browser window to return to the signup screen, everything you entered so far will be gone! If you make this mistake — which is all too easy to do — repeat Steps 4 through 8.

   Once you click Submit This Form, you'll be taken to a new Web page, titled Build Your Own Web Site. Read all about it in the next section.

You can reach the GeoCities Web site by typing the URL www.geocities.com into your browser's address window. The address is automatically remapped to geocities.yahoo.com/home. Web sites often give simpler Web addresses to the public, but remap them to other internal Web addresses for their own convenience. You can continue to use the www.geocities.com address as a starting point for your own ease of use.

Begin Building Your Web Site

Once you're signed in, the Build Your Own Web Site page will appear, as shown in Figure 3-3. Follow these instructions to get started.

1. **Under Free Web Site, choose Sign up now!.**

   The Free Web Site option will give you a free home page with the URL www.geocities.com/*yourname*, where *yourname* is your Yahoo! User ID. You may want to use one of the paid options later, but you will probably want a free Web site to use for practice in any case.

   Once you click Sign Up Now, the Sign up for your Home Page page appears.

2. **Choose a topic for your Web page.**

   Carefully choose a topic for your Web page. Yahoo! will display advertising relating to this topic on your Web page, so choose carefully. (The right kind of advertising can actually "ad" value to your page — pun intended.)

3. **Enter the security code shown onscreen.**

   As in the Yahoo! User ID signup, this helps Yahoo! make sure a real person is signing up.

4. **Click the Submit This Form button.**

   A Congratulations Web page appears, as shown in Figure 3-4.

5. **Write down your Yahoo! ID and password and your new home page's Web address.**

   Yahoo! will send you an e-mail explaining steps to take to begin creating your Web page. In the next section, we'll start giving you our own take on the process.

6. **Click on the link, Build your page now!.**

   The front page of the Yahoo! GeoCities Web site will appear, but this time with your user name in the upper-left corner and your Web page's URL in the upper right. Follow the steps in the next section to begin building your Web page.

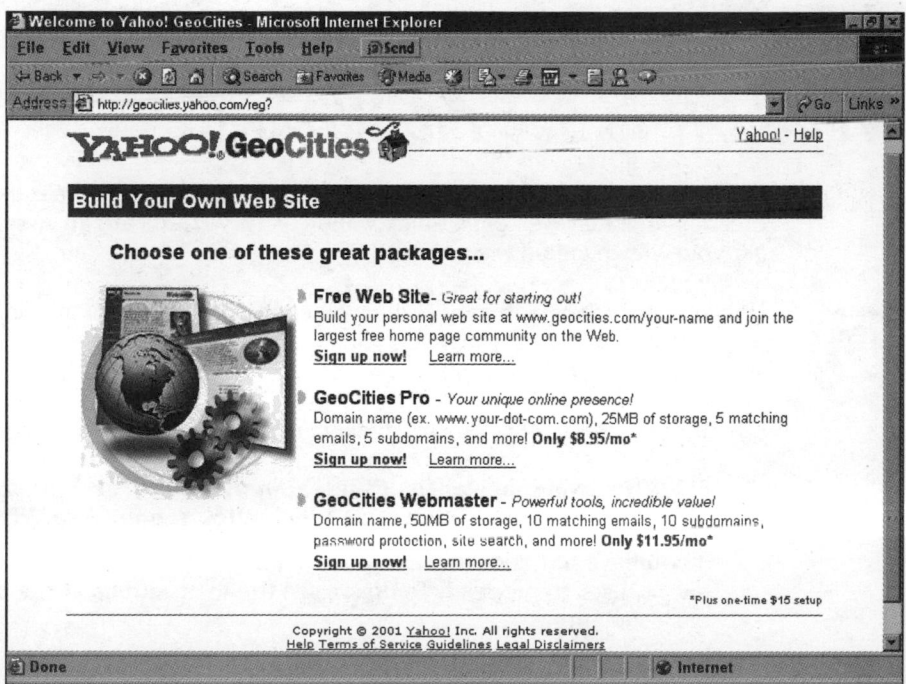

Figure 3-3: Choose the freebie!

Figure 3-4:
When you
see this,
you're in.

We're Off to See the Wizard

GeoCities has recently introduced a new feature, Yahoo! PageWizards, for creating an initial Web page quickly and easily. Wizards are an easy way to get your Web page off the ground.

Unlike many other Web page tools, you cannot enter HTML tags in the text within Yahoo! Wizards. However, you can edit your Web page later and add HTML tags, as described in Part II.

Use the Yahoo! PageWizards to quickly create your initial Web page:

1. **From the front page of GeoCities, at** www.geocities.com, **make sure you're signed in (see above) and then click Yahoo! PageWizards.**

   If you have not done so already, you'll have to become a registered Yahoo! user to proceed. To do so, see the instructions at the beginning of this chapter.

   If you're a registered user, the Yahoo! PageWizards page, part of which is shown in Figure 3-5, appears.

Figure 3-5:
We're off
to see the
(Page)
Wizards.

2. Click the Personal Page link.

Getting the right wizard can save you a lot of time, so it's worth looking at as much information as possible before choosing. For the purposes of this chapter, we'll describe how to use the Personal Page Wizard; if you want to try a different wizard, roughly the same steps will apply, but you'll need to work around the differences.

The choices, at this writing, include

- **Photo Page:** If you have a few digital photographs handy — or can get your local photo processor to convert your next roll to digital format — this is a fun choice to start out with.

- **Quick Start:** A group of page templates with roughly the same information about you but each with a distinctive look.

- **Sanrio Themes:** Copyrighted cartoon graphics liven up these simple page designs. These are great for kids to use.

- **Baby Announcement:** Great if you just had a little one; not much use otherwise. If you do this, make sure to include a picture! See Chapter 9 for details.

- **Birthday or Party Invitation:** This is fun to do, but online invitation services such as eVite (www.evite.com) will also help you put up an event Web page, plus help you handle the inevitable e-mail messaging back and forth. Either this wizard or the eVite-type approach is a good option.

- **Personal Page:** This is the best choice for most people who want to quickly create their own page. You have four choices of color — and yes, you can replace the little stick figure with a picture.

3. **Click the link, Launch Yahoo! PageWizard.**

   The Build Your Personal Page screen, shown in Figure 3-6, will appear. It shows the six areas that you'll be customizing: Your name and e-mail address, your image (or you can keep the stick figure!), a brief personal description with your hobbies and interests, a list of favorite links (up to four), and a list of friends and family links.

4. **Click on the Begin button.**

   A screen that allows you to choose a look for your page will appear: green, blue, yellow, or pink. Choose one.

5. **Choose a color and then click Next.**

   Now you're ready to actually create your page. The next section tells you how.

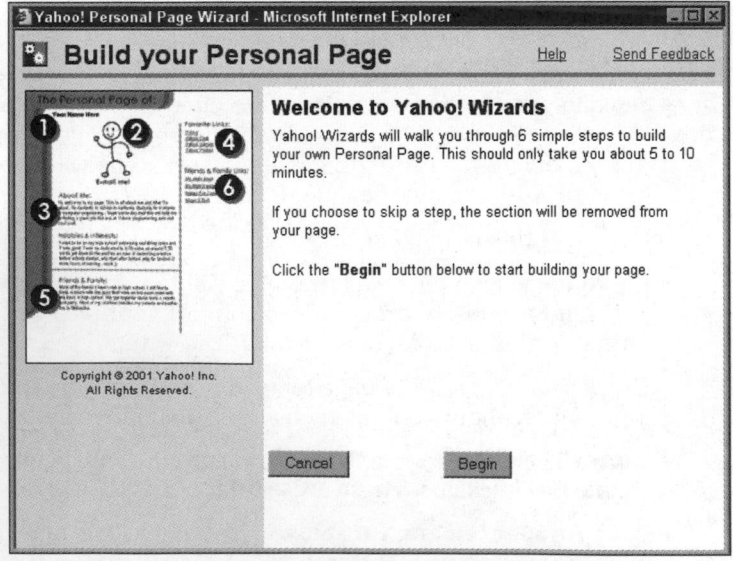

Figure 3-6: Six items, six minutes, one home page.

Six Steps to Success

Once you launch Yahoo! PageWizard, as described in the previous section, you're just six quick and easy steps away from having your own Web page. Let's get going:

1. **Enter your name and the e-mail address you want to have appear on your Web page, and then click Next.**

   If you don't want to publish your work e-mail address, or heavily used personal e-mail address, on the Web — where it might be copied into spammers' lists — consider creating a Yahoo! e-mail account for the purpose of publication. Go to mail.yahoo.com to sign up; if you do create a new address, remember to check it.

   At any point in the wizard process, you can preview your page as you build it. Just click the Preview button where it's available. You can close the preview when you're finished with it; just don't close the underlying Personal Page Wizard browser window!

   After you click Next, the Pick Your Picture Web page appears.

2. **Choose a picture — a picture you upload, the default stick figure image, or no picture. Then click Next.**

   If you want to upload a picture, GeoCities allows you to pick any image from your hard disk in any of the following Windows formats: .jpg (JPEG), .gif (GIF), .tif (TIFF), .bmp (Windows Bitmap), or .png (Portable Network Graphics). See Chapter 9 for more on these formats and on obtaining images. (Once you've uploaded one or more pictures, you can use them by choosing them from the "Pick from GeoCities" drop-down menu.)

   Don't publish an image you don't have rights to on your Web page. No sense in inviting a call from someone's lawyer.

   After you click the Next button, the Describe Yourself Web page appears.

3. **Enter a description to appear under the header "About Me" and a list of your hobbies to appear under "Hobbies and Interests," and then click Next.**

   In the description of yourself, leave out hobbies and interests; they're in the next section. You may want to include where you were born and live, what kind of work you do, and similar information. Don't give too much information, though; a scam artist can get credit in your name with just a few pieces of data such as your full name, address, and mother's maiden name.

In the Hobbies and Interests text box, keep it brief, for now, but make it interesting; your hobbies and interests may be as individual to you as your fingerprint.

After you click Next, the Enter your favorite links Web page appears.

4. **Enter a description and the URL for up to four of your favorite Web links and then click Next.**

Enter several favorite links. And don't worry about the small number of links; you can change the links later, or add more links using other tools.

After you click Next, the Describe your friends and family Web page appears.

5. **Type in a description of your friends and family, and then click Next.**

Say something about your family — the one you came from, as well as your spouse and kids, if you have such. Emphasize anyone who has a personal Web page that you can link to — or anyone who will be especially thrilled to see their name on the Web, such as kids. Again, be careful about giving too much detail that scam artists could use.

After you click Next, the Enter your friends and family links Web page appears.

6. **Type in links to friends and family members' Web pages. Then click Next.**

You can link to family members' Web pages. If you don't know of any, just leave all the entries blank.

After you click Next, the Name your page Web page appears.

7. **Enter a page name for your personal page. Then click Next.**

The name you enter becomes part of your Web page's Web address. For instance, if you use the default name, personalpageblue, the Web page's complete address will be `www.geocities.com/yourname/personalpageblue.html`. We suggest you rename it something shorter, such as "mybluepage."

If you want to make this your site's home page, name it `index.htm`. (Not a bad idea; if you do this, the URL someone needs to type to reach your page is simpler: `www.geocities.com/yourname`). You can always move the page around within your site later if needed. When you click Next, the wizard will tell you that there is already a page by that name, and ask if you want to replace the page. Choose Yes.

After you click Next, the Congratulations! page appears.

8. **Click on the link to view your new Web page.**

   Your new Web page will appear in a window, as shown in Figure 3-7.

9. **Write down or save your Web address, and then return to the wizard and click Done.**

You will probably want to improve your Web page quite a bit from here, but you're off to a great start. See Chapter 5 for information on how to expand your initial Web page. But for now, send your new Web address to your friends, and take a well-deserved break!

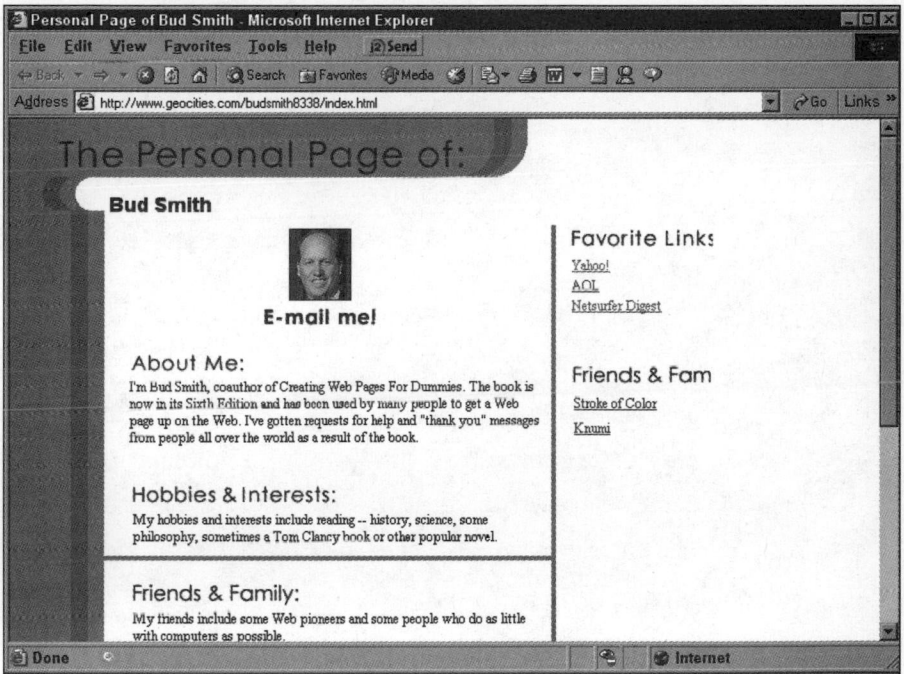

Figure 3-7: Houston, we have a Web page.

Chapter 4

Introduction to HTML

• •

In This Chapter

▶ Making it all work
▶ Understanding HTML
▶ Examining key HTML tags
▶ Creating a blank page with HTML
▶ Browsing your own little Web

• •

*K*nowing the basics of HTML is a *good* thing. HTML is the code that connects the text content of your Web page with the graphics, links, and appearance users see in a Web browser. If you know the basics of HTML, you'll understand why Web pages look and work the way they do, and you'll understand how you can create and improve your own Web page.

Why bother with HTML basics?

More and more Web authoring tools try to hide HTML from the user; you can use one of these tools to create a Web page without knowing a thing about HTML. But here are several reasons to figure out the basics of HTML:

✔ **Because everyone else is:** Bad reason. Next!

✔ **To understand how the Web works:** This understanding is pretty valuable if you're a heavy Web user (or a light one), especially if you plan to publish on the Web. Some of the Web's limitations, such as "what you see is not what you get," are hard to understand if you don't know something about HTML.

✔ **To use free Web tools:** Many free Web tools enable you to enter HTML tags directly to

jazz up your text. Knowing a few tags can go a long way.

✔ **To work directly in HTML:** Many Web pros tire of managing HTML tags by hand and start using a tool that hides the tags. Others swear by HTML. Everyone swears at HTML, at least some of the time. But the only way to have a choice is to know some HTML.

✔ **To do better work using a tool:** When you're using a tool that hides the gory details of HTML from you, it's actually an advantage to know enough HTML to understand what's going on "behind the scenes." In fact, tools that hide the HTML almost all have a mode that lets you see and work in HTML when you choose to, for just that reason.

Trying to figure out a lot of HTML right away is a *bad* thing. Spending hours and hours going over all the details of HTML is likely to slow your quest to becoming a Web publisher. And becoming a Web publisher quickly can, again, be a *good* thing. So don't let a bad thing get in the way of good things; use this chapter to find out just enough about HTML to help you create some basic pages and get them on the Web.

Get Ready: A Refreshingly Brief Description of HTML

HTML (Hypertext Markup Language) is a specific way of adding descriptive tags to regular text so that all the formatting, linking, and navigational information you need in a Web page is contained in the same file with the regular text. HTML is designed to be something that humans can read *and* that machines can process, a kind of common ground for human-to-machine communication.

Suppose you want to add bold to a word in your text, such as:

```
You can use HTML to specify that a word is bold.
```

To add formatting to a sentence using HTML, just take the regular sentence and add a couple of tags to specify where bolding starts and stops. Here's the above line in HTML:

```
You can use HTML to specify that a word is <b>bold</b>.
```

When you display the sentence with the HTML tags in a Web browser, the browser displays all the words, but not the *tags* — the information between angle brackets. The Web browser uses the tags to do extra things to the text, such as add formatting to it. In this case, the formatting is simple: Start using bold text after the word "is," and stop using bold text after the word "bold."

Because HTML tags exist alongside the text that users see on your Web page, a document with HTML tags in it is called *HTML-tagged text*. That simply means text with HTML tags in it. A file with HTML-tagged text in it is called an HTML file and usually has the extension .htm or .html at the end of the file-name. If you look at HTML-tagged text in a text editing program, you see the angle brackets and HTML commands; if you look at it in a Web browser, you see text with formatting, links, and so on.

TECHNICAL STUFF

Examining the HTML script

Take a closer look at the term for which HTML is an acronym, Hypertext Markup Language. You may already know that hypertext is text that has links in it. A *link* is just a connection to another file. So far, so good. But what's a *markup language*? (It's not that confusing language that car dealers speak when they decide how high to jack up the price!) A markup language is simply a way to put information about a document — for example, information about hypertext links and formatting — in the document itself. Markup languages often use tags — labels placed within text that give display instructions. So Hypertext Markup Language — HTML — is a specific way of using tags to convey information about a document.

Most tags in HTML come in pairs: One starts a change and the other ends it. In the following sample sentence, the first tag, `<B>`, means start displaying text in a **bold** typeface; the second tag, `</B>`, means stop using bold.

Here's how the sentence looks when "marked up" with HTML tags:

```
That's a <B>good</B> idea.
```

Here's how the sentence looks when displayed on-screen:

```
That's a good idea.
```

The browser reads the original, text-only sentence — `That's a <B>good</B> idea.` — and says to itself, "I'll display `That's a`, turn bold on, display **good**, turn bold off, and display `idea`." The person who created the original sentence puts in the HTML tags, the browser interprets them, and the user only sees the effect — in this case, the word good displayed in boldface type.

The `<B>` and `</B>` tags are *formatting tags* that describe how a browser displays text. The other kind of tag in HTML is the *linking tag.* Linking tags specify outside information to be brought into a document. Here's some complicated-looking HTML text that shows examples of formatting and linking tags:

```
To learn about <I>Pokemon</I>,
the "pocket monsters" so
popular with kids today, go
to the official Web site
for <A HREF="http://www.
pokemon.com">Pokemon</A>.
```

The text appears on-screen as follows:

```
To learn about Pokemon, the
"pocket monsters" so
popular with kids today,
go to the official Web site
for Pokemon.
```

The `<I>` and `</I>` formatting tags specify that the word *Pokemon* is to be displayed in italics. The `<A>` and `</A>` linking tags specify that Pokemon is displayed as an *anchor* — that is, the starting point of a link. On most browsers, as here, anchors are underlined. So what does the extra text — `HREF="http://www.poke-mon.com"` — inside the `<A>` tag mean? HREF is short for *Hypertext REFerence.* If you click the anchor, your browser looks for the URL that serves as the hypertext reference, which in this case is the Pokemon Web page address that appears after the equal sign.

The idea of a machine or procedure that reads a piece of input, uses that input to make a decision, carries out the decision, and then reads some more input is centuries old and has been thoroughly studied. Such a machine or program — a browser, for example — is called a *finite automaton.* (Pronounced to rhyme with "fly night oughtomaton.") Try dropping that term into your conversation the next time the Web comes up!

A document with no formatting — such as italics and other formatting added by a word processor — is called a *plain text* document. HTML-tagged text documents are considered plain text documents because the characters you see onscreen are the only characters in the document. Word processing documents that aren't plain text documents have additional formatting codes embedded in them to tell machines how to display and print the text.

You can add HTML tags to regular text to create your own Web documents in any text editor or word processing program. Or you can use a Web editing tool that hides the gory details of HTML tags.

This chapter gives you enough background to know what you're seeing when you look at text that includes HTML tags and to make a few changes in HTML-tagged text if you need to. We don't burden you with hundreds of pages of HTML tags, tips, and tricks. You can find some of the more technical details and background in the sidebar called "The helter-skelter growth of HTML." (Try it; you'll like it.) After you publish a few Web pages, you can take the time to find out more about HTML. At that point, you may want to buy yourself that 400-page HTML book.

If you like to know everything that's going on before you roll up your sleeves and plunge into things, you may want to start by looking at *HTML For Dummies*, 4th Edition, a comprehensive guide to HTML by Ed Tittel et al (Hungry Minds, Inc.).

Viewing HTML documents

You can see HTML anytime you use the Web. Just pull up a Web page in your browser and choose View➪Source for Internet Explorer, or a similar command for other browsers. A new window opens, the contents of which are the HTML source code that underlies the Web page. Figure 4-1 shows the home page of the For Dummies site and its HTML source code as an example.

Having the ability to instantly view a document's HTML code naturally leads to the temptation to borrow attractive documents from the Web, save them to your disk as HTML files, and then use them as templates for your own work — kind of a magpie approach to Web page building.

Borrowing someone else's material is okay for basic HTML formatting, but for more sophisticated formats that are distinctive and embody a great deal of work, get permission before you use them. Simply contact the Webmaster at the site you admire, describe how you want to use the format, and request permission. You may be surprised how many people say yes — without even exacting a promise from you that you hand over your firstborn.

The helter-skelter growth of HTML

HTML is a markup language that follows rules stipulated in a more complex specification — SGML (Standard Generalized Markup Language). HTML has evolved to Version 4, and most, but not all, browsers and Web authoring tools support all the features of HTML 4. Many users never upgrade the browser they get with their computers, so old versions of browsers stick around for a long time. And some users

access the Web through devices like WebTV, which don't support advanced features such as frames and Dynamic HTML (DHTML). For the widest possible audience, stick with older tags, such as those in the HTML 3.2 specification or earlier. Nearly all the capabilities described in this book are from the most widely supported, early versions of HTML; we'll point out the few times we use more advanced features.

Figure 4-1:
The For Dummies site is made of HTML and graphics.

Creating HTML documents

You can create HTML documents in a word processing program, in a text editor, or by using an HTML tool. Each method has its advantages:

✔ **Word processing program:** Most newer versions of popular word processing packages include "save as HTML" capability. You can open and edit a document in the word processing program and then save it as HTML-tagged text that makes up a Web page. However, the conversion process between the many features that a word processor supports and the smaller range of features supported by HTML is less than perfect. Ironically, you can only use your familiar word processing program to edit HTML documents if you understand what formatting HTML supports directly, which you find out about in this chapter.

✔ **Text editor:** A text editor is a program that edits regular text, such as the dull, boring, plain text that most people send e-mail messages in — no fonts, no bold or italic text, and no styles. You can use a text editor to create a file with HTML tags in it. When you save a file from a text editor, it saves as plain text, with no added, hidden codes for formatting. Although most text editors lack the advanced features found in word processing programs, many HTML experts swear by them. (You can also create a file in a word processing program and then save it as a text file to achieve the same effect, but you have to remember not to save it as a word processing file.)

✔ **HTML tool:** An HTML tool hides some of the details of HTML from you. However, you have to go through a learning curve for any HTML tool, and few tools completely hide HTML. So the basics we present in this chapter will help, even if you plan to use a tool. By knowing the basics, you can make better use of the tool and have some alternatives if the tool doesn't do everything you need it to. (And what tool does?)

After you create an HTML file, save it with the extension .HTM. The extension enables the Web browser to recognize the file and interpret it correctly. If you use the extension .HTML instead, not all systems will recognize it as an HTML file.

Every computer allows different kinds of filenames. But for your Web pages to work on the widest possible range of systems, you should keep your Web filenames short, and within the 8 x 3 filename limits of DOS. (FILENAME.EXT is an example of an 8 x 3 filename; up to 8 characters before the period, up to 3 characters after.) HTML files should end in the characters .HTM. Also, leave spaces and special characters such as colons or apostrophes out of the name. This way, your filenames are valid regardless of the type of computer that ends up being the Web server for your pages.

One of the most frustrating problems that beginning HTML authors run into is the fact that word processing programs now try to function as HTML editors and make it hard for you to work directly with HTML tags. These programs want to hide the tags from you and "let" you work in a formatted document where you don't see the tags directly, which is easier at first but gives you less control. If you work in Microsoft Word or Wordpad (which comes with

Microsoft Windows), and save the file in text format each time, you can have direct access to the HTML tags. You must be persistent, though; Word or Wordpad will ask you repeatedly if you want to save the file as a formatted document. Just say no!

Previewing HTML documents

However you create your HTML file, you need to see what it's going to look like on the Web. Some HTML tools offer special preview modes, but you can get the best idea of how your HTML file will look on the Web by using your Web browser.

While working in your text editor or word processing program or while using an HTML tool, simply save your file to disk. (Remember to save the file using the .HTM extension.) Then open your Web browser. In Netscape Navigator, choose File⇨Open Page to open the file you just saved. In Internet Explorer, choose File⇨Open, click the Browse button to find the file, and then open it.

The file appears in your browser just as it would if the file had been posted on the Internet. If you're connected to the Internet, you can even click links in your document to see the appropriate graphic or Web page. However, what you see may not be what other people would see when they open the file; other people may use different browsers, and they may specify different fonts for displaying Web pages. And accessing a file from your hard disk is much faster than accessing the same file from the Internet. But at least you get an idea of how the page looks.

If you can run your editing tool and your browser at the same time, all the better. (In Windows, use the Alt+Tab key combination to shift quickly between applications. On the Mac, use the application pull-down menu in the upper-right corner of the screen.) You can change the document in your editing tool, save the file, and then use the Reload command or similar command in your browser to see the changes. (Kind of like those bumper stickers you may have seen on the freeway that say "Keep Honking, I'm Reloading.") This way, you never need to be surprised by what you see after something you created is published on the Web.

If you're tricky, you can size and arrange the windows on your screen so that you can see both the HTML file you're editing and the browser window that displays the resulting Web page at the same time!

But don't stop there. See what your document looks like on different browsers before you publish on the Web. You can get copies of the top browsers from the Web sites of the browser companies, as described in Chapter 5, and pre-view your document in them as well.

Get Set: HTML Horse Sense

People used to refer to common sense as "horse sense." Most things about HTML fall under the realm of horse sense. After you see HTML tags a few times, most of the rules "feel right," and you will have little trouble remembering or using them most of the time. You will occasionally make mistakes, though; don't be surprised *to see that most of a document's text is in italics because you forgot to add a </I> tag to end italics.* (Having these last several words in italics was the authors' idea of a joke.)

Basic HTML rules

Here are a few basic HTML rules and some "gotchas" to watch out for:

- **Most HTML tags work in pairs.** (Does that make these dynamic duos "tag teams"?)

    For example, if you want some text to appear in bold, you have to put <B> at the front of the text that you want to have appear in bold, and you have to put <B> at the end of the text. If you forget the <B> at the end, you can easily end up with a document that looks fine at the start but then switches to bold somewhere in the middle — and this bold continues all the way through to the end.

    So remember to use paired tags and to check your document for unpaired tags before you publish it. If you still end up seeing italics or bold all over your document, you know what to look for.

- **HTML tags should be written in ALL CAPS.**

    Convention says to put HTML tags in ALL CAPS so that they stand out from the text they're embedded in. But inside an anchor, put the hypertext reference (such as a URL) in the case it would normally have (upper or lower) if you were using it elsewhere. The following example illustrates this use of capitalization:

    ```
    <A HREF="textver.htm">Text version.</A>
    ```

    The parts of the tag that are predefined HTML tags, such as A, /A, and HREF, are in ALL CAPS. The filename is in all lowercase letters, a convention used by UNIX (a type of operating system) that may save you some problems if your Web page ends up on a UNIX server. You can capitalize the text between the tags, which appears on the Web page as link text, in whatever way makes sense for your Web page's readers.

UNIX machines are case-sensitive: If you call one file MyFile.txt and another file myfile.txt, they are saved as separate files. The Macintosh and PC are case-insensitive and treat the names MyFile.txt and myfile.txt the same. Because you may end up putting your Web files on a Web server that's a different kind of machine from the one you create them on, you need to pay attention to the use of upper- and lowercase. The easiest rule is the one followed by UNIX users: Always use lowercase letters for filenames. (Some UNIX users go to extremes and use lowercase for everything, including all the text in personal e-mail messages they send.)

✔ **HTML ignores paragraph symbols and tabs in your text.**

One of the most confusing things about HTML is that it ignores the paragraph markers created in your text when you press Enter, as well as tabs. When displaying HTML, the browser automatically breaks lines to fit the current window size. And the browser makes a paragraph break only when it sees the paragraph tag, ⟨P⟩, or some other tag that implies the start of a new line (such as a top-level heading tag, ⟨H1⟩).

✔ **HTML needs you to put paragraph tags (⟨P⟩) between paragraphs.**

No matter how many times you hit Return while typing your text, you won't prevent the text from showing up as a big blob on your Web page unless you put paragraph tags (⟨P⟩) between paragraphs.

✔ **Basic HTML looks different on different types of browsers.**

Basic HTML doesn't give you much control over the appearance of your document. (Newer versions of HTML allow more control but aren't supported by older versions of popular browsers, so we suggest that you avoid the new stuff.) Different browsers handle the same tags differently. For example, a top-level heading (specified by the ⟨H1⟩ and ⟨/H1⟩ tags) may look much larger in one browser than in another browser.

✔ **Some tags don't work on some browsers.**

Some browsers (such as Netscape Navigator) support tags that other browsers can't handle. We recommend that you stick with basic tags to avoid the chance of giving users nasty surprises when they view your documents. We use only those tags in this book.

✔ **Users configure their browsers differently.**

As if the differences among different browser versions weren't enough, users can configure their browsers differently. Users who have bigger monitor screens tend to look at documents in a bigger window. But because these users sit farther back from their big screens — remember your mother telling you always to sit at least six feet from the TV? — they may also use larger font sizes to display text. Some users set their browser to display all graphics as the page transmits; others turn off graphics. All these idiosyncrasies can make your document look different to different users. Figure 4-2 shows the Web page for the For Dummies site, displayed with different option settings. As you can see, the figure doesn't look like the normal Dummies page.

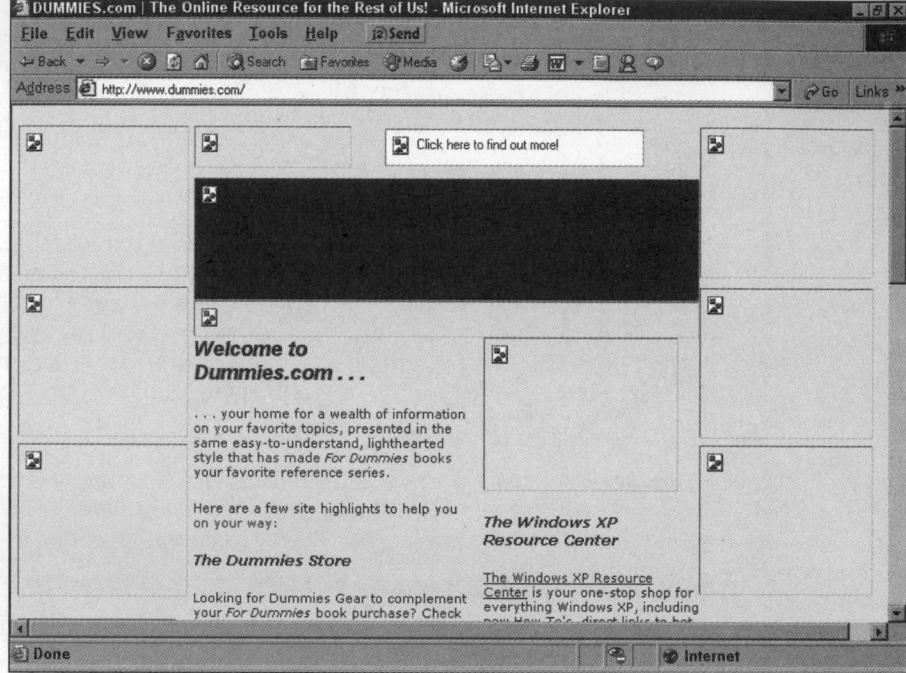

Figure 4-2:
The
Dummies
home
page with
graphics
turned
off and
different
font
settings.

Ten key HTML tags plus one

The Cheat Sheet at the beginning of this book shows an example of an HTML document, which is just regular text plus tags — those funny things with the angle brackets around them. If you haven't already, tear out the Cheat Sheet so you can look at the sample HTML document while you read this section. Table 4-1 summarizes the tags we use in this chapter.

Table 4-1	Key Tags to Use
Tags	*Tag Location*
`<HEAD>`, `</HEAD>`	Put these tags around the `<TITLE>` and `</TITLE>` tags at the start of the document.
`<TITLE>`, `</TITLE>`	Put these tags around a short title that describes the document and that appears at the top of the browser window. (For more information about the `<HEAD>`, `</HEAD>`, `<TITLE>`, and `</TITLE>` tags, see the section "Head users your way to win" in this chapter.)

Tags	Tag Location
`<BODY>, </BODY>`	After you add the `</TITLE>` and `</HEAD>` tags to end the title and header area, you surround everything below them in the document with the `<BODY>` and `</BODY>` tags.
`<H1>, </H1>, <H2>, </H2>,...`	Put the initial heading at the top of your document between the `<H1>` and `</H1>` tags. Then use higher-numbered tags for progressively lower heading levels. You can go down six levels (`<H6>, </H6>`), which is a lot — this book uses only three heading levels. If a book that weighs in at 350-plus pages needs only three levels, you have to create something pretty detailed before you need five or six.
`<B>, </B>`	Surround text you want to display in bold with these tags.
`<I>, </I>`	Surround text you want to display in italics with these tags.
`<P>, </P>`	You don't need to place the paragraph-break tag at the end of headings and in some other places, such as within a list, but you do need the tag everywhere else. Besides the anchor tags (`<A></A>`), `<P>` may be the easiest common tag to misuse. The end paragraph tag, `</P>`, is basically optional for beginners.
`<HR>`	The horizontal rule tag displays a horizontal line that is good for separating sections of documents.
`<A>, </A>`	The anchor tags define hypertext links and contain hypertext references, somewhat complicated information about where the link goes to. Link text — the text that gets underlined to indicate a hypertext link — goes between the tags. When the user clicks the underlined link text on a Web page, the display changes to show the Web page indicated by the hypertext reference.

(continued)

Table 4-1 *(continued)*	
Tags	**Tag Location**

`<A HREF="http://www.`
`aSite.edu"> My kid's`
`site. </A>`
	The `<A>` and `</A>` tag pair defines an anchor. HREF indicates a hypertext reference — in this case, a pointer to a Web site's URL. The link text is `My kid's site`; the user sees this text, underlined, as part of the Web page. See the section on anchors near the end of this chapter for details on these and other kinds of hypertext links.

`<IMG SRC="BudPic.gif">`	The `IMG` tag brings in an image in a format that the browser understands, either GIF or JPEG, and displays it as part of the Web page. The `SRC` part of the tag tells the browser where to find the file. In this example, the filename is `BudPic.gif` and is in the same directory or folder as the HTML file that the `<IMG>` tag is in. (You can tell it's in the same directory because the filename doesn't have any pathname information in front of it, such as \images\BudPic.gif.) In addition to this chapter's description of this tag and other key tags, you can find a further description of the `<IMG>` tag in Chapter 7.

For an example that uses these tags, see the Cheat Sheet. For a quick list of basic HTML tags, see Appendix C.

Go: Create a Web Page with HTML

Yes, you are just about ready to create a Web page with HTML. However, the whole secret of using HTML is knowing what tags to use and when. So now that you know what a tag is, what more do you need to know? Well, tags can be divided into three kinds:

✔ **Tags that contain meta-information about your document:** *Meta-information,* such as the title in the header section of your document, doesn't affect what shows up within the body of the Web page; instead, this information is used by various Web tools, such as search engines, that look at the title to see what your document is about. (And we never "meta" Web tool we didn't like!)

- **Tags that format characters in your text:** These tags (<B>, </B> and <I>, </I>, for example) do nothing but modify the way your text looks when the browser displays it.

- **Linking tags:** These tags connect the user to different kinds of information and even to other documents. The section "Look back (and forward) in anchor," in this chapter, explains linking tags in detail.

After you create and save an HTML file with text and these different kinds of tags, pat yourself on the back. You've just created a complete HTML document, and you're well on the way to being a tagger yourself! (Not the kind that puts graffiti on buildings, but the kind that expresses himself or herself electronically on the Web.)

Create a blank file for your HTML

HTML files should include only plain text — no hidden formatting codes from your word processing program. And the name of the document should always end with .HTM. So start by creating a text-only file to hold your Web page's text and HTML tags.

To create a blank plain-text document that you can insert HTML code into, follow these steps:

1. **Start your text editor or word processing program.**

2. **Open a new document.**

   Some programs automatically open a new document when you start them. In that case, you can skip this step.

3. **Start the process of saving your document so that you can name it.**

   If you use a word processing program, use the Save As or similar command and choose Text as the type of file.

   Don't choose the Text with Line Breaks option; line breaks make the document harder to edit. The good ol' Text option will do.

4. **Name the document.**

   Put **.HTM** at the end of the name.

5. **Save the document.**

   In most programs, you click a Save button or press Enter.

The steps enable you to create a blank HTML document — which wouldn't be very interesting if you were to put it on the Web! So now you want to start filling in your document by adding heading information.

Recent versions of Microsoft Word and other word processing programs may try to "help" you in a way that interferes with what you're trying to accomplish. For instance, when you tell Word to save your file as a text file, it will automatically change the suffix to .txt. Change it back to .htm and save the file normally.

Head users your way to win

First, some bad news: You start your HTML documents with some tags that don't really do much for the appearance of your Web page. In fact, the tags add a few more things to worry about. And you thought that you could finally start getting some real work done!

Now, the good news: These tags make the Web a better place. They contain introductory *meta-information* — descriptive information about your document that doesn't affect how the user sees your document. But although the user doesn't see these tags directly, the tags support search tools and other tools that make finding a Web page — hopefully, finding *your* Web page — so quick and easy that users can get to it straight away. (Of course, looking at a lot of other things in between can be half the fun of using the Web.)

- <HTML>, </HTML>: These tags surround everything in your document and identify the document as being in HTML. As the Web supports more and more different types of files, these tags become increasingly important.

- <HEAD>, </HEAD>: These tags go around the title of your document and any other information that doesn't appear within the Web page itself. For now, that just means the title.

- <TITLE>, </TITLE>: These tags go around the title of your document. The title is a short phrase that describes your document and doesn't appear within the body of your Web page. It does appear, however, within the strip at the top of the document window when your Web page is viewed.

- <BODY>, </BODY>: These tags go around everything in your document that isn't part of the head. The <BODY> tag goes just after the </HEAD> tag, which goes just after the </TITLE> tag.

 If you use a tool that creates a Web page for you, such as the free services described in Chapters 2 and 3, or Netscape Composer, described later in this chapter, you don't need to put these introductory tags in because the tool does it for you. However, you may need to add the <TITLE> and </TITLE> tags, and put the title of your Web page in between them yourself.

Look at this well-mannered, albeit nearly empty, HTML document to see what the top should look like:

```
<HTML>
<HEAD>
<TITLE>A Brief Introduction to Electric Guitars</TITLE>
</HEAD>
<BODY>
Some introductory information about electric guitars.
</BODY>
</HTML>
```

Popular Web tools use these tags. The Advanced Search option of the AltaVista Web-searching service enables users to search specifically by words in the title; just enter the phrase "title:" followed by the text you want to search for in the title. To access the AltaVista search engine, go to www.altavista.com.

Netscape Navigator and Microsoft Internet Explorer use the title of your document — the phrase between the <TITLE> and </TITLE> tags — as the document description in their Bookmarks menu. (No, we don't keep mentioning these products because we own stock in Microsoft and America Online, the companies that develop those products; this is just one of those cases where the best products and the market leaders are the same.) The title also appears in the title bar of the browser window when the page is displayed.

To give yourself a head start each time you want to begin a new HTML document, create a text-only document in your word processing program or text editor with the head, title, and body tags already in place. When you're ready to begin a new HTML document, start by making a copy of this document.

Follow these steps to create a text-only document that contains the introductory tags:

1. **Open a new document.**

2. **Save your document as a text-only document with the name you want, ending with .HTM.**

3. **On the first line of the document, enter the tag** <HTML>.

4. **On the second line of the document, enter the tag** <HEAD>.

5. **On the third line of the document, enter the tags** <TITLE> **and** </TITLE>.

   Don't enclose anything within the <TITLE> and </TITLE> tags for now. After you copy this text-only document to create an HTML document, you can enter the material that you want to use as the "title."

   When you are deciding what to include between these tags, remember that many Web tools use the information between these tags when searching for documents.

6. **On the fourth line of the document, enter the tag** `</HEAD>`.

7. **On the fifth line of the document, enter the tag** `<BODY>`.

8. **Leave the sixth line of the document blank.**

   The main content of the document goes here.

9. **On the seventh line of the document, enter the tag** `</BODY>`.

10. **On the eighth line of the document, enter the tag** `</HTML>`.

    Whatever else you do in your document, `</HTML>` is always the last tag.

11. **Save the document.**

Get a heading and some body

Underneath the headings, your document needs some content — just plain old words, maybe highlighted with **bold** and *italics* where needed.

Don't overuse the bold and italic tags. Like early desktop publishers, who put *three* different fonts on every **line** of text, HTML novices tend to put **lots of bold** *and italics* in their documents. (The formatting in the previous sentence was meant to be funny, please don't blame the printers!) When you preview your document in your Web browser, look for areas where you overuse bold and italic formatting. And when in doubt, don't use bold and italics. Your Web page's visitors will thank you.

Here's how to put a top-level heading and some basic text into your Web document:

1. **After the** `<BODY>` **tag, and before the** `</BODY>` **tag, put in your top-level heading. Surround the heading with the** `<H1>` **and** `</H1>` **tags so that the browser knows that the text is a level-1 heading.**

   You may also use your top-level heading between the `<TITLE>` and `</TITLE>` tags, as many Web publishers do.

2. **After the heading, type some text.**

   For optimal use by Web search tools, the first paragraph in your document should be a brief summary of the document's contents.

3. **At the end of each paragraph, put in a** `<P>` **tag.**

   No matter how many times you press Enter in your document, your dense browser doesn't get the message. It only understands that you want to end a paragraph and start a new one when it sees the `<P>` tag.

4. **Surround text with the** `<B>` **and** `</B>` **tags to make it bold.**

   Don't overdo the use of the `<B>` and `</B>` tags! Starting out, use bold once or twice just to get a feel for it.

5. **Surround text with the** ⟨I⟩ **and** ⟨/I⟩ **tags to make it italic.**

   Don't overdo italicizing, either! Use italics a few times in your first document or two for practice.

6. **Try adding a horizontal rule.**

   Add the ⟨HR⟩ tag in one or two places to create horizontal rules. (Not to start an argument with those who think that vertical or diagonal rules.)

   As with headings and other elements of your document, put the ⟨HR⟩ tag on a line by itself so that you can find it easily later to move or remove it.

7. **After you're done, check your tags.**

   Paragraphs should end with a ⟨P⟩ tag to start the next paragraph. All ⟨B⟩ tags should have a matching ⟨/B⟩ tag, and all ⟨I⟩ tags should have a matching ⟨/I⟩ tag.

   The most effective way for many of us to check tags, believe it or not, is to print out the document and then cross out pairs of tags with a pencil. In the old days, computer programmers called this kind of exercise "desk-checking."

8. **Save your document.**

   If you use a word processing program rather than a text editor, be sure to save your document as text-only.

The Cheat Sheet at the front of this book shows a simple sample Web page.

Add a little list

One of the best ways to "break up" your Web page is to insert lists. HTML supports bulleted lists, numbered lists, and lists of definitions or descriptions. Although HTML makes creating lists easy, it doesn't give you direct control over how lists look. (Repeat after me, "Trust your browser, trust your browser. . . .")

- **Unnumbered lists** (often called bulleted lists): Unnumbered lists display as lists with bullets next to them and are "appropriately" indented (the indentation varies with different browsers and browser settings). The list you're reading now is a bulleted list, but it uses check marks in place of the bullets.

- **Ordered lists** (often called numbered lists): These lists are similar to bulleted lists, but with — you guessed it — numbers in place of the bullets. You can rearrange the items in the numbered list as much as you like. The browser automatically keeps things in order by putting in the right numbers when it displays the list.

- **Definition lists:** These lists usually alternate terms and their — duh — definitions. The term goes where the bullet goes in a bulleted list, and the definition goes next to it or on the line immediately below.

You create all lists in basically the same way: You start the list with a beginning tag, such as <UL> for an unnumbered list. You then tag each item separately to let the browser know that it's a separate item. You use the tag <LI> at the beginning of each item in both unnumbered and numbered lists; you don't use an end tag for individual list items. The list finally ends with a closing tag — </UL> to end an unnumbered list, for example.

The formatting in HTML lists often looks different than how you want it to look. For instance, many browsers display a bulleted HTML list with a blank line before the list items, but no blank lines between them. You can't change this formatting with standard HTML commands — and trying to change it by using tricky HTML is a very difficult process. Better to get used to the way HTML displays lists.

The following instructions describe how to create an unnumbered (bulleted) or ordered (numbered) list:

1. **Put in a tag to start the list: <UL> for an unnumbered list, <OL> for an ordered list.**

2. **Put in an <LI> tag to indicate a list item.**

3. **Starting on the same line, enter the text for the list item.**

   "Red Hot Chili Pepper Potato Chips" is a good way to start.

4. **For the remaining items in the list, enter the <LI> tag followed by the item text. Press Enter at the end of each line to visually separate the items onscreen as you edit.**

   You don't need to use an end tag for list items. Also remember that hitting Enter at the end of a line causes the cursor to move to a new line onscreen but doesn't cause line breaks to be put in the HTML-tagged text; the browser starts a new line when it sees a new <LI> tag or a </UL> tag. The <LI> tag is one of those rare tags that doesn't come as part of a pair.

5. **Enter a tag to end the list — </UL> to end an unnumbered list or </OL> to end an ordered list.**

To create a definition list, follow these steps:

1. **Enter the <DL> tag to start the definition list.**

2. **Enter the <DT> tag to indicate a definition term.**

3. **Enter the text for the definition term.**

4. **Enter the <DD> tag to indicate definition data — the description of the definition term.**

5. **Enter the text for the definition data.**

6. **For the remaining items in the list, enter the** ⟨DT⟩ **tag followed by the definition term and then enter the** ⟨DD⟩ **tag followed by the description of the term. Press Enter at the end of each line to visually separate the items on-screen as you edit.**

As with other list items, you don't need to enter an end tag for definition terms or definition data.

7. **Enter the** ⟨/DL⟩ **tag to end the list.**

Figure 4-3 shows an example that includes the three kinds of lists. Because people use the Web to find out new things and to look things up, lists are some of the most important formatting elements in HTML.

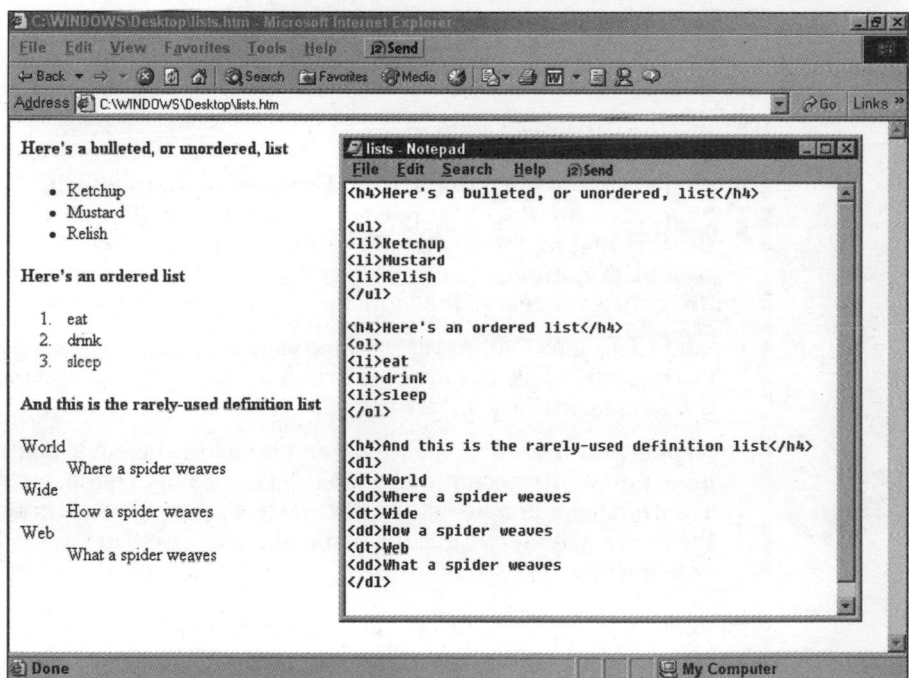

Figure 4-3:
Using lists
in your
Web page.

Look back (and forward) in anchor

Remember that HTML stands for Hypertext Markup Language? Well, applying all those tags is the markup part. Now hang on to your hat: Here's everything you need to know about the hypertext part. In this section, we demonstrate how to use hypertext to create links between information in your document and information in other documents. This stuff is a bit confusing at first, but after you understand it, you'll think of many exciting ways to use hypertext in your Web pages.

In HTML, every hypertext link has two ends, which are called *anchors*. (Some people think that putting anchors into a Web page makes them anchorpersons — but sorry, no seven-figure salary.)

When you define an anchor, you use tags to specify two things:

- ✔ The text or image that is highlighted as the place you click to follow the link
- ✔ The other anchor that you want to go to when you click the link

Anchors are among the most complicated tags in basic HTML. But you don't want to say "Anchors away," as the old movie had it, because anchors expand the possibilities of your Web page tremendously. The following is an example of an anchor:

```
<A HREF="http://www.listentoyourdog.com">How to train dogs</A>
```

Here are the parts of an anchor:

- ✔ `<A>`, `</A>`: These tags go around text that you want highlighted as a hypertext link (`How to train dogs` in the preceding example). Try to use text that represents the thing that you want to link to, such as "Adobe Corporation" or "my résumé." The better this text describes the thing that you link to, the more helpful the text is to the user.
- ✔ `HREF`: This information falls within the `<A>` tag. When the user clicks on the hypertext link, the browser brings up the Web location indicated by the pathname that appears after `HREF`.
- ✔ **Hypertext reference:** These characters follow the equal sign in the `HREF` part of the anchor and should be enclosed in quote symbols. They are the pathname of the document that you link to. In the example, the hypertext reference is the name of a Web site: `"http://www. listentoyourdog.com"`.

When you post an HTML file on a server, some anchors in the file can point to Web documents on the same Web server as the HTML file, while other anchors point to Web documents on other Web servers. When the document is on another server, the anchor contains the document's full URL, in the same form as you type it in your browser. For example, an anchor pointing to the For Dummies Web site looks like this:

```
<A HREF="http://www.dummies.com">"For Dummies"</A>
```

When the document that's pointed to by the initial anchor is on the same machine, the anchor contains the pathname of the document. The pathname specifies the file's location on the machine.

For simple Web sites that you create, put all the documents in the same directory or folder so that you have simpler anchors. Then you don't have to worry about pathnames!

The pathname looks different depending on where the second document is in relation to the HTML document that contains the link. If the two documents are in the same directory or folder, the pathname is simply the filename. But if the second document is in a different directory, you can use two methods to specify how to reach it: absolute addressing and relative addressing. In *absolute addressing,* you use the path from the lowest-level, or *root,* directory of the server to the second document. In *relative addressing,* you start with the location of the HTML file that's currently being viewed. You then use the path from the HTML file to the second document.

To specify an absolute address, start with a forward slash (/) to indicate the root directory of the Web server. Then specify the full pathname from the root directory to the file. The following example shows an absolute address:

```
/photoshp/samples/sunrise.gif
```

To specify a relative address, start with the directory of the HTML document that the anchor is in and then enter the path that leads to the desired file from there. A pair of dots (..) specifies the directory one level above the current one.

For example, if you have an HTML file called sunset.htm in the directory /mysite/html, and you need a GIF graphics file that is in /mysite/html/pix, a subdirectory of the current directory, the relative address is the following:

```
pix/sunset.gif
```

If you also need a file that is in /mysite/trial/pix, you use the .. characters to specify the subdirectory above this one and then go back down the directory tree to the needed file. Put a slash after the dots. In this case, the relative address is as follows:

```
../trial/pix/moonrise.gif
```

Starting at the beginning of the path, ".." means "the directory above the current one." The words separated by slashes, "/trial/pix/," are the names of the directory and subdirectory in which the file is stored. And "moonrise.gif" is the filename.

Usually, you create your Web site on one machine, then publish it by copying the files to another machine, the Web server. It's very easy to forget to copy all the files needed to the Web server. If you keep all the files in one overall folder — that doesn't have any files in it that aren't part of the Web site — you'll have a fighting chance of making the transfer successful.

Table 4-2 shows examples of anchors.

Table 4-2	Examples of Hypertext Links (Anchors)
Destination	**Sample Anchor**
Web page on same server, same directory	`<A HREF="MyDoc2.html" >link text</A>`
Web page on same server, different directory; relative addressing	`<A HREF="Personal/ Resume">link text</A>`
Web page on same server, different directory; absolute addressing	`<A HREF="/Maya/Personal/ Resume">link text</A>`
Web page on a different server	`<A HREF="http://www.mycorp. com/Job Requirements">link text</A>`

The simplest way to handle addressing, and the one least likely to cause errors, is to put all documents in the same directory or folder. The next simplest way — best used for more complex Web pages or Web sites — is to use relative addressing. This makes it easy for others to bundle up all the files needed for your Web pages and move them around on a Web server. Absolute addressing is the most error-prone.

Link for yourself

Absorbing all this knowledge about hypertext links is pretty useless if you don't actually use the knowledge yourself. Here's a description of how to create a link; note how we cleverly work several different types of links into the instructions:

1. **Open an existing HTML document.**

2. **Move to the place in the document where you want to insert a link.**

3. **Start the link by entering the opening tag, including the hypertext reference that you want the link to lead to.**

   For a link to a Web page in the same directory, enter the filename in quotation marks, as in `<A HREF="AnotherDoc.HTM"></A>`. ("AnotherDoc.HTM" is the filename.)

   As described previously in this chapter, you can enter a relative or absolute address for a document that's in a different directory within your Web site.

For a link to a file in the graphics subdirectory of the current directory, enter the pathname: `<A HREF="graphics/dancers.gif">Dancers</A>`.

For a document that's on a different server, enter the document's URL (for example, `<A HREF="http://www.ACoolSite.com"></A>`).

If you don't enter a specific filename, the browser looks for the default file: index.htm or index.html.

4. **After the opening tag, enter the link text.**

5. **Don't forget the closing tag!**

    After the opening tag and the link text, enter the closing tag.

Link from within

That's a lot of stuff to absorb! Just one more thing to consider: What if you want to link to a specific spot *within* the same Web page?

To link to a specific spot, you need a pair of anchors. The first is at the spot from which you want to link, just like we described above. This first anchor is just like the external links, but it has one more element — the name of a second anchor that's at the spot to which you want to link. You have to put the second anchor into the Web page you're linking to, at the spot where you want the link to go. For example, the following anchor links to a spot that's named "Bebak," within the same file as the first anchor:

```
<A HREF="#Bebak">Bud's coauthor</A>
```

The pound sign, #, denotes an anchor within a Web page. The second anchor, also called the link, is at the spot to which you want to link. The second anchor exists only to specify that spot and doesn't cause the link text to show up as underlined on the user's screen. Here's the link for the second anchor:

```
<A NAME="Bebak"> </A>Arthur Bebak<P>
```

The link doesn't need a pathname, but the anchor that links to it needs a pathname if the anchor and link are in different files. And you don't need any text between the anchor's beginning and ending.

Try using internal links in an HTML document on your own machine, and test the links in your browser. Experiment with different kinds of relative addresses, or pathnames. Trying different links and pathnames gives you the experience you need to easily use these features in your "real" Web pages.

Linking to specific spots in your own Web page is common. Many Web sites have long Web pages that include clever internal links that move the user around in the page. Linking to specific spots in other people's Web pages is less common. Why? Because it's hard to control where the other page's author chooses to put link anchors — and harder still to make sure that link anchors don't get moved around on you unexpectedly, rendering your anchor invalid. How would you like it if, for example, you defined a link to a serious essay on home wine making and later discovered that the essay had been replaced by a discussion of Greek philosophy? (Though much of the latter may have been inspired by consumption of the results of the former.) Sheesh!

Browse your own weblet

Here's the moment you've been waiting for: Whether you've followed all the previous steps, or just some, you now have a ready-to-use little HTML document. To see whether you did it right, all you have to do is try it in your Web browser. That's right — you can view your very own HTML document in your very own browser!

Not only can you view your HTML document from your browser, but you can even follow the links to other HTML documents on your local system and from your system out onto the Web. (We assume that your browser is connected to the Web at the time. If not, following a hypertext link to a Web URL will be a short trip!) Using the Back command in your browser, you can even return to your own document.

There's only one limitation to this testing: Other Web sites can't link to your HTML document because it's only saved on your local machine, not on a Web server. And that's the one thing that's stopping your HTML document from being a Web page: It's not hosted on a Web server. Details, details — we take care of that little omission in Chapter 12.

For now, you need to figure out how to view your HTML document in your browser. This is something you do every time you work on HTML documents. Start a document; view it in your browser. Change the document; view it in your browser. And on and on . . . (Maybe it's finally time to buy that 20-inch computer monitor you've been thinking about so that you can see both documents at once as you switch back and forth.)

Can your browser handle it?

An anchor can link the current document to another HTML file or to some other type of file, such as a graphic, a sound, a video clip, or almost anything else. Most browsers know how to handle HTML files and GIF or JPEG graphics files automatically. Different browsers may handle other types of files in different ways — automatically, or by the user's specifying a program to handle them. So for these examples, we stick with links to HTML files and GIF and JPEG files because we know that those files work with just about any browser.

To view your HTML document in your browser:

1. **Start your browser.**

2. **Select the Open Page command (for Netscape) or Open command (for Internet Explorer) under the File menu. In the Open dialog box that appears, click Browse.**

3. **Find your HTML document on your hard disk and open it.**

4. **View your own HTML document in your own Web browser.**

   You can even follow links by clicking them. Use the Back command in your browser to return to your HTML document.

5. **Look for problems in your HTML document or things you want to add.**

   So half of your document is in *italics* and the rest <u>is underlined as if it's all part of a link</u>. Who cares?! Go fix it!

6. **Open the HTML document in your text editor or word processing program and fix it.**

   You don't need to close your browser to work on the HTML document. Note that the earlier sections of this chapter may be of some help here.

7. **Save the changed HTML document.**

   If you forget to save the document, your changes don't show up in your browser, and you wonder whether your changes "took" or whether you're losing your sanity.

8. **Use the Refresh command or a similar command in your Web browser to reload the fixed HTML document.**

   If you forget to reload the document, your changes don't show up in your browser, and, again, you wonder whether your changes "took" or whether you're losing your sanity.

   If you forget to save the document after you make changes, or forget to reload the document in your browser, the changes you just made don't show up. Anytime you think that this may have happened, just go back to your text editor or word processing program, save the document, return to your Web browser, and reload. The changes will appear.

9. **Repeat Steps 5 through 8 until done.**

   (*Done* can mean until the HTML document is done, as in finished, or until the HTML document's author is done, as in toast!)

   Don't forget to use the Refresh command when you're done modifying your document and want to look at it again in the browser.

Advances in HTML

Since the Web first became widely (and wildly) popular in the mid-1990s, several advances in HTML have taken place. These advances build on the solid base of the original HTML specification and add new capabilities. However, they also make HTML much more complicated and add many more issues for those who design Web pages.

The biggest changes are the additions of tables, frames, and Dynamic HTML. Tables not only display information in table form, but also are widely used to help precisely position text and graphics. Frames allow a Web page to be divided up into independently controlled sections. They are somewhat widely used, but not as popular as tables.

We describe how and when to use these advanced features in Chapter 11. However, you can go far with the basic HTML specification that is usable by all browsers, so we stick with that version in nearly all of this book.

Look to the next HTML steps

The parts of HTML that we cover in this chapter represent just the basics. As you create, test, and deploy your own Web pages, you may want to understand more about HTML.

If you use Netscape Composer, which we describe in Chapter 5, or an online Web page service like the ones we describe in Chapters 2 and 3, you may be protected from the gory details of HTML. But you never know when you may end up back in "raw" HTML to add a feature or fix a problem. You can find lists of HTML tags on the Web at sources such as w3.org. And don't forget that *HTML 4 For Dummies*, 3rd Edition, by Ed Tittel et al (Hungry Minds, Inc.) is an excellent source for more detail on HTML.

Part II
Building Pages

The 5th Wave   By Rich Tennant

"Well, it's not quite done. I've animated the gurgling spit-sink and the rotating Novocaine syringe, but I still have to add the high speed whining drill audio track."

In this part . . .

It's time to tackle a couple of tools that let you do anything you want with your Web pages. Learn how to enrich your page with formatting and links. And now, META tags are an arcane art no longer. Help Web searchers find your pages!

Chapter 5

Choosing Your Tools

• •

• •

*Y*ou can use online tools, like those we discuss in Chapters 2 and 3, to create your initial Web page using a template. However, at some point, you will want to go further with your Web page than a template allows. To do this, you will have to move away from the online tools and create your own Web page on your own hard disk. Then you can upload tried-and-tested Web pages to any number of different Web hosts, including Yahoo! GeoCities and AOL.

This chapter describes how to create your initial Web page locally, on your own hard disk. The next few chapters describe how to improve your Web page and how to extend your Web page into a multi-page Web site. Chapter 12 tells you how to publish one or more Web pages that are on your own machine onto the Web.

This chapter helps you choose the tool you want to use and then shows you how to create your initial Web page.

Yahoo! GeoCities and AOL each have advanced tools that will let you go pretty far with your Web page. However, these tools lock you into having your hosting done on the service that provides them. If you feel comfortable keeping your Web page on the same host for a long time to come, you may want to continue using these advanced tools. The approach we describe in this book, however, gives you more opportunities to keep costs low and flexibility high.

Choosing Between WYSIWYG and Plain Text

You can use a couple of different approaches to create and edit Web pages on your own computer. One approach is to use a WYSIWYG Web page editor. WYSIWYG is pronounced "whizzywig," and stands for What You See Is What You Get. A WYSIWYG Web page editor is like a word processing program — what you see onscreen is at least close to what you get when you publish your Web page and look at it online.

The problem with this is that WYSIWYG doesn't work perfectly on the Web. As we described in Chapter 4, different Web browsers can interpret the same HTML tags differently. Also, users can have different browser settings, which means the same page can look different for different people. This variability undermines your efforts to make your Web page look just so. To work around these problems, and to create Web pages that work well on the widest possible range of different kinds of computers and different browser versions and settings, it really helps to know what's going on with the underlying HTML.

For this reason, many Web page publishers work directly with HTML tags. Others work with a WYSIWYG editor, but frequently check what the underlying HTML-tagged text — usually just called "the HTML" — looks like.

We recommend that you either work directly in HTML or use a simple WYSIWYG tool that doesn't try to do too much for you, and look frequently at the underlying HTML. If you do want to use a tool, we recommend Netscape Composer.

Pluses and minuses of text editors

The reasons in favor of editing HTML directly in a text editor are fairly simple. You work directly in HTML — never anything else. You're always looking directly at the HTML tags. Any time you want to add a feature to your Web page, you're forced to learn the HTML tags for that feature and use them, which means you're gradually learning the underlying language of Web pages.

The reasons not to work directly in HTML using a text editor are fairly simple as well. It's quite difficult to imagine what your Web page is going to look like when you're just looking at text and tags. It's easy to make mistakes in the construction of your Web page when you're working directly with the tags — and easy to get lost in looking at the HTML-tagged text when you're trying to remember where to make an addition or change.

Figure 5-1 shows a simple Web page as it appears when being edited in a text editor and the Netscape Composer editing window. You may be able to tell just from looking at the picture which kind of environment you prefer to work in. If not, try both, using the instructions in this chapter, and see which you prefer.

Pluses and minuses of Netscape Composer

Using a WYSIWYG editor such as Netscape Composer has its trade-offs too. WYSIWYG editors shield you from the underlying HTML, so you can see what your page is likely to look like on the Web. But the underlying HTML tags are hidden from you, so you don't know exactly what's going on. The more capable WYSIWYG editors support newer, more advanced HTML functionality as well — which is good if you want to use those functions, but makes it all too easy for you to create Web pages that don't work well on all Web browsers.

Netscape Composer has most of the advantages of an HTML tool, with few of the disadvantages. Here are its six key advantages as an HTML tool:

> ✔ **Netscape Composer is free.** Netscape makes Composer available for free along with Netscape Navigator, the first widely popular browser for the Web.

Figure 5-1:
You can compose in a text editor or Composer.

- ✔ **It's easy.** Netscape Composer is very easy to use. It leaves out some complex editing functions in favor of drop-dead simplicity.

- ✔ **Its functions match HTML tags.** The functions available in Composer are the functions available in HTML — and only those functions. So you don't do things in your Web page that won't be supported by Web browsers.

- ✔ **It uses "generic" HTML.** The only functions available in Composer are those supported by all widely used versions of HTML. Web pages that you create with Composer are likely to be usable by all major Web browsers.

- ✔ **It lets you see and edit HTML.** Netscape Composer gives you one-click access to the HTML tags underlying your Web page. You get ease of editing in WYSIWYG mode but can still always see and edit the underlying HTML-tagged text.

- ✔ **It's part of Netscape Navigator.** Composer comes with Netscape's browser, the second-most-popular browser for the Web. You need to have the Netscape browser, along with Internet Explorer, available on your system anyway for testing your Web pages before you publish them. Since you need the Netscape browser anyway, it's convenient that Composer comes with the Netscape browser.

These features of Netscape Composer place it comfortably between using a text editor and working directly with HTML tags, which can be frustrating and lead you to make mistakes in the look and layout of your page, or the more advanced HTML editors, such as FrontPage and Dreamweaver, which may overwhelm you with functionality.

So we recommend that most beginning Web publishers use Composer, and check the underlying HTML frequently to see what's really going on. As you get more knowledgeable with HTML, you may wish to buy and use a more advanced HTML editor — or go the low-tech route and use a basic text editor.

We recommend that you consider using Composer initially even if you own a more advanced HTML editor such as Dreamweaver or FrontPage. The functionality of Composer is simpler, making it easier to learn the core features of HTML, and you'll be able to follow along better with this book.

If you already have Netscape software installed, you may already have Netscape Composer on your computer. Check Start⇨Programs⇨ Netscape⇨Netscape, or similar folder and filenames, to see if Netscape Navigator, Netscape Communicator, or Netscape 6.*x* is already there. If so, check to see if Composer is available, either as a separate program or as an option within the Netscape browser. If Composer is there, you can run the software you already have or upgrade using the instructions in this chapter.

What if you use AOL or Compuserve?

AOL and CompuServe each have built-in Web browsers that run within the program, somewhat muddying the distinction between the online service itself and the open Web that anyone can access.

It used to be that if you ran AOL, you could only use the Web browser built into the program. However, with new versions of AOL software, you can run a regular Web browser alongside the AOL client software. (You've been able to do this for years with CompuServe.) We recommend that you do use a "real" Web browser alongside the AOL or CompuServe client software.

Simply install the latest versions of Internet Explorer and Netscape software. (This chapter describes how to install Netscape software; for general instructions about installing Internet

Explorer, see the sidebar "What if you need IE?" later in this chapter.)

Start your AOL or CompuServe software and connect to the Internet. Then start your Web browser. (You can even start one browser, then the other; recent versions of IE and Navigator can both run at the same time.) The figure shows AOL and Internet Explorer running at the same time. Use your Web browser to look at Web sites, including for testing your own Web site under development. And use Netscape Composer to create Web pages.

You can also test the Web page(s) you're developing in the built-in AOL or CompuServe browser to make sure you don't have problems. However, doing this is less important than testing in the IE or Navigator browsers, which are more widely used.

Working with Netscape Composer

Netscape Composer has all the important basic features that you need to build basic Web pages. Using these features, you can

- ✔ Create and edit Web pages without seeing HTML tags.
- ✔ Drag and drop links to other Web locations without typing the URL or pathname.
- ✔ Cut and paste graphics into your Web page, resize graphics, and add alternate text.
- ✔ Create and edit tables.
- ✔ Create and edit *forms* — interactive data entry fields commonly found on Web pages.

You can also insert multimedia files and computer programs into your Web page. However, not all users can play back those files or run those programs because they may not have the appropriate browser or the right plug-ins installed. If you add advanced elements, such as multimedia files or computer programs, into your Web page, be prepared to test your pages with several different browsers and to tell your Web visitors what to expect.

Netscape Composer supports forms, but it can't give you the CGI scripts, also known as CGIs — short for Common Gateway Interface scripts — that you need to make the forms work. These CGI scripts process the data that the user enters into a form; if you can create CGI scripts, you're probably ready for a more advanced tool than Netscape Composer. However, if you don't want to mess with creating these scripts, you can get CGIs from others on the Web.

Netscape Composer doesn't support *frames* — advanced HTML elements that split up a Web page into separate, scrollable pieces. Designing Web pages that work well with frames isn't easy, so it makes some sense that Netscape Composer, as a free tool, doesn't support frames.

Though Netscape Composer doesn't support frames, it does enable you to add any HTML tags that you want directly into your Web page. However, the whole point of using a tool is to reduce the amount of HTML coding that you have to do; if you find yourself coding directly in HTML to avoid the limitations of Netscape Composer, consider buying a more capable tool, such as FrontPage 2000 or Macromedia Dreamweaver.

Where Netscape 6.2 runs

At this writing, the current version of Netscape software is called Netscape 6.2. (See the sidebar "What to call Netscape software" for details.) You can choose which parts of the suite to download; you can get all the pieces that used to be in the Netscape Communicator suite, such as the e-mail application, or just the browser (including Composer), or any mix you want. For more about Netscape 6.2, go to `http://home.netscape.com/browsers/6`, which is shown in Figure 5-2:

Figure 5-2:
Find out about Netscape's benefits.

In this chapter, we tell you how to get the basics that you need for Web authoring: the Netscape 6.2 browser and Composer. You can download more pieces of the suite if you choose. Follow the instructions in the next section.

In order to run Netscape 6.2, you need one of the following system setups:

- ✔ **Windows:** You can run Netscape 6.2 on Windows 95 or any later version of Windows — Windows 98, Windows ME, Windows NT 4.0, Windows 2000, or Windows XP. You need a 233 MHz or faster Pentium, 64MB of RAM, and 26MB of free hard disk space. (You can actually run Netscape 6.2 on a somewhat lesser system configuration — except you need enough hard disk space to install the parts of Netscape 6.2 that you download — but performance will suffer.)

- ✔ **Linux:** Netscape 6.2 runs on Linux on Intel-architecture machines (usually called PCs). You need Red Hat Linux 6.0 or later — 6.1, 6.2, or 7.0 with X11 R6. Hardware requirements are the same as for Netscape running on

Windows — a 233 MHz or faster Pentium, 64MB of RAM, and 26MB of free hard disk space. As with Windows, you may be able to get by with a slower Pentium or less RAM, but performance will be slow.

✔ **Macintosh:** For the Mac you need a fairly recent version of the operating system: Mac OS 8.6, 9.*x,* or Mac OS X. Hardware requirements are similar to those for the PC: A 266 MHz or faster PowerPC 604e, G3, or G4 chip, 64MB of RAM, and 36MB of hard disk space.

If you have a UNIX workstation (not using an Intel microprocessor and Red Hat Linux), or a PC or Mac that doesn't meet the requirements above, you can probably get an earlier version of Netscape software that will meet your needs. Find the older software at `http://home.netscape.com/browsers/4/index.html`.

What to call Netscape software

If you're considering using Netscape's software — which has been known by many names over the years — you might want to know a bit about the history of this famous company. Netscape was launched by Jim Clark, who brought a small fortune from his co-founding of Silicon Graphics, and Marc Andreesen, a leader of the team that created Mosaic, the first popular Web browser. Netscape brought out a new browser, Netscape Navigator, which quickly replaced Mosaic as the best way to surf the Net.

Netscape Navigator was wildly popular for several years, until Microsoft brought out Internet Explorer. The first versions of Internet Explorer — "IE" for short — were not very good, but gradually, Microsoft's software caught up. Microsoft also got advantageous distribution deals for IE from many computer manufacturers, and got a version of IE built into America Online's software as well.

Netscape expanded Navigator into a suite of related applications (such as e-mail, an address book, and a calendar) and named the suite Netscape Communicator. The last version of the Communicator suite was Netscape Communicator 4.7. Communicator remained popular for a while, but Internet Explorer gradually gained market share.

Now Internet Explorer is the most-used browser with about 80 percent of the market, and Netscape has almost all of the remainder. Netscape was purchased by America Online, but it remains a separate company within AOL.

Now Netscape calls its software "Netscape," followed by the version number — the current version is Netscape 6.2. The Netscape software includes all the functions of the old Netscape Communicator, except for the calendar, but you can pick and choose which pieces you want. The Netscape browser remains the core of the package, and at this writing Netscape Composer — the program we recommend for Web authoring — always downloads with the browser.

When you hear someone talk about "Netscape," "Navigator," "Communicator," or "Netscape 6 point" 1, 2, or 3, they're usually talking about the same thing: Netscape's browser software, with or without add-on tools.

If you need to use an older version of Netscape software, follow the onscreen instructions for installation. They will be similar to the instructions for installing Netscape 6.2, below, but not exactly the same.

Getting Netscape Composer

You may already have Netscape Composer, Netscape's free Web authoring software, on your system. You may have the old Communicator suite, which includes the Netscape Navigator Web browser plus an e-mail package, AOL-compatible Instant Messenger functionality, an address book, and other software. Or you may just have the stand-alone Netscape Navigator browser without the other parts of the Communicator package. In either case, you probably want to upgrade to the current version of the software, which at this writing is called Netscape 6.2.

The instructions in this section tell you how to get the newest version of Netscape software (including Composer) only, not the remaining pieces of what used to be called the Netscape Communicator suite. That's because getting Navigator only makes the download quicker and means you have a simpler software package that takes up less hard disk space. We'll show you where to click a different button if you want the other parts of the suite as well.

Be sure to upgrade your software if you have Netscape Composer or Netscape Navigator Version 6.0. Netscape 6.0 was widely disparaged as buggy, slow-loading software. Later versions, such as 6.1 and 6.2, don't have the same problems.

If you're in a networked business, organizational, or school environment, check to see if your company, organization, or school has a preconfigured, approved version of Netscape software available for you to install. Doing so will save you configuration hassles that you might otherwise have relating to the interaction of Netscape software and the network.

Download procedures for Netscape software may change due to changes in the Netscape Web site. If the steps below don't match what you see onscreen, check for updates on the Web page for this book on the For Dummies Web site at www.dummies.com.

Follow these steps to get the current version of Netscape Navigator:

1. **Go to the Netscape Web site at** www.netscape.com.

    The Netscape Web site will appear — slowly, if you're not on a fast connection, because it's a complicated page with many small graphics. This site is the default home page for the Netscape Navigator browser.

2. **On the Netscape home page, click the Download button in the upper-right corner.**

   The Download page appears, as shown in Figure 5-3.

3. **On the Download page, click the Download button — the one next to the Order CD! button.**

   You have a choice of downloading Netscape software or ordering a CD-ROM. The download is lengthy — about an hour long even if you choose a near-minimum set of options — but it still doesn't take several weeks, which is how long it may take the CD-ROM to reach you. Also, downloading is free, whereas ordering the CD-ROM costs several dollars.

   The File Download dialog box appears.

4. **In the File Download dialog box, click the radio button, Run this program from its current location. Then click OK.**

   It's easy to miss this, since the default option for the File Download dialog box is Save this program to disk. If you keep this option, you'll go through an unnecessary step of erasing the installation program.

   The installer program downloads into a temporary folder and a dialog box appears.

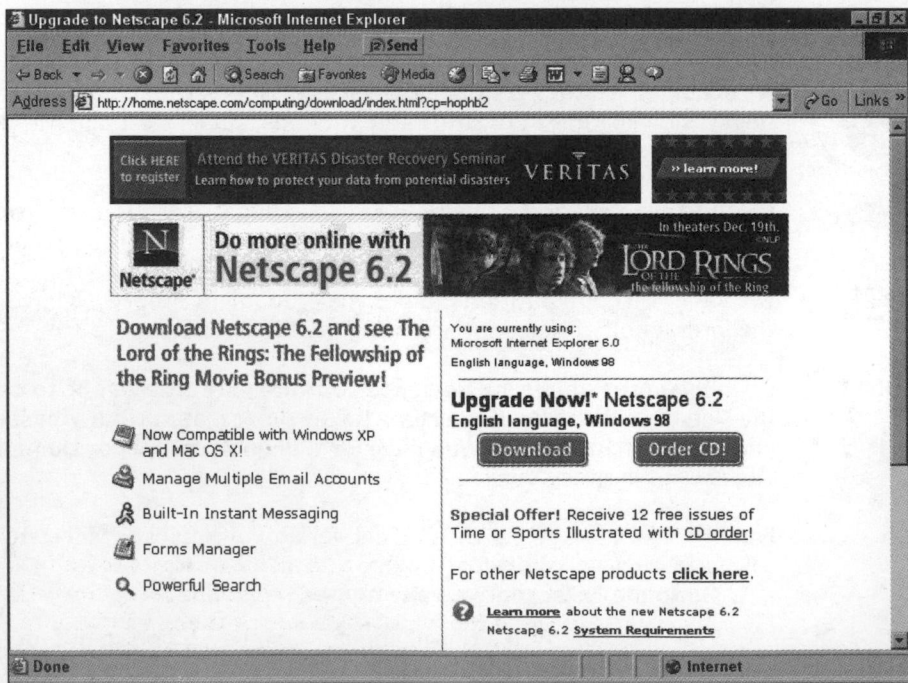

Figure 5-3: Get ready to download Netscape software.

5. **In the dialog box, you are asked whether you want to install and run N6Setup.exe. Click Yes.**

   The Netscape 6 Setup Welcome dialog box appears.

6. **In the Welcome dialog box, click Next.**

   The license agreement appears.

7. **Click Accept to accept the license agreement.**

   The Setup Type dialog box appears.

8. **In the Setup Type dialog box, choose Custom and then click Next.**

   The Select Typical Components dialog box appears, as shown in Figure 5-4.

Figure 5-4:
Just get
Navigator
and the
spell
checker.

9. **In the Select Typical Components dialog box, clear the checkboxes for Mail and Instant Messenger, unless you need these programs for reasons other than Web page authoring. Leave the Spell Checker checkbox checked. Click Next.**

   The Mail program adds about 1.5MB to your download size and hard disk requirements, and Instant Messenger adds another 460KB or so. Spell checker adds about 470KB and helps keep you from making embarrassing spelling mistakes on your Web pages.

   The Select Additional Components dialog box appears.

10. **In the Select Additional Components dialog box, shown in Figure 5-5, we recommend that you clear all the checkboxes if you're in a hurry. If you want to consider including some of them, read about the size and purpose of each, as explained below, and decide which ones to keep. Then click Next.**

Figure 5-5:
Clear most
or all of the
Additional
Compo-
nents.

We recommend that you don't download additional components unless you are sure you need them for Web sites you plan to visit using Netscape Navigator, or unless you plan to add the relevant media type to your own Web site and therefore need the component for testing. The additional components are

- **Sun Java 2 (7.7MB):** Fewer and fewer Web sites use Java, partly because it's prone to security problems. So unless you plan to use Java in your own Web site, and therefore need the component for testing, don't add nearly 8MB to your Netscape download.

- **Quality Feedback Agent (340KB):** This is software that allows you to fill out a bug report if Netscape software crashes on you. You don't necessarily need to do the company's debugging work for it.

- **AOL ART Extensions (380KB):** This allows you to view AOL-formatted graphics in your Web browser. Rarely needed.

- **Net2Phone (760KB):** Software for making phone calls over the Net, not needed for Web authoring.

- **Macromedia Flash Player (180KB):** Drop this for the fastest possible download. However, some sites do use Flash, so you may want to keep this relatively small player. (This download doesn't help you create Flash animations; go to the Macromedia Web site at www.macromedia.com for tools to do that.)

- **RealPlayer 8 (3.6MB):** RealPlayer is a big download, but if you don't already have a relatively new version of RealPlayer, you may want this. You'll find lots of RealPlayer multimedia on the Web, but it's unlikely you'll put RealPlayer-formatted audio in your own Web site because the requirements for doing so are fairly onerous, as we explain in Chapter 13.

- **WinAmp (1.7MB):** WinAmp is good for playing back MP3 files, so include this if you plan to put MP3s on your Web site. More on this in Chapter 13.

- **HP Printer Identifier plug-in (30KB):** You may want this if you have an HP printer, though printing will probably still work without it.

- **Classic Skin (380KB):** Keeps the old Netscape look. Skip it unless you're used to that look.

- **Canadian, Latin American, and UK Region Packs (about 60KB each):** You need only one of these if a majority of the people using your Web page is likely to have it, so you can see what they see. But since these options are so buried in the installation dialog, it's unlikely your users will have one of them, even if they're primarily in Canada, Latin America, or the UK, respectively. So we recommend you skip all of these.

When you click Next, the Select Program Folder dialog box appears.

11. **In the Select Program Folder dialog box, keep Netscape 6.2, the default choice, and then click Next.**

When you click Next, the Quick Launch dialog box appears.

12. **Enable Quick Launch if you plan to run Netscape Navigator as your everyday browser, otherwise leave the checkbox unchecked. Click Next.**

Quick Launch moves part of the Netscape Navigator startup code to your computer's startup process, which means some of the work of loading the program is already done when you launch Navigator itself. This costs you a few seconds every time you start up, and uses system resources that other programs might need, but saves you a few seconds every time you start Navigator. The tradeoff is worthwhile if you plan to use Netscape Navigator as your daily browser, and isn't if you plan to use Internet Explorer or another browser, such as the built-in browser in AOL or CompuServe software, instead.

The Download Options dialog box appears.

13. **In the Download Options dialog box, leave the option Save Installer Files Locally unchecked. Click Next.**

If the installation works properly, you won't need to run it again.

The Start Install dialog box appears.

14. **In the Start Install dialog box, review the choices you've made. If you need to make a change, click Back as many times as needed, make the changes, and then work your way back to this point. Then click Install.**

When you click Install, the Download dialog box appears. If you chose the minimal download we recommend above — Netscape Navigator plus the spell checker — the downloaded file will be about 8.4MB in size, and will take a minute or two to download over a fast connection, about 45 minutes to download over a 56K modem, or about an hour over a 28.8K or 33.6K modem.

Once the install is complete, the Netscape 6.2 folder opens on your desktop.

What if you need IE?

Over 80 percent of Web users these days use Internet Explorer as their first-choice browser. However, you may be one of the few who doesn't have Internet Explorer, or you may have an old version that needs updating. If so, go to the Microsoft Web site at www.microsoft.com and click on the Downloads link. Use the instructions there to download and install the current version of Internet Explorer; the process is similar to the process for downloading and installing Netscape Navigator described in this chapter.

One caveat: You may not wish to upgrade your version of Internet Explorer if you have an older version that includes FrontPage Express. FrontPage Express is a Web page editor that Microsoft offered with old versions of Internet Explorer, but no longer offers with newer versions. If you have a version of Internet Explorer with FrontPage Express, you'll probably have to avoid upgrading if you want to keep it — some newer versions of Internet Explorer won't coexist on your computer with some older versions.

Using Netscape Composer

Throughout the remainder of the book, we'll describe how to use Composer to make specific kinds of changes in your Web site. But before that, follow these steps to start Netscape Composer and get oriented to using it:

1. **Start Netscape Navigator.**

   Start Navigator from the Start menu by choosing Start⇨Programs⇨ Netscape 6.2⇨Netscape 6.2.

   The Navigator window opens, as shown in Figure 5-6.

   The Netscape Navigator browser has a toolbar on the left side, called My Sidebar, that reduces the space available for Web page content. The presence of My Sidebar makes it difficult to use Navigator to test your Web page to see if it fits in a normal Web browser window. You can get rid of the toolbar by clicking on the handle between the arrowheads embedded in the right edge of the sidebar. (You can also bring the sidebar back by clicking on the same handle.) Figure 5-6 shows the toolbar and the location of the handle.

   The Netscape Navigator browser will start and the Netscape Web site will appear — slowly, if you're not on a fast connection, because it's a complicated page with many small graphics. This site is the default home page for the Netscape Navigator browser.

   In the list of programs in the Netscape 6 folder, as well as on your desktop and in your Start menu, you'll see a yellow icon named Get $$$ — Refer a Friend! If you find this icon tacky, as we do, simply right-click on it wherever you find it, then choose Delete to delete it.

2. **Start Composer by choosing Tasks⇨Composer.**

   The Composer window opens, as shown in Figure 5-7.

Figure 5-6:
Navigator
lets you
handle the
sidebar.

Figure 5-7:
Composer
helps you
create
noteworthy
Web pages.

3. **Pull down the menus and look at the flyout options and buttons to see what options are available.**

Composer's options are only those supported by HTML, so you can get a good idea of what you can do on a Web page by looking carefully through Composer's menu options. The remaining chapters in this part of the book go into detail about how to create a Web page using Composer.

Using a Text Editor

If you want to use a text editor, you have the following choices:

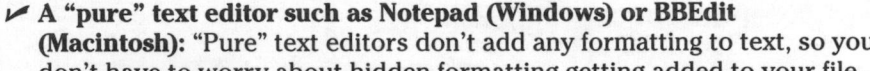

✔ **A "pure" text editor such as Notepad (Windows) or BBEdit (Macintosh):** "Pure" text editors don't add any formatting to text, so you don't have to worry about hidden formatting getting added to your file.

The CD-ROM for this book includes BBEdit, a Macintosh text-editing program, along with a set of BBEdit extensions for Web-page editing.

For the PC, you may want to see if you can find a freeware or shareware text editor with Web editing features; a good place to look is C|NET's download.com at `www.download.com`.

✔ **A word processor:** You can use a word processing program such as Windows Microsoft Word, WordPerfect, or some other full-featured word processor. Windows WordPad, which comes free with Windows, is a simple word processing program, not a true text editor.

When using either a word processor or a text editor, you should save your Web page files with the suffix `.htm`. When using a word processor, you additionally have to use a pull-down menu or other option setting to tell the word processor to save your file as a text file — with none of the normal word processor formatting.

The trade-off between using a pure text editor versus a word processor can be summed up as the trade-off between two different kinds of convenience. A pure text editor never adds word processor formatting to your document — the file is always a text file. And the pure text editor is simple — it doesn't offer you a bunch of formatting options that may or may not be supported by HTML.

A word processor, on the other hand, is familiar. You know exactly how to work with features like the spell checker (which already has any words you've added to the dictionary), formatting, and print options. This can be a real plus when you're working with a long and complicated Web page file.

Many spell checkers choke on HTML tags, so they aren't very usable for Web pages. Composer's spell checker works on the text that will appear in the Web page, so it doesn't have this problem.

You can use either a text editor or a word processor, but our experience is that the text editor is a better choice. Almost every serious Web page pro we know uses a text editor for some of their work, and a real Web page creation tool like FrontPage or Dreamweaver for the rest.

If you do use your word processor for editing Web pages, you may find that it has an option for working directly on Web pages. In our limited experience, this is more confusing than helpful. However, you may wish to try this option if you feel most comfortable in the word processing environment.

Chapter 6

Creating Your Home Page

· ·

· ·

Creating your Web home page is a lot of fun — and may be the occasion for some anxiety. After all, your home page will be published on the World Wide Web — it's like putting something you wrote onto a billboard on the busiest street in town!

Knowing what to say on your home page can be hard, but and we'll give you some ideas in this chapter. Luckily, the mechanical part — creating your first Web page and putting it on the Web — is fairly easy. This chapter will tell you how to create the page itself; the next chapter will tell you how to add graphics. Other chapters tell you how to improve your page further. And in Chapter 12 we tell you how to publish your page on the Web.

What to Put in a Home Page

Many people think the most important thing about publishing their first Web page is learning HTML. They may take an HTML course, or pick up a book like this one, and feel ready to create their first Web page. Only then do they find out that the real problem in creating their first Web page is knowing what to say!

The "what to say" problem is easier to solve if you think of your Web page as a set of blocks of content. Each block covers a specific thing you want to describe on your Web page. For instance, a set of links relating to your hobby is one block of content; your résumé would be another block. By figuring out which blocks of content you want to put up first and then figuring out what to say in each block, you cut the overall problem of what to put on your Web page into easier-to-manage pieces.

Using blocks of content also helps you move smoothly from having a single Web page to having a multi-page Web site. Your first Web page might be a long page with several blocks of content. When you're ready to move to a multi-page Web site, as described in Chapter 15, you can take the blocks of content and move several of them onto separate Web pages.

The great thing about Web publishing is that you can always change your Web pages later. "Just do it" — get something up that you're at least sort of proud of — then continually improve your Web page as you learn more.

You may have your own ideas for what to put on your initial home page, and if so, that's great. But in case you're stuck, the next few sections offer a few ideas to get you started.

Me and my interests

The easiest and most fun thing to put on your first Web page is a description of yourself and the things you're interested in. This is a good type of Web page to put up for fun, and also works well for certain specific purposes, such as applying for college or online dating (don't laugh, it's a big deal — at least here in Silicon Valley). Figure 6-1 shows an example of this kind of personal Web page.

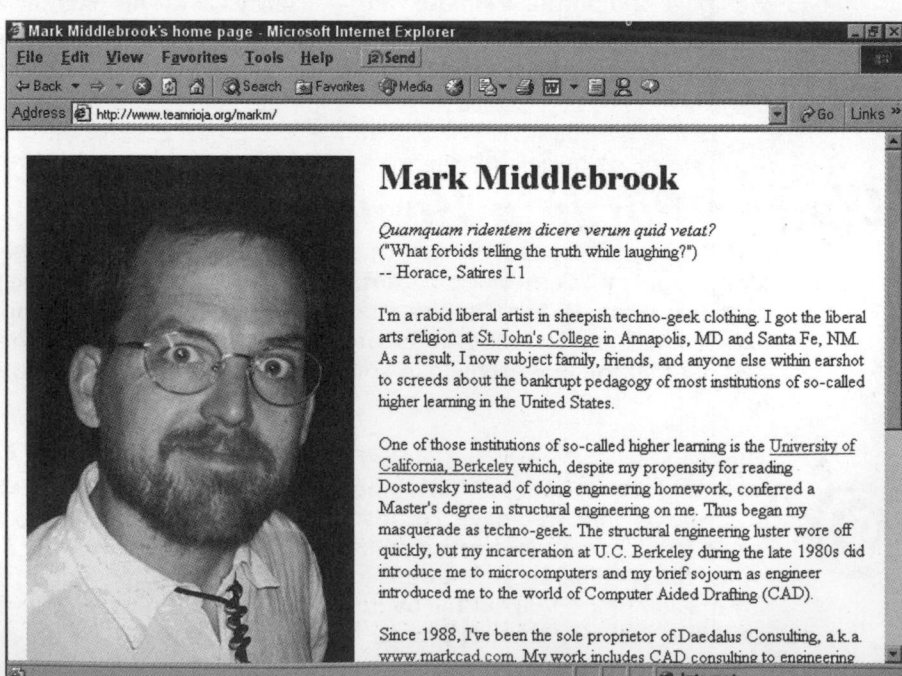

Figure 6-1: Get personal with your first Web page.

Here are some of the blocks of content you may want to include in an interests page:

- ✔ **A brief description of yourself:** Briefly describe yourself — name; age or age range; what you do; where you work, go to school, and live; and a bit of your personal history.

  Don't give too much detail about yourself, or you may become a victim of identity theft. See the sidebar, "Maintain your identity," for details.

- ✔ **A photo of yourself:** You can use a photo of yourself as part of your self-description. We'll tell you much more about how to get a photo of yourself onto the Web in Chapter 9.

- ✔ **A description of your interests:** Your Web page may focus on one of your interests, but it's nice to have a brief list of all your major interests — this makes someone visiting your Web page feel like they really know you.

- ✔ **A description of your work or school:** Describing how you spend your days is an interesting part of a rounded picture of you. Include a link to the Web site of your company or school, if there is one. (We tell you how to do this in Chapter 8.)

- ✔ **Favorite links, by interest:** (One or more blocks.) Many people put their favorite links on their Web site, but the list tends to be both obvious and confusing — a mishmash of things thrown together and including obvious sites like Yahoo! or Amazon, which almost all Web surfers know about already. Create short lists of your favorite sites on one specific interest at a time — and precede it with a brief description of why you have that interest.

- ✔ **Detailed link descriptions:** For each link you provide, give a description of the site and what you find valuable about it. Link to specific pages in the site with the best stuff, rather than just linking to the site's front page.

You can create this kind of Web page as a simple, long, scrolling page with no navigation — just one block of content after another. For this kind of Web page, it doesn't even matter much if the formatting and look of the page are kind of rough around the edges — interesting content is enough to make the Web page stand on its own.

Me and my family

A popular use of a Web page is to put up photos of yourself, your spouse or significant other, your kids, your pets, and other important people in your life. (We know pets aren't people, but many pet lovers don't.) This kind of Web site helps families and friends keep in touch. See Figure 6-2 for an example.

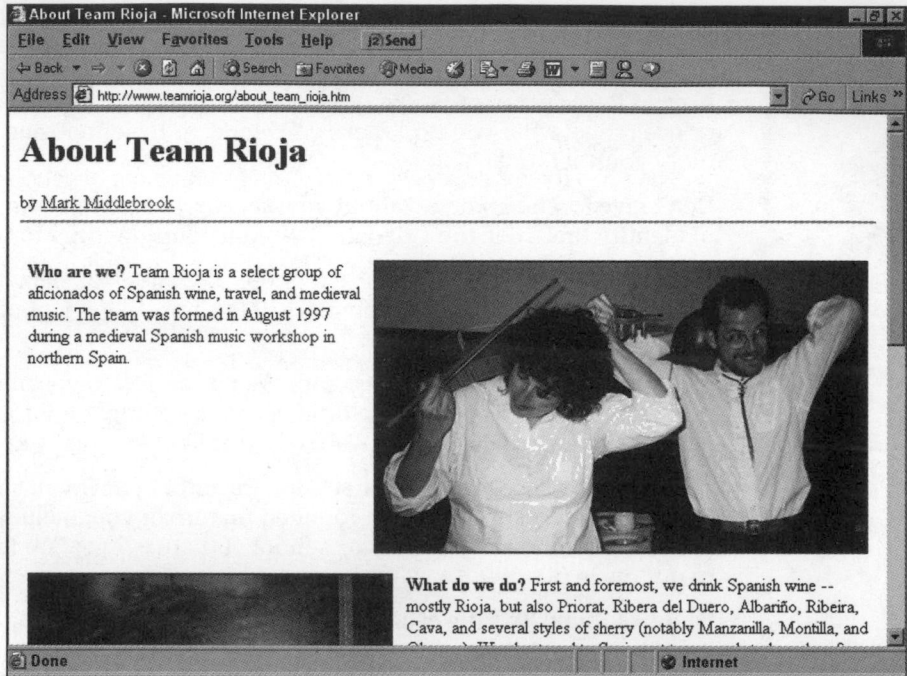

About Team Rioja - Microsoft Internet Explorer

File   Edit   View   Favorites   Tools   Help   Send

Back   Search   Favorites   Media

Address   http://www.teamrioja.org/about_team_rioja.htm   Go   Links

About Team Rioja

by Mark Middlebrook

Who are we? Team Rioja is a select group of aficionados of Spanish wine, travel, and medieval music. The team was formed in August 1997 during a medieval Spanish music workshop in northern Spain.

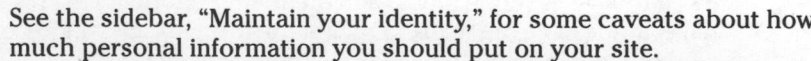

What do we do? First and foremost, we drink Spanish wine -- mostly Rioja, but also Priorat, Ribera del Duero, Albariño, Ribeira, Cava, and several styles of sherry (notably Manzanilla, Montilla, and

Done   Internet

Figure 6-2:
Make the
Web a
family affair.

Such pages can grow into fairly large Web sites as additional pages are put up for each family member and each birthday party or vacation that gets memorialized on the Web site. For your initial, simple home page, though, consider the following content:

- ✔ **A brief description of yourself and other family members:** Have each person in the family briefly describe themselves — name, age or age range, work or school details, where he or she lives, and a bit of personal history.

  See the sidebar, "Maintain your identity," for some caveats about how much personal information you should put on your site.

- ✔ **A photo of each person:** Include a group photo or a photo of each person. Don't use too many photos, or photos that are too large, or your Web page will load very slowly. See Chapter 9 for more on photos and other graphics.

- ✔ **Descriptions of everyone's interests:** A brief list of each person's major interests is a nice touch on a family Web page. This can also give relatives a clue as to what to get each person in the way of birthday and holiday gifts, without your being too obvious about saying what you want.

✔ **A description of each person's work or school:** It's nice to see — or to be reminded — how each person in your family spends his weekdays. Include a link to the Web site of each person's company or school, if available. (We tell you how to do this in Chapter 8.)

✔ **Favorite links, by person:** (One block per person.) A list of each person's top five or seven sites gives visitors an idea of each family member's interests without making the page too lengthy.

Like a personal page, a family page can be a simple, long, scrolling page with no navigation, and the look can be whatever you want it to be — no professionalism needed. This kind of page is more fun the more you put into it, without worrying too much about appearances.

Me and my work

You can put up a brief Web professional page describing your professional background and interests — kind of an illuminated résumé. This kind of page can be tilted toward sharing your professional interests, or more narrowly focused on helping you get a job.

Some of the blocks of content you may want to include in a work-related page:

✔ **A brief description of yourself:** As in a personal page, described in the previous section, a brief description of yourself is interesting. Talk about yourself — leave your professional interests to their own section.

✔ **A photo of yourself?:** A photo of yourself is a nice addition to a professional site. But if you're going to be using your professional page for getting a job, you may want to leave the photo off. Why? Because employers who are concerned about discrimination issues won't accept a résumé with a photo in the early screening stages; they simply ignore any such résumés. So leave the photo off your professional site if you're looking for work.

✔ **A description of your professional interests:** A professional Web page should list your major professional interests. You should probably leave personal interests for your personal site, unless you have a leadership role in a volunteer organization or some other work-relevant personal involvement.

✔ **Favorite links, by interest:** (One or more blocks.) A well-organized list of links to areas of professional interest to you can be a real resource for others with similar interests. Create a separate list for each of your major areas of interest.

✔ **A formatted, printable résumé:** If you are considering using your professional site as a resource for a job hunt, or if you just want people to be able to see all the work experience that's summed up in your résumé, then add a formatted résumé to your Web page.

A work-related site can be a single Web page at first, but you'll probably want to have your résumé as a separate page before too long. We describe how to add additional pages to your Web site in Chapter 15.

As for appearance, it's not too important that your professional page look real sharp, but you don't want it to be out-and-out ugly either. See Chapter 11 for details on creating an attractive site.

We suggest that you not create a Web site for your business — even a small business — as your first Web publishing effort. It's very important that a business Web page have an attractive look, a good balance of text and graphics, and correct spelling and grammar. This is a lot of requirements to meet in your first Web publishing effort. We suggest you create a personal Web page — either for yourself as an individual, for your family, or for your work interests — to start. Later you can use your newly acquired skills to tackle the tougher job of creating a business Web site. (We describe how to in Chapter 15.)

Maintain your identity

When creating your personal Web page, avoid giving out specifics that a thief could use to steal your identity. It takes surprisingly little personal information for someone to fill out a credit application in your name and get credit while posing as you. The identity thief can then run up thousands of dollars of charges against your credit in a few days, all without your knowledge. Cleaning up after this kind of attack on your credit can be very difficult, expensive, and time-consuming.

The main thing to avoid is giving specific names and numbers: Your driver's license number, your Social Security number, and credit card numbers are strictly off limits, which may seem obvious. But you should also avoid giving other numbers: Your street address and your personal phone number are good things to leave out, as are your exact age and your birthdate. You

might even want to leave these details off an online résumé; just include your name and e-mail address for people to use in making an initial contact with you.

Don't give a lot of details about family members, and specifically avoid giving your mother's maiden name — a bit of information that's commonly used to verify identity. Staying vague about family members protects them as well as you.

Be especially careful to avoid giving details about kids, especially information that could allow someone to identify and find a child. For instance, you may decide to put your address and phone number on your site — but don't also include a picture of one of your kids and his name, or your kids may get the attention of the wrong kind of people.

Starting Your Page

Okay, so you're ready to create your first personal Web page. How do you actually do it?

Just fire up your Web page editor — whether it's a text editor or a Web page editing program like Composer — and start writing. Use HTML commands, if in a text editor, or the commands that your Web page editor makes available to format your text as you go along.

One way to make Web publishing easier is to separate the "what do I say" part from the Web publishing part. Consider creating a mock-up of your home page first in your favorite word processing program. Get the text right, insert a picture, and so on. Then, when it's time to actually create your Web page, copy and paste the text from your word processing program into your Web page editor.

When you bring content from a word processing program into a Web page editing program, be ready to redo your formatting — and to rewrite some of your text to make it more Web-friendly. Short, punchy text with lots of headings, bulleted lists, and numbered lists is the recipe for easy-to-read Web writing.

Creating your initial page using HTML

In this section, and following sections, we tell you how to create your Web page using HTML in a text-editing program. This allows you to really get to know the HTML tags by using them directly.

In alternating sections we describe how to do the same thing using a Web-editing program like Netscape Composer. This allows you to concentrate more on your content and less on the mechanics of HTML.

The steps in this section are for Windows Notepad, but a similar process will work for any text editor — or even for a word processing program, if you're careful to save the file as text, then add .htm to the end of the filename to indicate that it's an HTML file.

In this section, we describe very specifically how to get your HTML file started — if you do it right, life will be easy, but if you make even a small mistake, it will be hard to edit and preview your file. Follow these steps to create an initial Web page in HTML:

1. **Open your text-editing program. For instance, to use Windows Notepad as your text editor, choose Start⇨Programs⇨Accessories⇨Notepad.**

   Your text-editing program will open a new document.

2. **Add required header and other tags to your document: The** `<HTML>` **and** `</HTML>`, `<HEAD>` **and** `</HEAD>`, `<TITLE>` **and** `</TITLE>`, **and** `<BODY>` **and** `</BODY>` **tag pairs.**

   Enter the following lines in your HTML file:

   ```
   <HTML>
   <HEAD>
   <TITLE>Bud Smith's Personal Web Page
   </TITLE>
   </HEAD>
   <BODY>
       <!--The main content of your Web page goes in the body
           section.-->
   </BODY>
   </HTML>
   ```

   See Figure 6-3 for a display of these HTML tags in a Notepad document.

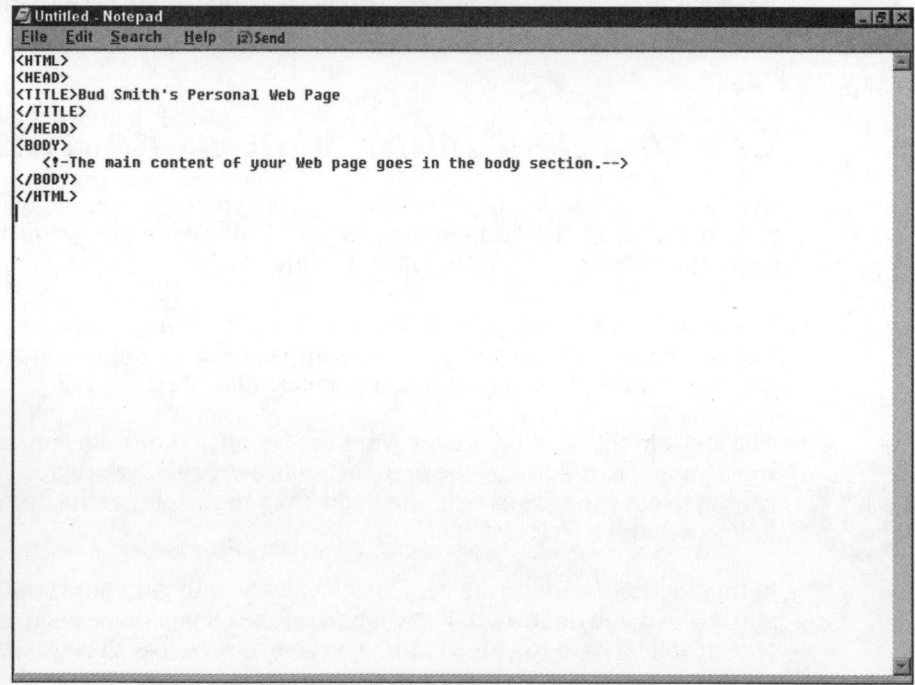

Figure 6-3: Get the HTML into your document.

The main part of your Web document will go between the <BODY> and </BODY> tags. The tag with an exclamation point, <!-- The main content... -->, contains a comment. The browser ignores this tag and its contents, and doesn't display them in your document, but using this tag allows you to make notes to yourself in the HTML text.

The text between the <TITLE> and </TITLE> pair of tags is the title of the document. It's displayed by a Web browser in the top of the file window.

3. **Begin the process of saving the file by choosing File⇨Save.**

The Save As dialog box will open.

Both the Save and Save As commands open the Save As dialog box when you're saving a file that hasn't previously been saved.

4. **Create a new folder for your Web page files. Use the pull-down file menu at the top of the Save As dialog box to navigate to the spot where you want to create your new folder. Then use the Create New Folder icon — the folder with the star on it — to create the new folder. Name it according to the rules in the sidebar, "How to make Web filenames." Then open the new folder so your file will be saved into it.**

See the sidebar, "Files of a feather," for details on why it's important to keep all the files that make up your Web page or Web site in one place.

5. **Use the pull-down menu, Save as type, to specify that your file should be saved as a Text document.**

Get in the habit of saving your HTML files as text documents. That way, even if you work on the file in a word processor, your file will be saved in text format, without any word processor formatting codes.

6. **Enter the File name you want to use, followed by the suffix .htm. For example, you can call the file mypage.htm.**

See the sidebar, "How to make Web filenames," for details on why it's important to save your file as a text file, and to end your HTML files' filenames with .htm. Using the .htm suffix will allow you to easily open the file in a Web browser program to review it.

7. **Click the Save button.**

Notepad will save your file as a text document with the filename you gave it, including the suffix .htm.

8. **To preview your Web page in a Web browser, open a browser such as Internet Explorer.**

Now's a good time to get in the habit of having a browser window open so you can check your HTML work as you go along. Every time you save your HTML document, you can open the saved document in your Web browser to see how it will look as a real Web page.

9. **In your browser, choose File⇨Open to bring up the Open dialog box. Click the Browse button to open a dialog box that will allow you to find your file. Navigate to where your file is and click on its name to select it. Then click Open.**

10. **Your file will open in the browser. Figure 6-4 shows the text file and the browser open next to each other. Note that the title specified in the HTML document is shown in the Web browser's file window.**

Web page authors commonly use this way of working, with your HTML document and a Web browser open at the same time, to keep track of the changes they're making in a document.

To see changes you're making in your HTML document, you have to save the HTML file and then click the Refresh or Reload button in your browser. Refreshing the contents of your browser makes the browser go get a new copy of the page from the Web server — or, in this case, from your computer's hard disk.

Title in HTML document   Title displayed in Web browser

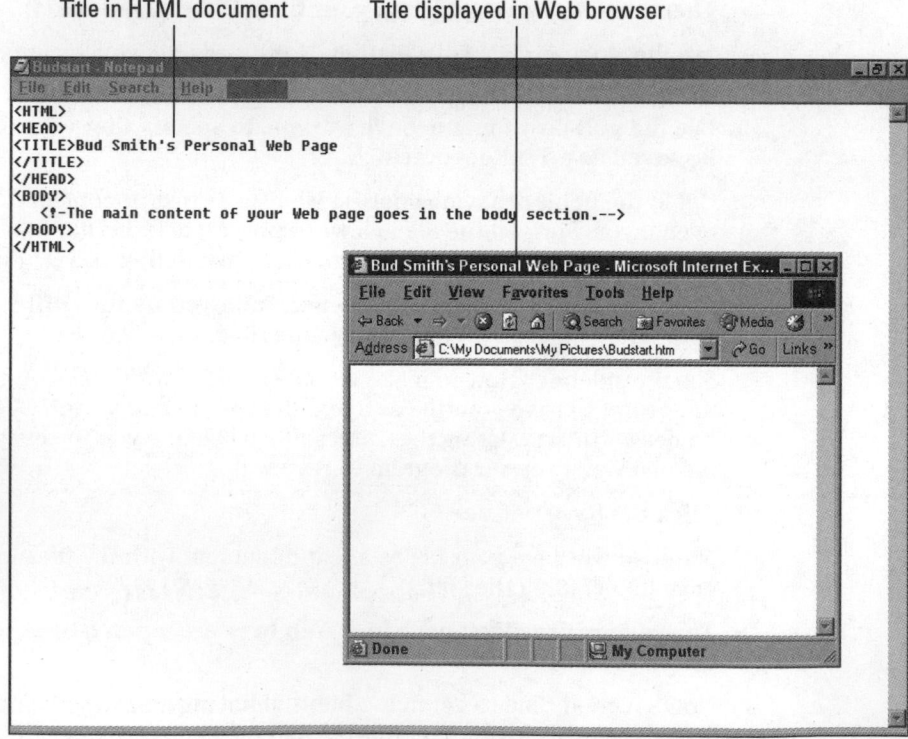

Figure 6-4:
Only the title has been changed to protect the emptiness.

How to make Web filenames

Here are a few things to keep in mind when naming your files for the Web:

✔ When you tell a Windows program to save your file as a text document, it saves just the actual text characters that you see onscreen, without any formatting commands. The Windows program also assigns the suffix `.txt` to the file, unless you tell it otherwise. The filename's suffix, which is usually hidden from you by Windows, helps Windows figure out what kinds of programs the file "belongs" to. When you name your file with the suffix `.htm`, it overrides the `.txt` suffix.

✔ When your file ends in `.htm`, Windows recognizes it as an HTML file. This allows you to easily open the file from a Web browser program such as Internet Explorer. By doing this, you can preview your file as you work on it — and, more importantly, other people will be able to open your file as a Web page when you put it on a Web server.

You may also see some Web pages with filenames ending in `.html`; this suffix works on some servers. However, you should not end the filenames of your Web pages with `.html` because some programs that you may use to edit your file or to transfer it to a Web server will truncate the suffix to `.htm`. This will break any links you have to the document, since they'll refer to the file using its original suffix, `.html`. Save yourself potential headaches and always use `.htm` as the suffix for your HTML files.

✔ It's also important to not put spaces in your Web filenames, to keep them eight characters or less in length, and to use only lowercase letters in the filenames. Why? Because your Web page might be published on a UNIX server, or on a server that runs an old version of Windows. Different servers have different filename rules. Only a filename with its main part eight characters or less, with `.htm` as its suffix, and with no uppercase characters can be sure to be kept intact when you publish your Web page onto a Web server.

You should also keep your folder names all lowercase and eight characters or less, for the same reasons. If your folder name changes when you transfer your Web page to a server for publication, links to the Web pages and graphics files in the folder can be broken. There's not much that's more frustrating — or embarrassing, especially if you're creating a Web page for a company or other organization — than having your hyperlinks break when you move your Web site from your own machine to the Web.

Creating your initial page using a Web editor

Using a text editor, as described in the previous section, allows you to get up close and personal with HTML tags. Using a Web editor such as Netscape Composer, as described in this section, allows you to worry less about HTML tags and more about your actual content. (Don't worry that you won't learn HTML — we'll have you look at the HTML-tagged text underlying your document frequently.)

The steps in this section are for Netscape Composer, but a similar process will work for other Web page editors such as Microsoft FrontPage or Dreamweaver. These full-featured editors have all the features of Composer, and then some, so you'll be able to follow the steps given here in the more capable programs.

Follow these steps to create your initial Web page in Composer:

1. **Open Composer (which you can only start from within Netscape Navigator). First open Netscape Navigator by choosing Start⇨ Programs⇨Netscape 6.2⇨Netscape 6.2. Then choose Tasks⇨ Composer.**

   Netscape Composer will open with an empty window.

   Once Composer is open, you can close Navigator, and Composer will still stay open.

2. **Give your document a title by choosing Format⇨Page Title and Properties.**

   The Page Properties dialog box will open

3. **In the Page Properties dialog, enter the title for your document. (A Web browser in the top of the file window will display the title.) Optionally, you may want to enter your name and a file description in the Author and Description areas. Click OK when finished.**

   The Author and Description fields are most useful if you're working with others on the same machine or on the same Web site. They help identify who on a team has been working on a document and what each HTML file is for.

4. **Preview your document's HTML by choosing View⇨HTML Source or clicking the <HTML> Source tab at the bottom of the editing window.**

   Your document's HTML source will appear, as shown in Figure 6-5. Note that you have no actual content in your document, but already you have almost a dozen HTML tags! Don't worry, most of the work you do from here on will have results that are directly visible in your Web page.

   Note the sets of tag pairs that are standard in any HTML document: the `<HTML>` and `</HTML>`, `<HEAD>` and `</HEAD>`, `<TITLE>` and `</TITLE>`, and `<BODY>` and `</BODY>` tag pairs.

   Also note the META tags. For a brief description of META tags, see the section, "I Never META Tag I Didn't Like," later in this chapter.

   The main part of your Web document will go between the `<BODY>` and `</BODY>` tags. The tag with an exclamation point, `<!-- The main content... -->`, contains a comment. This tag and its contents are ignored by the browser and not displayed in your document, but the comment tag allows you to make notes to yourself in the HTML text.

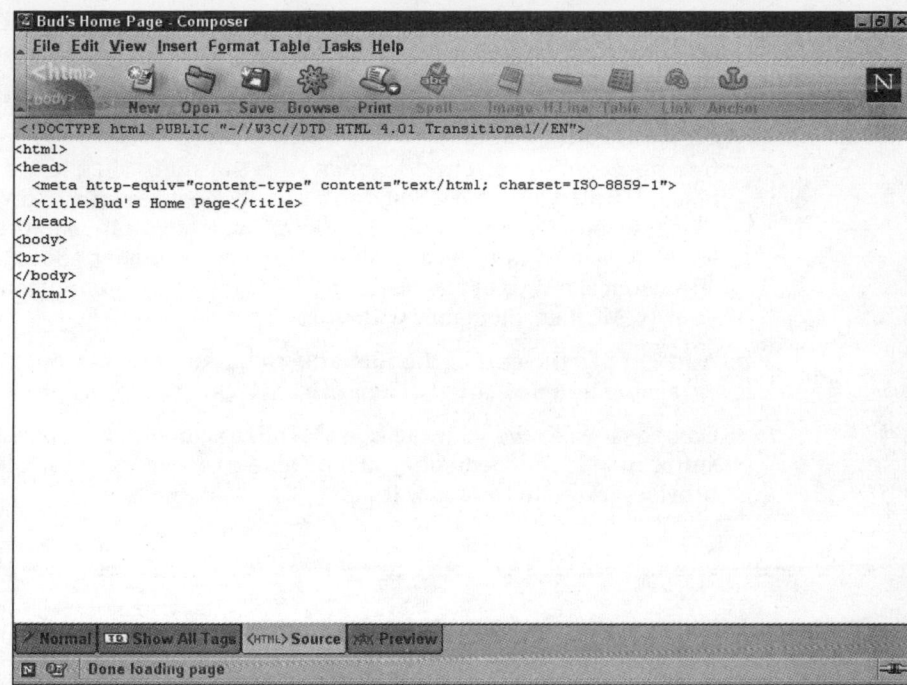

```
Bud's Home Page - Composer
File  Edit  View  Insert  Format  Table  Tasks  Help
<html>
<body>       New   Open  Save  Browse  Print   Spell   Image H.Line Table   Link  Anchor    N
<!DOCTYPE html PUBLIC "-//W3C//DTD HTML 4.01 Transitional//EN">
<html>
<head>
  <meta http-equiv="content-type" content="text/html; charset=ISO-8859-1">
  <title>Bud's Home Page</title>
</head>
<body>
<br>
</body>
</html>




 Normal  Show All Tags  <HTML> Source   Preview
 N      Done loading page
```

Figure 6-5:
Composer
lets you
go to the
(HTML)
source.

The text between the <TITLE> and </TITLE> pair of tags is the title of the document. The Web browser in the top of the file window displays it.

5. **Return to a normal view of your Web page by choosing View⇨Normal Edit Mode or by clicking the Normal tab at the bottom of the editing window.**

Your empty editing window appears. Note, however, that your Web page's title appears at the top of the editing window.

If you don't give your document a title before you save it, Composer will prompt you to enter a title before saving.

6. **Begin the process of saving the file by choosing File⇨Save.**

The Save Page As dialog box will open.

Both the Save and Save As commands open the Save Page As dialog box when you're saving a file that hasn't previously been saved.

7. **To create a new folder for your Web page files, use the pull-down file menu at the top of the Save Page As dialog box to navigate to the spot where you want to create your new folder. Then use the Create New Folder icon — the folder with the star on it — to create the new folder. Name it according to the rules in the sidebar, "How to make Web file-names." Then open the new folder so your file will be saved into it.**

See the sidebar, "Files of a feather," for details on why it's important to keep all the files that make up your Web page or Web site in one place.

8. **Use the pull-down menu, Save as type, to specify that your file should be saved as an HTML Files document.**

Composer will save your document with the suffix `.htm` to indicate that it's an HTML document. (You don't usually see the suffix of a Windows filename, but it's how Windows "knows" which icon to use when displaying a file, and what programs should be able to open it.) See the sidebar, "How to make Web filenames," for details on why it's important to end your HTML files' filenames with `.htm`.

9. **Add `.htm` to the end of the filename to make sure it is given the .htm extension and not `.html`. Then Click the Save button.**

Composer will save your file as an HTML document. Because it has the suffix `.htm` in the filename, you'll be able to easily open the file in a Web browser program to review it.

Files of a feather

Keep all the files for your Web page, or for a small multi-page Web site, in a single folder. The Web publishing process will be much easier.

✔ **For a Web page:** It's important to keep the HTML file for your Web page and all the images that are used in your Web page in a single folder. Why? Because the hyperlinks are much simpler if you just have to give the filename. If you put image files in a separate folder, the hyperlink (see Chapter 4) has to name the folder and its relationship to the folder. Trust us, you don't need the hassle.

There's yet another reason to keep your HTML file and your image files in one folder. When you publish your Web page, you'll be moving your HTML file and the image files onto a different machine — the Web server that will host your Web page. If you keep all your files together, doing this transfer correctly will be much easier.

✔ **For a multi-page Web site:** Hyperlinks to images and to other Web pages in your site are easier to specify, and transferring the site to a Web server is easier, when you keep all your files in a single folder.

This reasoning breaks down, though, when a Web site gets larger and more complicated. When you have more than a couple of dozen files, keeping them all in one folder becomes difficult to manage. At that point you'll have to break your site into a group of folders, one per Web page, plus a folder for shared graphics. And then you get to change all your hyperlinks so they work across the new folder hierarchy (see Chapter 4 for more about hyperlinks).

You should also keep extraneous files that aren't part of your Web page out of your Web page's folder. Why? These extra files will most likely be moved, along with your Web page, to a Web server when you publish your site. And who needs the extra files?

If you want your Web page to be easily found by search engines, put key information — like your full name, for a personal page, or your business name, for a business page — in the title, in the first heading within your document, in the first 20 or so regular-text words of your document, and in META tags (described in the next section) in your document. When a spider indexes your page, it will look in some or all of these places, and people searching for your name or your business name are very likely to see your page in the search results.

I Never META Tag I Didn't Like

One of the most interesting, and controversial, tags in HTML is the META tag. That's because META tags affect how your Web page appears in search engines, and some people go to great lengths to have their pages rank high in search engine lists. The META tag is used for *meta-information* — information about your Web page, rather than information that is displayed in your Web page.

The META tag is used only in the header area of your site. The header area is all about meta-information, so that makes sense. (The <TITLE> tag is supposed to be meta-information, for use only by spiders, but Web browsers also display the title in the top of the file's window.)

The META tag has one main purpose: To better describe your Web page to the spider programs that gather Web information for search engines. Some search engines depend heavily on the contents of META tags to decide how to index pages for use in search results, and to find a description of the page to use in the search results themselves.

In some cases, if a user is searching for Ukrainian Frisbee teams, and the words in your META tag include "Ukrainian" and "Frisbee," your page will come up first in the search engines! Other search engines, though, largely ignore the content of META tags. For more on how to place your site high in search engine results, see Chapter 15.

META tags consist of three pieces: The word META, a field that describes the content of the META tag, and the information that goes in the field. Here's the META tag that Netscape Composer puts in all your Web pages:

```
<meta http-equiv="content-type" content="text/html;
        charset=ISO-8859-1">
```

What a bunch of junk! But this is simply three fields of data. The first tells a Web spider that this is a META tag. The second says that it's the "content-type" version of a META tag. The third says that the content of this Web page is text, in HTML format; it uses the character set ISO-8859-1, or standard English-language ASCII characters. You can add this META tag to any document you create.

There are three other META tags you really should put in your Web page: the author, description, and keyword versions of the tag. Examples follow:

✔ `<meta name="author" content="Bud Smith">`

The author version of the META tag simply states who created the page. This is mostly useful for internal purposes — so someone who knows you, or who works in the same organization you do, knows who to go to with questions or comments about this particular Web page.

✔ `<meta name="description" content="Bud Smith's own Web page">`

The description version of the META tag is simply a brief description of the Web page. Put in it any Web page that you want to have show up in search results. Some search engines use the DESCRIPTION version of the tag as the actual description that shows up in the search engine listings, so write the content carefully.

✔ `<meta name="keyword" content="Bud Smith, Web authoring, Dummies, For Dummies">`

The keyword version of the META tag is a list of keywords that you want search engines to associate with your page. Your results will be better, overall, if the keywords listed in your META tag are also within the title, first header, or first 20 or so ordinary words of your Web site.

For additional information about META tags, check out Search Engine Watch at `http://searchenginewatch.com/webmasters/meta.html`. This Web site has the latest and greatest information about Web search engines. Its information about META tags is written in an understandable way, and it has a lot of other great search engine information as well.

Adding META tags with HTML

It's very easy to add META tags to your HTML document:

1. **Open your Web page in your text-editing program.**

   For instance, to use Windows Notepad as your text editor, choose Start➪Programs➪Accessories➪Notepad, and then choose File➪Open to choose the file to open.

   Your Web page will open in Notepad or your text editor of choice.

2. **Add the author, description, and keyword META tags to your document in the header area, between the** `<HEAD>` **and** `</HEAD>` **tags:**

```
<meta name="author" content="xxx">
<meta name="description" content="yyy">
<meta name="keyword" content="zzz">
```

xxx should be your name; yyy should be the description of your Web page that you want to have appear in a search engine's results; and zzz should be keywords related to the content of your page. For a personal Web page, good keywords are your first name, last name, your full name, and keywords relating to the interests described on your page.

3. **Save your document, and then exit your text-editing program.**

You can't preview this change in a Web browser, since META tags don't appear in your Web page. So simply save your document and exit.

Adding META tags with Composer

Most changes to your Web page are easier with Composer than with HTML in a text editor. However, since adding META tags involves adding HTML code directly to your document, it's actually a bit complex:

1. **Open your Web page in Composer.**

Choose Start⇨Programs⇨Netscape 6.2⇨Netscape 6.2 to start Netscape Navigator. Then choose Task⇨Composer to start Composer. Finally, choose File⇨Open to open your Web page file. Your Web page will open in Composer.

2. **Within Composer, choose Format⇨Page Title and Properties.**

The Page Properties dialog will open, as shown in Figure 6-6.

Figure 6-6:
Paging all
Properties.

Page Properties

Location:	[New page, not saved yet]
Last Modified:	Unknown
Title:	Bud's Home Page
Author:	
Description:	

Advanced users:
To edit other contents of the <head> region, use "HTML Source" in the View Menu or Edit Mode Toolbar.

[OK] [Cancel]

3. **Enter or modify the contents of the Author and Description field. Don't be afraid to write a long description, even though there isn't much space for it in the dialog box. (You can also take this opportunity to modify the title of your Web page if you want.) Click OK when finished.**

Composer automatically generates the author and description META tags for you and places them in the Header area of the HTML document you're creating.

The description you enter may show up as the description of your Web page in the results page of a search engine.

The good news is, that was easy. The bad news is, you're not done yet. You still need to enter the keywords for search engines to associate with your Web page, and you have to work directly in HTML to do that.

4. **In Composer, click the HTML Source tab, or choose View⇨HTML Source.**

The HTML source for your Web page will appear, as shown in Figure 6-7. Note that the META tags for author and description are there, just as you entered them.

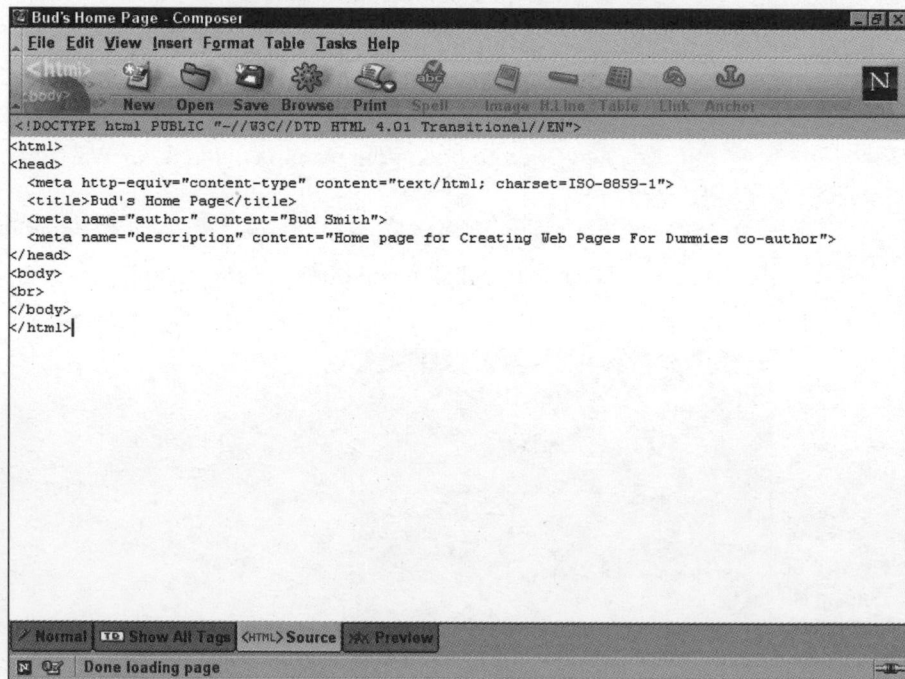

Figure 6-7:
You can go to the HTML source in Composer.

5. **Copy and paste the META tag for your Web page's description into the HTML source. (You should now have two identical DESCRIPTION lines.) In the second line, change "description" to "keyword". Then change the words after "content=" to the keywords you want your Web page to be associated with for search engines.**

   Editing a copy of existing HTML is often much easier than creating new HTML code yourself.

6. **Go back to the normal viewing mode by clicking the Normal tab, or by choosing View⇨Normal Edit Mode.**

   The content of your Web page will appear, with HTML tags hidden.

7. **Save your document, and exit Composer.**

   Your Web page now has appropriate META tags — many commercially created Web pages don't. Congratulations!

Chapter 7

Filling in Your Home Page

• •

• •

The previous chapter shows you how to get your Web page started. This chapter will show you how to put some text in it and get the text formatted so it looks good.

Along the way, we'll also talk about how to write for the Web. Web writing is a bit different than other kinds of writing. It's also kind of fun, once you get used to it.

Writing for the Web

Every new medium develops its own style. Magazine articles are often wordy and literary in style. Newspaper articles are brief, to the point, and written in a "pyramid" style that puts the most important information first. The Web has its own style. Learning to use it, even a little bit, can make your Web page much more interesting and effective.

Web realities

The new style of writing found online is based on three underlying realities about the Web:

✔ **The capabilities of HTML:** HTML allows you to specify some simple text formatting, headers, and lists. Newer versions of HTML also allow you to specify fonts and specific text sizes, but a user can easily override these specifications.

Result: Don't count on complicated formatting and specific layout to get your message across. Keep it simple.

✔ **The difficulty of reading from a computer screen:** A computer screen is a much lower resolution than a printed page — about 100 dpi versus anywhere from 600 dpi on up for most print. People's eyes get tired when they try to read long blocks of text onscreen. Figure 7-1 shows how far onscreen letters are from the smooth lines of printed text.

Result: Web writing shies away from long blocks of text. Write briefly, and break up what you write using headers, lists, quotes, and other devices. Then cut what you write down to the fewest words that do the job.

✔ **The ease of clicking away:** One of the most fun things for Web users is one of the most vexing for Web publishers: It's very, very easy to click away. Web content is free and voluminous, so users are always enticed to go elsewhere.

Result: In addition to keeping your text brief and broken up, you need to make it as interesting as possible. Take advantage of the ease of clicking away: Include relevant hyperlinks in your Web text.

Figure 7-1:
Zooming in shows how "chunky" onscreen letters are.

chunky

To further illustrate these difficulties, Figure 7-2 shows a Web page from the For Dummies site at www.dummies.com. This Web page shows content from the previous edition of this book. It's very well laid-out online, but the amount of content displayed is only about half of a printed page (remember, a book reader sees two pages at a time). The comparison to the Web is even more unfavorable for magazines or newspapers, which fit far more information on a page than a computer screen does.

The point is that the reader gets far more content for a given amount of effort from print than they do from online content. So when writing for the Web, you need to keep your text short, your layout simple, and your content interesting.

If you have something dense and detailed that you really want people to read, put it on a separate Web page and encourage people to print the page out. That will make it easier for them to carefully read the text rather than scan it, as most people tend to do with text on the computer screen.

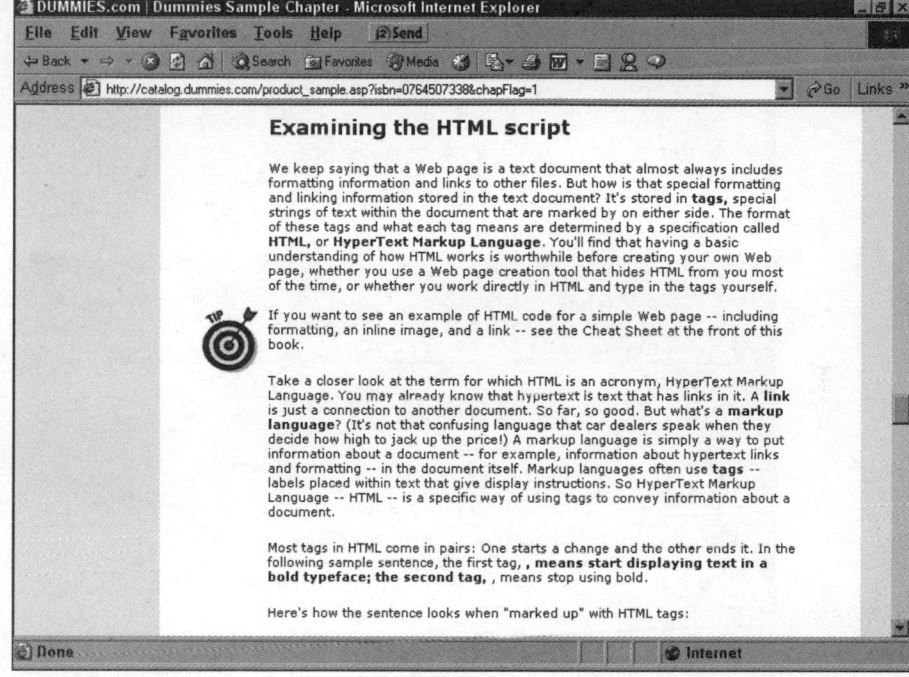

Figure 7-2:
An
onscreen
page has
fewer
words than
a printed
one.

Web style

Some characteristics of Web writing are based on physical realities. Others have evolved because of the way the Web evolved — beginning as a network for rapid communication among scientists and researchers, civilian and military. As a result, Web writing also has a couple of other characteristics that are interesting:

- **A lack of hype:** In the early days of the Web, commercial use of the Internet was expressly forbidden — though some business activity did sneak in. In the early 1990s, the Internet and the Web were opened to commercial activity. Even so, a calm, informative tone still dominates on the Web. Enthusiasm is encouraged, but hype, overly broad claims, and hucksterism seem odd and out of place on the Web.

- **An informal tone:** Web writing, like e-mail, tends to be casual in tone — like writing to a friend. Formality stands out like a sore thumb, but so does too much cuteness. The Web is a "cool" and informative medium. Figure 7-3 shows a page from Netsurfer Digest, published by Arthur Bebak, one of the authors of this book. It's cool, low key, informal, and informative.

✔ **A need for correctness and accuracy:** Informal doesn't mean inaccurate. It's true that early use of the Web was somewhat a way of connecting friends — people in the scientific and military communities who knew each other from conferences and via e-mail. However, they were highly educated and extremely literate friends. You need to be accurate in order to show people that you're one of the voices on the Web worth listening to.

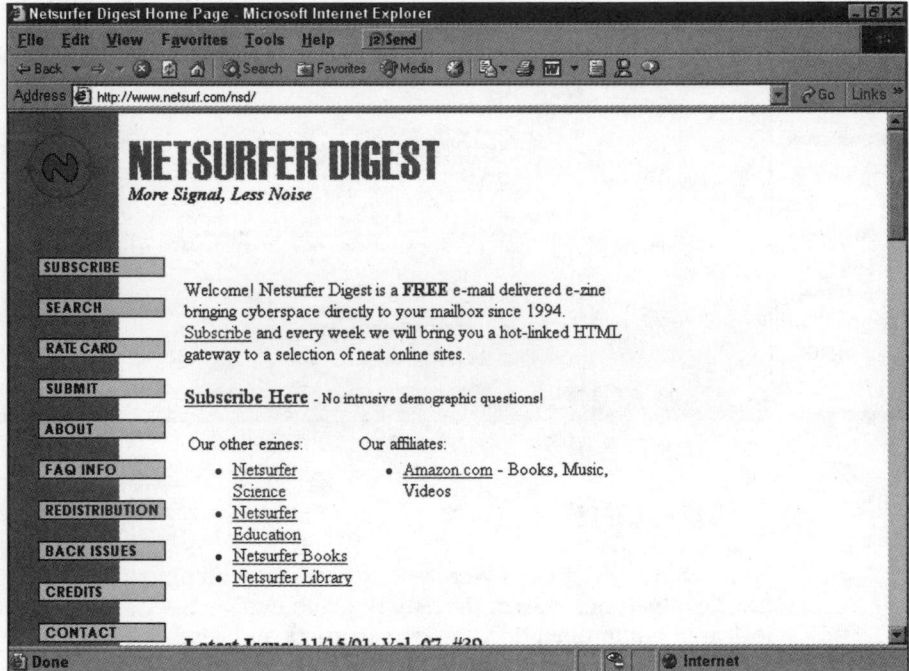

Figure 7-3:
Netsurfer
lacks hype.

Have fun

Writing for the Web is actually fun, once you start to get used to it. You can be informal, and you don't need to go on and on to belabor every obscure point you're trying to make. Just make your point, perhaps add links to a couple of Web sites that give relevant facts or support what you're trying to say, and move on.

Do check over what you've written before you publish it, though. People will feel like you're wasting their time if you don't make sure your spelling is correct, your grammar is passable, and your facts are accurate. (If you're not sure of your information on a given point, just say so.)

Many unhappy Returns?

One of the most disconcerting things about Web page editing when you work directly in HTML is the way HTML handles carriage returns and line breaks.

We're all used to hitting the Enter or Return key when we want to create a line break in a word processing document or an e-mail message. If we want more blank space, we hit Enter or Return more times. However, it doesn't always work that way when you're creating a Web page.

First is the issue of getting a carriage return into your document when you're working directly in HTML. (Netscape Composer and other Web page editors handle this problem for you.) When you hit Enter or Return when entering text in HTML, HTML doesn't notice the end-of-paragraph marker that gets placed in the text. So, if you enter several paragraphs of text, hitting Enter or Return after each, you end up with one big blob of text in your Web browser.

What's the solution? When working directly in HTML, you have to insert a <P> tag at the start

of each paragraph and a </P> at the end. Every time HTML sees a new <P> tag, it starts a new paragraph. (The </P> tag at the end of the paragraph isn't strictly necessary, but it's better to be safe than sorry.)

So if you need more white space between paragraphs, you just add a few more <P> tags, right? Well, no. Different browsers handle multiple <P> tags differently, but most ignore the second and succeeding <P> tags. No matter how many <P> tags you put in, you just get one paragraph break. (The same goes for the <BR>, or break, tag. The <BR> tag creates a line break without starting a whole new paragraph. This can be useful when you're working in a list, for instance, and want to insert a line break without starting a whole new paragraph, which might be indented differently.)

The solution is to insert a special character called a non-breaking space in each blank line you want. The tag for a non-breaking space is #nbsp;. Just put this tag after a <BR> tag and, in most versions of the major browsers, you'll get a full line break.

Formatting Web Text

The mechanics of formatting Web text are actually pretty simple. Later in this section, we'll show you how to use these capabilities either when using a text editor, using HTML directly, or using a Web page editor like Netscape Composer. First, here's a brief list of the text capabilities available for Web publishers, based on the HTML tags found in the most widely used versions of HTML:

- ✔ **Headings:** You can specify six levels of headings in HTML, using the tag pairs <H1> and </H1> for the largest, top-level heading; <H2> and </H2> for the next level; and so on down to <H6> and </H6>.

   Heading style: The ideal way to use headings is as intended — <H1> for the most important heading and so on, down to <H6>. However, you may notice the heading you should be using seems too large in comparison to the text beneath it. Many people use <H4>, for instance, for a second-level heading, or use text size commands and bolding to create their own header styles. Try using the intended headings first, and then use your own formatting if you need a specific look.

✔ **Font sizes:** HTML allows you to specify font sizes that are larger or smaller than medium, or standard, size. You can go two sizes smaller or three sizes larger than medium. This formatting works even if the user has specified a font size or style in their browser setup or in Windows. (As people get older, and their eyes weaken, they resort to various tricks to make using the computer easier — as one of the authors knows from experience.)

Font sizes style: You don't want your Web page to look like a hostage note, but font sizes can be a good way to make a point (with a larger font size) or fit a lot of text into a small space (with a smaller size). Using font sizes is one of the few formatting tricks that almost always work well on Web pages.

✔ **Character formatting:** You can make text bold or italic using the <B> and </B> tags to start and stop bolding, and the <I> and </I> tags to start and stop italics. You can also underline text, but we don't recommend it, because it is too easy for users to get confused when they see HTML links that are underlined.

Character style: You should use bold and italic to make it easy to find your point, but don't overdo it. Structured use of bold and italics, like the bolding used to highlight items in this list, is one good solution. As for underlining, avoid using it on the Web — people will confuse it with the underlining (and use of a color, usually blue) used for hyperlinks. See the sidebar, "What color is your hyperlink," for details.

✔ **Advanced character formatting:** Using tags that aren't supported by all browsers currently in use, you can specify the fonts used in your Web page, as well as font colors. There are lots of problems with doing this, though. Some users have older browsers that don't support this kind of formatting. And some folks have their browsers set to use specific fonts, regardless of what you specify. Yet others have specified large fonts in Windows, which will make some parts of your Web look much different than you intended.

Advanced character style: We don't recommend using advanced character formatting because it's complicated and because, just when you start to depend on it, you find it doesn't work for many of your users. Using font and link colors can cause problems because users are accustomed to seeing only standard colors used for text and for links. Stay away from this kind of formatting unless you're working at a professional level, with the design help and testing resources needed to make it work well for all your users.

What color is your hyperlink?

HTML allows you to use colored text on your Web page. We generally don't recommend this.

Why not? (This is a book about all the things you can do on a Web page, after all!) The reason is that people are very used to monotone text, usually black, on a contrasting background. People have adjusted to the use of colored text on Web pages, but mainly in the form of standard hyperlink colors: blue for a link the user hasn't clicked on yet, and purple for a recently visited link.

Some Web page authors customize these colors to fit better with the color scheme of their

Web pages. The problem is, research into making Web pages easier to use and less confusing has found that users subconsciously count on blue underlined text to indicated unvisited links and purple underlined text to indicate visited links. Any change in these colors, or any use of blue or purple text or underlining for other purposes, causes deep confusion.

So we recommend that you don't use colored text, don't change link colors, and don't use underlining except in links. The people who visit your Web page will have a better time using it as a result.

Figure 7-4 shows these options for Web text formatting in a single example. Use it as a resource when deciding what formatting to use in your own Web page.

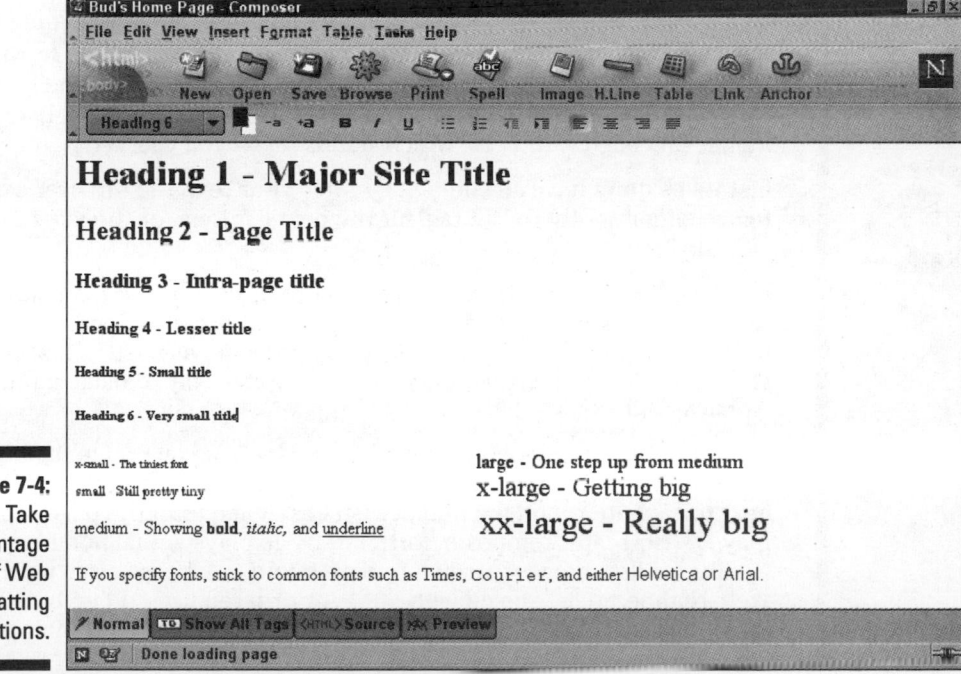

Figure 7-4:
Take
advantage
of Web
formatting
options.

Using HTML Lists

People really like lists. David Letterman's Top Ten lists are the highlight of his *Late Night* show and have been the subject of several books. Everywhere you look, you see lists. Here are our top three reasons why — in a list, of course:

- ✔ **Lists are interesting to look at.** Writing pros are always telling people to use lots of white space to vary the appearance of their pages so they're not just featureless blobs of text. Lists do this; they break up text.

- ✔ **Lists are easy to scan.** As we mention earlier in this chapter, people are more likely to scan text on the Web than to read it carefully. Lists are very easy to scan. With the key points highlighted, people can go in depth by carefully reading the points that interest them and skimming the ones that don't.

- ✔ **Lists make the writer get to the point.** When you write a list, you have to cut and condense what you're trying to say. You may end up replacing a page of boring, monotonous text with three or four points in a half-page bulleted list. All this extra work you have to do greatly benefits the reader, especially the reader who's reading from a computer screen.

HTML and Web page editing programs based on HTML (such as Netscape Composer) offer three kinds of lists, but only two are used much.

- ✔ **Bulleted lists:** Bulleted lists are by far the most widely used kind of list on the Web. And why not? Bulleted lists are flexible and fun, both to write and, more importantly, to read. You start a bulleted list with the `<UL>` tag, which stands for *unordered list*. You end it with the `</UL>` tag. Each list item is preceded with `<LI>`, which stands for — you guessed it — *list item*.

    List items don't have an ending tag. After your text, the browser expects to see either another `<LI>` tag, for the next list item, or the `<UL>` tag to end the list.

    Bulleted lists style: You can convert many, or even most, long blocks of text into a bulleted list — and make the text shorter, easier to read, and more interesting in the bargain. If you have to move existing text to the Web, consider "bulletizing" parts of it as a quick way to make it more Web friendly.

- ✔ **Numbered lists:** Numbered lists look weird when you create them in some Web editing programs — the program puts a number symbol (#) next to each item, and the number isn't assigned until the page is displayed. (Netscape Composer, fortunately, displays actual numbers.) Numbered lists are very useful, but are found much less often on the Web. Numbered lists begin with `<OL>` for ordered list, end with `</OL>`, and — like bulleted lists — use the `<LI>` tag to mark the beginning of each list item.

Netscape Composer or a free trial package?

Although offerings change with time, you can usually get a free trial version of excellent Web page editing software such as Microsoft FrontPage or Macromedia Dreamweaver from the companies' Web sites or an online download site like CINET's download.com (at `www.download.com`, natch). Why use Composer instead of a free trial version?

✔ **Truly free:** Composer is truly free for as long as you want to use it. You don't need to worry about paying anyone money when your trial version expires, which is usually just when you're getting going as a Web publisher.

✔ **Truly easy:** Because it's designed as an introductory program, Composer has only basic features — not too much complexity, which you don't need most of the time, to make things confusing.

✔ **Truly HTML-compatible:** As an introductory program, Composer only supports features that work on just about any Web browser out there — using all the features in FrontPage or Dreamweaver often means that you've added things that don't work in older browsers or within AOL or CompuServe.

And, of course, our argument is that you can better follow along with the instructions in this book if you're using the software that we use for many of our examples and figures.

If you're sure that you're going to be using FrontPage or Dreamweaver soon, or if you already have a copy, you may want to use a trial version of the program that's in your future. Even then, you may want to use Composer for easy work, and the full-featured program for advanced features. If you do work in a full-featured Web page editor, most of the steps in the sections of this book dedicated to Composer will still work for you — you just need to substitute the specific commands for your program in place of the instructions and illustrations for Composer.

Numbered list style: Anytime you have a list that has an order in terms of importance, sequence in time, or any other reason, make it a numbered list. Putting your list items in order makes them even easier to scan than a regular, bulleted list.

✔ **Definition lists:** *Definition lists* give a term and then a definition for the term. They're rarely used, though it's a good exercise to find a use for them in your Web page. A definition list starts with <DL> and ends with </DL>. Each term is preceded by <DT>, for *definition term,* and each definition is preceded by <DD>, for *definition data*.

Definition list style: The appearance of definition lists in your Web page is a bit funny — most Web browsers put the term on one line and then the definition, indented farther in, on the next line. You can help make it easier for the reader who's scanning to find the terms by making them bold, as in the list you're reading here. People like definition lists, but not necessarily formatted the way most Web browsers do it. Use definition lists where you can, or use bolding and bulleted or numbered lists to create your own definition-type list.

✔ **Lists within lists:** You can insert or *nest* one list inside another. The nested list can be the same kind of list, or a different kind, than the list that contains it.

List-in-list style: It's a bit complicated for the reader to keep track of where they are in the overall list if you start throwing sublists at them as well. We believe that putting one list within another is usually a case of something that's technically possible, but not editorially desirable. (We look forward to one of you proving us wrong by coming up with a good use for nested lists.)

Figure 7-5 shows different list options. Pick and choose the right ones for you when creating your Web pages.

Figure 7-5:
List all your options and then choose one.

Entering Text in HTML

Entering text directly in HTML is a challenge at first because you have to spend a lot of time thinking about HTML tags instead of about what you want to say. After awhile, though, you get used to it, and working with the HTML tags — while still tedious — becomes routine. The good news is that working this way gives you hands-on control of what your HTML is doing.

This section shows you how to use HTML to accomplish the following simple Web authoring tasks and fill in your initial Web page:

- ✔ Enter some text.
- ✔ Format the text.
- ✔ Make some of the text into a list.
- ✔ Check out how the text looks in a Web browser.

The rest of this section shows you how to accomplish these tasks with HTML in a text-editing program; in the next section, we show you how to accomplish the same tasks with Netscape Composer.

Entering and formatting text

The best way to get used to working with HTML is to jump right in:

1. **Open or create an HTML document in a text editor. Give your document a title and then add META tags, as described in Chapter 6.**

2. **In the editing window, enter some text.**

   The example in this chapter's figures includes the following text:

   ```
   I just got a new portable computer.
   I'm extremely happy with it.
   My favorite things about it are:
   1.2 GHz Pentium MMX processor
   20GB hard disk
   128MB of RAM (I wish it had 256MB though)
   It's much faster than my old portable computer.
   ```

3. **Start by surrounding lines of regular text with the paragraph tags (`<P>` and `</P>`).**

   In the sample text, we placed the paragraph tags before and after the first three lines and the last line.

4. **Find the text that you want to format.**

   In the sample text, we highlighted "extremely" in the phrase "extremely happy."

5. **Put formatting tags, such as `<B>` and `</B>` or `<I>` and `</I>`, around the text to format it.**

   The tags appear around the text. It will show up as formatted when you look at it in a Web browser. In the sample text, we made the word "extremely" bold.

   Be sure to apply the closing tag, where one is needed, for each new tag you start.

Making a list

Making text into a list works in much the same way as applying paragraph formats, such as Heading 1, but you have to work with several lines at once:

1. **Identify the lines of text that you want to make into a list.**

    In the sample text, we make a list out of the lines about processor, disk, and RAM.

2. **Surround the selected lines with the** `<UL>` **and** `</UL>` **tags for a bulleted list, or the** `<OL>` **and** `</OL>` **tags for a numbered list.**

3. **Precede each item in the list with the tag** `<LI>` **to identify it as a list item.**

    Here's how the example looks now:

```
<P>I just got a new portable computer.</P>
<P>I'm <B>extremely</B> happy with it.</P>
<P>My favorite things about it are:</P>
<UL>
<LI>1.2 GHz Pentium MMX processor
<LI>20GB hard disk
<LI>128MB of RAM (I wish it had 256MB though)
</UL>
<P>It's much faster than my old portable computer.</P>
```

    The text immediately appears as a list.

    See Figure 7-6 to see how the screen appears at this point in the example.

    For more on HTML terms, such as numbered list or bulleted list, see Chapter 4 for HTML basics, and the sections earlier in this chapter for details about when to use which kind of list.

Looking at the Web page

When working in a text document using HTML, which allows you to be constantly reminded of the HTML tags you're using, it's useful to be reminded of what the actual Web page will look like — and to look for any problems as you go along. Here's how to keep an eye on what your final Web page will look like as you work in HTML:

1. **Choose File⇨Save to save your document.**

2. **Open a Web browser, such as Internet Explorer.**

3. **Use the File⇨Open command in your browser to open a file. In the Open dialog box, navigate to the file you just saved, and select it. Click Open to open the document.**

    Your Web document appears in the browser window as a Web page.

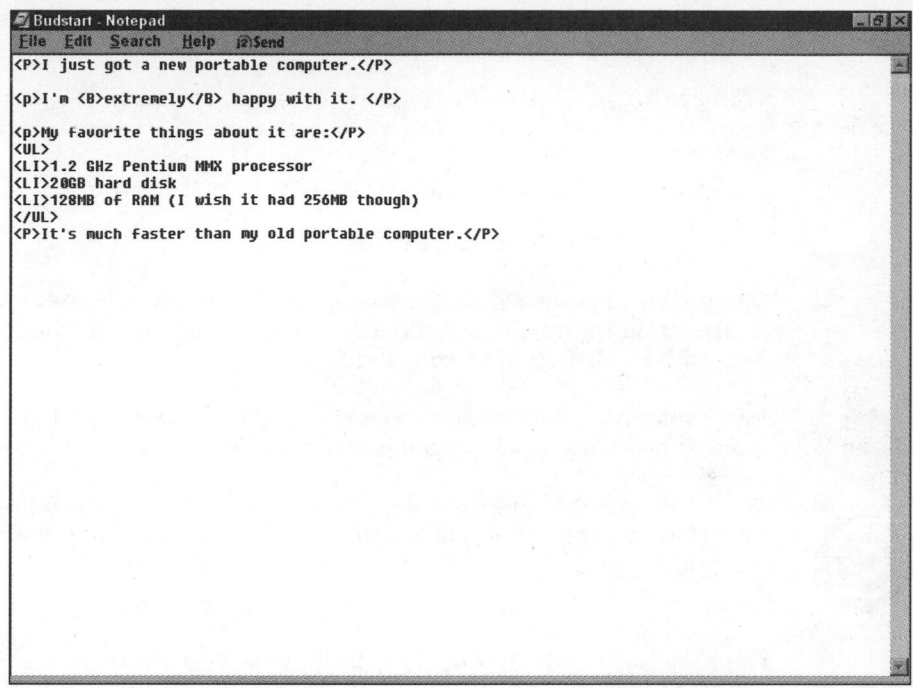

```
Budstart - Notepad
File  Edit  Search  Help  Send
<P>I just got a new portable computer.</P>

<p>I'm <B>extremely</B> happy with it. </P>

<p>My favorite things about it are:</P>
<UL>
<LI>1.2 GHz Pentium MMX processor
<LI>20GB hard disk
<LI>128MB of RAM (I wish it had 256MB though)
</UL>
<P>It's much faster than my old portable computer.</P>
```

Figure 7-6:
Use tags to
get your list
right.

4. **In your text editor, make a visible change in your text.**

   Try adding a new sentence, with or without formatting.

5. **Save the file.**

   If you don't save the file to your hard disk, you won't be able to see the changes when you look at it in your browser.

6. **Click the Refresh or Reload button in your Web browser.**

   The updated Web page appears in your browser.

7. **When done, save your document and exit Windows Notepad or the other text editor you're using.**

Entering Text in Netscape Composer

Filling in your initial Web page with Netscape Composer is fun because you can easily do most of the things that you may want to do with a Web page, though Netscape Composer doesn't let you do much beyond the basics. As you experiment with Netscape Composer, you'll find that you can use all the basic text features of HTML, without having to worry about HTML tags.

This section shows you how to accomplish the following simple Web authoring tasks and fill in your initial Web page:

✔ Enter some text.

✔ Format the text.

✔ Make some of the text into a list.

✔ Look at the underlying HTML-tagged text.

This section shows you how to accomplish these tasks with Netscape Composer; in the previous section, we show you how to accomplish the same tasks with HTML tags in a text editor.

See Chapter 5 for information about how to get Composer, and Chapter 6 for information about how to create your initial Web page in Composer.

You can learn HTML quite quickly by working in Composer and then clicking the HTML Source tab periodically to see the actual HTML tags underlying your Web page.

Entering and formatting text

Editing text for Web pages by using Netscape Composer is easy and fun because you can use the formatting options that are allowed on Web pages — and only those options. That means you're instantly seeing the same thing your Web page visitors will see — and not wasting your time with options that won't translate to the Web. Follow these steps to type and format some text:

1. **Open or create a Web document and give it a title. Then add META tags, as described in Chapter 6.**

2. **Type in the heading that you want at the top of your Web page.**

   For example, we entered Sierra Soccer Club as the first heading.

3. **Move the cursor to the same line as the heading text.**

4. **From the far-left pull-down menu, choose Heading 1.**

   The heading text reformats into Heading 1 style.

   Any HTML styles — paragraph-level formatting commands — that you choose affect the entire paragraph of text in which the cursor rests.

5. **Move the cursor to a new line.**

6. **Type some text introducing your Web page.**

When someone searches for your Web page by using a search engine, the search engine may display the Web page title, as described in Chapter 6, and the first few words that appear in the document. So make the first few sentences of text that follow the title an introduction to the entire page or Web site.

In the document we created for this chapter, we typed:

```
Sierra Soccer Club is a boys' soccer club that practices
and plays at the highest altitude of any in the United
States. If you meet the following qualifications, you
may be eligible to become a member of Sierra Soccer Club:
Born in 1993 or 1994. Sierra Soccer Club has played
together since its founding members were 5 and 6 years
old, and will stick together as they grow up. All our
club members must be born in 1993 or 1994.
Some soccer experience. If you have played in organized
leagues before, or if you're a skilled school player,
we may be able to help take your game to new levels.
Good academic record. We are proud that our club members
maintain good standing in school as well as in soccer.
```

7. **Highlight any text that you want to format.**

In our document, we highlighted the words Sierra Soccer Club at the beginning of the first sentence.

8. **Click the button for the formatting style that you want: the B button for Bold, the I button for Italic, or the U button for Underline.**

In our example, we made Sierra Soccer Club bold. The highlighted text takes on the formatting you choose.

Making a list

Formatting items into a list works in much the same way as applying paragraph formats, such as Heading 1. Just select the lines of text and then pick the effect that you want:

1. **Highlight the lines that you want to make into a list.**

In our document, we highlighted the lines that begin:

```
Born in 1993 or 1994
```

```
Some soccer experience
```

```
Good academic record
```

2. **From the pull-down menu, choose the list style that you want: Bulleted List or Numbered List.**

   The text instantly reformats into the list style that you choose, as shown in Figure 7-7.

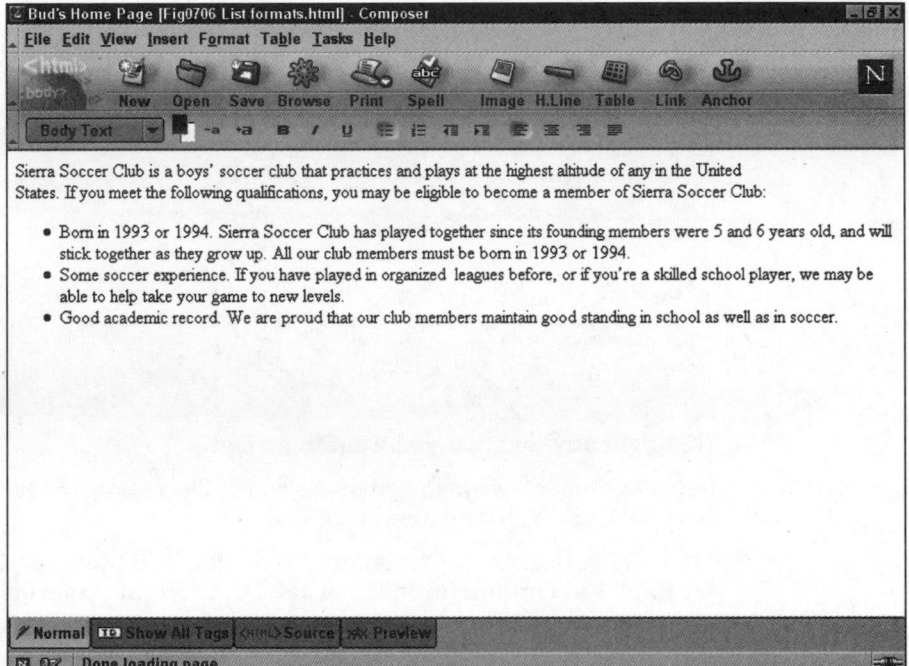

Figure 7-7: Composer makes listing easy.

For more on HTML terms, such as numbered list or bulleted list, see Chapter 4 for HTML basics, and the sections earlier in this chapter for details about when to use which kind of list.

Looking at the HTML

When working in a WYSIWYG (What You See Is What You Get) tool such as Netscape Composer, you often want to look at the underlying HTML code. Doing so enables you to find out how HTML works and gives you the chance to make adjustments in the HTML tags that affect the way your page looks and works on the Web. Here's how to check out your page's HTML code in Netscape Composer:

1. **Choose View⇨HTML Source, or click the <HTML> Source tab at the bottom of the window.**

   The HTML source for your page appears.

2. **Make any changes that you want in the HTML.**

   You can change the HTML directly — the changes will be reflected when you go back to normal editing mode.

3. **Choose View⇨Normal Edit Mode, or click the Normal tab at the bottom of the window.**

   The Netscape Composer window displays any changes you made in the HTML code that cause visible differences in your Web page.

4. **Save your document and exit Netscape Composer.**

Chapter 8

Adding Links to Your Web Page

• •

In This Chapter

▶ Finding out about linking basics

▶ Linking within a page

▶ Avoiding mistakes

▶ Linking to a Web page

▶ Creating a Mailto link

• •

*W*eb *hyperlinks* — the connections that let you go from one Web page to another with a single click — are the key to what makes the Web great. They're also a bit complicated to create, test, and maintain. We'll show you how to do it right in this chapter.

Hyperlinks, known as *links* for short, have a long and honorable history. They are the underlying concept behind *hypertext,* a kind of writing that takes advantage of computer and network capabilities to connect a spot in a piece of text to other information that supports, gives detail on, defines, describes, relates to, or even contradicts the information at the spot where the link is.

Hypertext was discussed and implemented in smaller systems long before the World Wide Web was invented. Ted Nelson invented the term in about 1960 and promoted the idea for decades. He wrote a famous book called *Computer Lib/Dream Machines* that described many different types of hypertext and uses for it. (The book is currently out of print.)

The idea of hypertext became popular within the computer industry throughout the 1980s, as more and more computers were getting connected to networks. The reason for the growth of interest in hypertext was simply the truth behind a rule called Metcalf's Law: The value of a network rises exponentially with the number of computers connected to it.

So it is with hyperlinks. Using a hyperlink, you can connect your Web page to any information on any other Web page out there. As the Web has grown, the total number of available hyperlinks has grown rapidly with it, to the point that now the number of links is seemingly infinite. Clicking around the Web via hyperlinks is so much fun that the term "surfing the Web" is used to describe it.

Hyperlinks also work to bring information into your Web page. The graphics that appear embedded within a Web page are really separate files; hyperlinks in the HTML document that defines a Web page point to each graphic. It really doesn't matter to the Web whether the graphics within your Web page are on the same machine or scattered across the Web, though download time for your Web page might be inconsistent if the various files are scattered around.

We'll describe these different kinds of hyperlinks separately, and show you how to use each type in your own Web page. And we'll tell you how to avoid some of the problems that all too often arise with hyperlinks in your Web page.

Linking Basics

Before you plunge into specific kinds of links, as described in this chapter, it's helpful to get an overview of how links work. The basic idea, remember, is for your HTML document — the core of your Web page — to refer to another file. The user is either going to see that file in your Web page, or click on something in your Web page to leave it and link to the other file.

One of the biggest problems users have on the Web is broken links. Encountering a broken link is very frustrating, and you, as the Web page publisher, may not find out about the problem for a long time. Create and test your links carefully and repeatedly to avoid broken links.

How links work

The basic mechanism for creating a link from one Web page to another is simple. You use the <A>, or anchor, tag to begin the link. Within the anchor tag, you can specify where the link goes to, using the HREF option to specify the Hypertext REFerence, or destination, of the link. Alternatively, within the anchor tag, you can specify a name for the link. Some text within your document usually follows the anchor tag. An </A>, or end-of-anchor, tag then follows that text.

Here's an example of a typical anchor tag within a sentence of text:

```
Visit the <A HREF="www.dummies.com">For Dummies site</A> for
                more information.
```

Here's how this would be displayed in a typical Web browser:

```
Visit the For Dummies site for more information.
```

Mouseover and out

Current Web browsers support a feature many users have learned to take advantage of: mouseover support. When your mouse moves over a link, the destination of the link shows up in the lower-left corner of the browser window. (Some versions of Internet Explorer have the status bar, where the destination appears, turned off by default; choose View⇨Status Bar to turn it on and see link destinations.) You can use this mouseover support to check your own links when you're testing your site, both before and after you publish it. Rest assured that your savvier users will take advantage of the mouseover feature to check out where a link is going before they decide to click on it.

In a typical Web page, the underlined text — called the *link text,* because it's where the user clicks to follow the link — would be displayed in blue as well as being underlined.

The other kind of link you commonly create in your Web page is an image link. You begin this kind of link with the image tag, `<IMG>`. You use the SRC option, which nearly always appears within the `<IMG>` tag, to specify where the image lives. For simple sites, the image should be stored in the same folder as the HTML file that links to the image. Then the SRC option is very simple:

```
<IMG SRC="myuglymug.jpg">
```

The next chapter gives many important details about graphics and graphics links. In this chapter, we focus on how to link to the image file that you want, whether it's on your Web server or another machine.

Links and URLs

Links have two main purposes: to help your user click on a link and go to another Web page, or to bring in a graphics file to display in your Web page. Whichever kind of link you're creating, you need to know how to specify where the file is located.

Most linking mistakes are made due to misunderstandings about the way URLs work when you're linking from the HTML file that is the core of your Web page to another Web page or to a graphics file. Understanding how URLs work will help you create more interesting Web pages and experience much less frustration as you create and test your page. Table 8-1 summarizes how you create the different kinds of links.

Table 8-1	URL	Web page example	Graphics example*
Same folder	*filename*	`<A HREF="mycv.html">text</A>`	`<IMG SRC="myface.jpg">`
Different folder at a lower level of the same path	*pathname/ filename*	`<A HREF="subpages/mycv.htm">text</A>`	`<IMG SRC="grfx/myface.jpg>`
Different folder on a different path	*pathname/ filename*	`<A HREF="../theotherpage/otherpage.htm>text</A>`	`<IMG SRC="../sharegfx/proface.gfx>`
Different server, home page (index.htm or index.html)	*domainname*	`<A HREF="www.largedomain.com">text</A>`	Unlikely to occur
Different server, interior page	*Domainname/ pathname*	`<A HREF="www.largess.com/files/bud.htm">text</A>`	`</IMG SRC="www.largess.com/gifs/icon27.gif">`
Link within a page	*Any of above +#anchorname*	`chor"></A>; NAME="myan<<A A HREF="www.largess.com/#myanchor>Go to my anchor</A>`	Doesn't apply

* This example leaves out the ALT option and other important graphics options, which Chapter 9 describes.

Linking to a file on another server

The easiest kinds of links are actually links to a spot on another Web server. That's because you can easily get the URL for the link — it's the same as the URL you see when you go to the site using your Web browser. When you're linking to a file on a different server than your HTML file, you can link to two kinds of URLs:

- ✓ **Different server, home page:** This is the easiest kind of URL: You just give the same domain name that you use to go to the home page of the Web site. For instance, if you know of a racing fan's Web site with the domain name `www.mygreenhorse.com`, you simply give that URL as the hypertext reference.

- ✓ **Different server, not the home page:** This kind of URL is easy too; it's just the URL, but the URL is a little longer, since it includes both the domain name and a path down to the specific file you want. There's a twist, though: When you're linking to a file on a large site, the URL is often a bunch of gobbledygook.

For instance, here's a URL from a search for Gumby on the Google search site:

```
http://www.google.com/search?hl=en&q=gumby+show
```

Figure 8-1 shows this search and its results.

The URL is not really a file location; it's a database query stored in a URL. Still, this isn't something you need to worry about. Just find the page you want, copy and paste the URL into your Web page, and you'll have an accurate link. (At least, until something on the site you're linking to changes.)

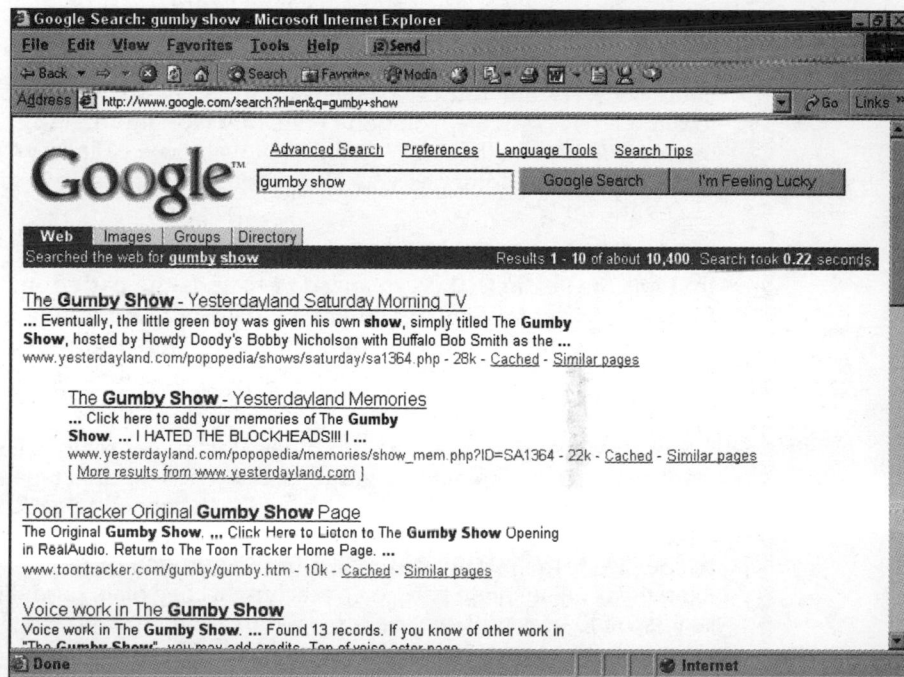

Figure 8-1:
A typical search generates a long URL.

You don't need to include the filename in the path for a Web page if the filename is `index.htm` or `index.html`. Most Web authors only use this filename for their site's home page, but others use it for major navigational pages within the site as well.

Don't worry if you don't see `index.htm` or `index.html` when you visit the Web site's home page; the site is automatically remapping the filename your browser expects to the one it wants to use. Try typing the URL without a specific filename; if that works, you don't need the filename in your link.

Linking to a file on the same server

It's harder to link to a file on the same server than to a file on another server. That's for two reasons: It's easier to get the path wrong when you are linking to a local file, because you can't just copy and paste a Web URL; and, the path you specify while testing on your own machine may change when you publish your Web site by moving it to a Web server. This can make the URLs you've been using wrong, breaking the links within your site.

When linking to a file on the same server, don't give the name of the server — just leave it off. Your Web browser knows to look on the same server as the Web page if no server name is specified in the path.

If you're linking to a file on the same server as your HTML file, there are three kinds of URLs you can link to:

- **Same server, same folder:** If a file is on the same server, and in the same folder as the HTML file, you don't need any path information. The pathname is simply the filename. To link to a Web page called `myresume.htm` that's in the same folder as your Web page, the pathname is just `myresume.htm`.

- **Same server, subfolder:** If a file is in a subfolder below the HTML file that has the link in it, then you need to include the path from the HTML file to the folder holding the other Web page or graphics file. For instance, if you have a folder containing your Web page and a subfolder, called `grfx`, with graphics files, the path to a graphic called `myface.jpg` would be `grfx/myface.jpg`.

- **Same server, not on same path:** Things start to get really tricky if you want to link to a Web page or graphics file that's on the same server, but on a different path. You can either give the absolute pathname that describes the path from the beginning of the server's directory structure to the file, or the relative pathname from your Web page to the file. An example of an absolute path, on a machine whose main hard disk is called `maya`, would be `maya/mypage/grfx/yourface.jpg`. An example of a relative path to the same file, from an HTML file stored at `maya/mypage/webpages/index.html`, would be `../grfx/yourface.jpg`.

Use the characters . . / to indicate going up one level in the current folder hierarchy. It's not very user-friendly, but simple enough once you get used to it.

Linking within a page

There's one more intricacy to pathnames that is easy to miss, but important: You can link to a destination within a Web page, as well as to the top of the page.

The only trouble is, HTML doesn't allow you to specify a location within the page using normal language — you can't say "link to the spot just below the picture of Britney Spears and just above the picture of Madonna." Instead, you need to create a special marker, called an *anchor*, to link to.

Technically, any link you create is an anchor, but people typically call them HREFs if you're linking out to a Web page or image references if you're linking in a graphics file. The term *anchor* is used most often to mean a special marker you create in an HTML file to give other HTML files a specific spot to refer to.

To create an anchor, you simply put the <A> and </A> tags into your Web page. For example,

```
<A NAME="aboveMadonna"></A>
```

You don't need to enclose any text between the <A> and </A> tags, because the anchor you are creating goes to the start of the next line of text below the anchor.

To link to the anchor, you add the symbol # and the anchor name to any other kind of URL. Let's say you've put in ten anchors into a Web page, one above each major header, and numbered them 1 through 10. Then a link to the third one, from within the same Web page, would look like this:

```
Check out the <A HREF="#3">third</A> wonderful reason to vote
            for me.
```

Avoiding mistakes

It's easy to make mistakes in your Web site when you're specifying links, and it's also easy for "good" links to become broken because of changes in the Web site you're linking to. Here are some ways to prevent problems, and to manage problems when they do come up:

- **Keep your whole Web page in one folder.** When your whole site is just one Web page, your only links are to the graphics images that display as part of your page. Put the graphics images in the same folder as the HTML file that defines your Web page. That way, your links to graphics files are simple — just the filename — and when you publish the site, you just move a single folder from your machine to the Web server.

- **Keep your whole Web site in one folder.** When you grow your Web page into a multi-page site, you can keep all the HTML files that define your Web pages, as well as all the graphics files they use, in a single folder, again simplifying links. This does get crowded after awhile, though.

  Here's an alternative for sites with more than a couple of dozen files: Create a very simple hierarchy in which each HTML file is in a folder with the same name as the HTML file, shared graphics are in a separate folder, and graphics used only by a specific page are stored with that page. This is still a whole new level of complexity, but at least you'll have some rules to operate by.

- **Avoid internal links to Web pages on other sites.** It's a lot of fun to link directly to a spot within a Web page on another site, but you're depending on an anchor that may go away as the Web page is updated. Try to use only internal links within your own site; that way you at least know who to blame if the anchor you're linking to is deleted or moved.

- **Check all links before you publish.** Before you publish your Web page or Web site, try every single page to make sure that graphics load properly, and try every single link to make sure it works correctly. If there's a problem, make the change while it's still easy and then recheck to make sure you got it right.

- **Check all links after you publish.** It's quite possible that some of your Web links — both links to graphics within the Web page and links to other sites — will break when you publish your site. Check to make sure. If you do find problems, fix them, test on your local machine, and then re-publish.

- **Check all links every couple of weeks.** It's easy for other Web publishers to make changes in sites you depend on — and it's a sure bet that the minute you decide that the site you link to will never change, it will. Keep checking your links every couple of weeks to make sure they're all good. (And update any out-of-date content in your site while you're at it.)

Linking to a Web Page

Here we'll summarize the different kinds of links you can create, and show you how to implement them in both straight HTML and in Netscape Composer. Actually, adding a link is quite different when working directly in HTML versus working with Netscape Composer.

Adding Web page links in HTML

To link to a Web page, just create an anchor tag and provide the path to the page you want (and any anchor that applies). Following are some examples:

- ✔ Linking to the home page of a site with its own domain name:

```
<A HREF="www.greatdomain.com">Go to the great domain.</A>
```

- ✔ Linking to a page within a site, giving the pathname and filename:

```
Read my review of <A HREF="www.greatdomain.com/reviews/
          budspeaks.htm">the great domain.</A>
```

- ✔ Linking to a page on the same server, and in the same folder, as your Web page:

```
I've created a <A HREF="gdlikes.htm">Web page</A>
          summarizing what I like about the great domain.
```

- ✔ Linking to a page on the same server, in a subfolder below your Web page:

```
I've created a <A HREF="/opinions/gdlikes.htm">Web page</A>
          summarizing what I like about the great domain.
```

- ✔ Linking to a named anchor within a Web page:

```
Now I don't like some things about <A HREF="www.greatdomain.
          com/news/policies.htm#payupnow">the great
          domain.</A>
```

In this last example, there has to be an anchor called #payupnow on the policies.htm page in the News folder of the Web site www.greatdomain.com. If not, the user's Web browser will take him or her to the right page, but will bring up the top of the page, not the desired spot within the page.

When you just enter a domain name for a hypertext reference, your browser looks for index.htm or index.html if it doesn't see a filename.

Adding Web page links in Composer

Creating a link in Composer can be a bit confusing. Follow these steps carefully to create a link in Composer without problems:

1. **Open Composer and your Web page, as described in Chapter 5.**

2. **Enter the text in which you want the link to appear.**

   Enter the text first, before you specify the link.

3. **Select the text that you want to use as link text.**

   Select the text you want to use as link text so that it's highlighted.

   Don't select the space before or after the text you want to use; it looks odd to have a link include leading or trailing empty spaces.

4. **Bring up the Link Properties dialog box by choosing Insert⇨Link or pressing Ctrl+L. Click the More Properties button to make all the options show.**

   The Link Properties dialog box will appear, as shown in Figure 8-2. The text you highlighted will appear at the top of the dialog box as the link text.

Figure 8-2:
Use the Link Properties dialog box to set up links in Composer.

You can also enter the link text by bringing up the Link Properties dialog box with no text highlighted and then entering link text in the Link Text box. When you're done, the link text appears on your page. However, anything you type immediately next to it will become part of the link text, which can be a hassle.

5. **For a link to another site, enter the URL that you want to link to. For a link to your own site, enter the URL manually, or click the Choose File button. Navigate to the file you want to link to, then click Open.**

Use a relative URL for most links to a Web page on the same server as the page that contains the link. See the section "Linking to a file on the same server," earlier for details on how to compose the URL (no pun intended).

The checkbox, URL is relative to page location, will automatically become checked or unchecked depending on which link location you enter. This helps you confirm that the link location you enter is absolute or relative (as described in Chapter 2), whichever you are trying to use.

6. **If you want to use an existing named anchor within the file you're linking to, select it from the list. For local files only: If the anchor doesn't exist, but you want to create one next to a heading, select a heading from the list. Netscape Composer will open the file and create an anchor next to the heading.**

   This is a lot for a free program to do for you!

7. **Click OK to accept the link properties.**

   The appropriate HTML code will be added to your Web page.

8. **Choose View⇨HTML Source or click the HTML Source button to check the underlying HTML.**

   The HTML code for your page will appear. Check it, using the information about links earlier in this chapter, to make sure it's okay.

Every so often, save your Web page to your hard disk, open it in a Web browser and test it and your links. Testing links is one of the most important kinds of testing you can do.

Creating a Mailto Link

Mailto links are a favorite trick on the Web. The good news is, they're fun to set up and fun to use. The bad news is, they don't work for all users.

A *mailto link* is a link that is supposed to automatically bring up the user's e-mail program and create a new mail message addressed to the e-mail address specified in the mailto link. The user only has to fill in the subject line of the e-mail message and the content, and then click Send.

However, some users will encounter problems with this scenario. Some older browsers don't support mailto URLs. Also, many users don't have their systems set up correctly so that the mailto link actually triggers their e-mail package. And finally, some users have multiple e-mail programs connected to different e-mail accounts; the e-mail program that automatically comes up is not necessarily the one that the user wants to use at that moment.

There are also some problems for you. Spammers — people who send unwanted e-mail — get e-mail addresses by creating spiders that search the Web for e-mail addresses. Any e-mail address that you put in a mailto link might end up being harvested and used to send you spam.

Create a separate e-mail account just for receiving e-mail from your Web site. That way, your personal or professional e-mail accounts aren't clogged with user mail and spam. Free services like Hotmail (at `www.hotmail.com`) allow you to create and use an e-mail account at no cost.

Users can get quite touchy if you ignore their e-mail messages. Make sure to check for user mail once or twice a day — even if you have to wade through a bunch of spam to find it.

One solution to all these problems is to not use mailto links and therefore not allow any user communication at all. However, we prefer two alternatives:

- ✔ **Create a form.** When asking for input, feedback, and so on regarding your Web site, use a form. A form allows you to structure your input from the user, if needed. And with a form you still get an e-mail message, but the user doesn't have to worry about what e-mail program (if any) gets launched, and you don't have to worry about spammers getting your e-mail address. (See Chapter 10 for a discussion of forms.)

- ✔ **Spell out the e-mail address when using mailto.** Users whose systems are set up in such a way that the mailto link doesn't work usually know it. If you spell out the e-mail address, as well as provide a mailto link to it, then users who can take advantage of the mailto link can click on it; users who can't take advantage of the mailto link can copy and paste the e-mail address into their e-mail program of choice. Figure 8-3 shows an example, with the e-mail address `budsmith2000@cs.com` marked as a mailto link. The following instructions show you how to do this.

Creating a mailto link in HTML

Creating a mailto link in HTML is easy; it's just like creating a regular link, but you don't have to worry about pathnames or local files versus files on other Web servers. Just add a line of text and HTML like the following:

```
If you'd like, send e-mail to Bud Smith, one of the authors,
        at <a href="mailto:budsmith2000@cs.com">
        budsmith2000@cs.com</a>.
```

Just as with a normal hypertext link, you use the anchor tag and the HREF option. Also like normal hypertext links, you surround the text that you want to highlight with the anchor tag in front and the anchor-end tag in back.

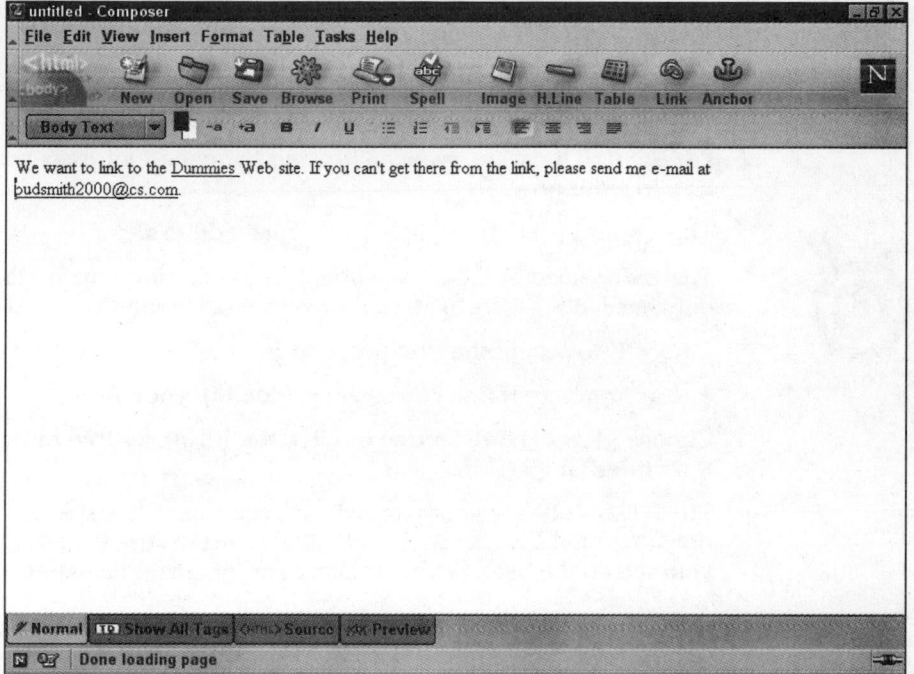

Figure 8-3:
Look to the
side to see
the mailto
URL.

Notice that in this example we gave the author's e-mail address explicitly, along with a link to it. Not only does this allow the user to cut and paste the e-mail address into the e-mail program of his choice, it also lets him see exactly where he's sending e-mail to before he clicks. In this case, users might appreciate seeing what looks like someone's personal e-mail address, instead of a generic address like feedback@budsmith.com or a Hotmail address that the author might not check very often.

Creating a mailto link in Composer

Creating a mailto link in Composer is just like creating a regular link, only simpler. Follow these steps:

1. **Open Composer and your Web page, as described in Chapter 5.**

2. **Enter the text in which you want the mailto link to appear.**

   Enter the text first, before you specify the link.

3. **Select the text that you want to use as mailto link text.**

   Select the text you want to use as link text so that it's highlighted.

4. **Bring up the Link Properties dialog box by choosing Insert⇨Link or pressing Ctrl+L.**

   The Link Properties dialog box will appear. The text you highlighted will appear at the top of the dialog box as the link text.

5. **For the link location, type** mailto: **and the e-mail address you want to link to, with no spaces.**

   This creates a link to the specified e-mail address.

   There's no need to look at the other properties for a mailto link; they're only needed for links to an anchor within a document.

6. **Click OK to accept the link properties.**

   The appropriate HTML code will be added to your Web page.

7. **Choose View⇨HTML Source or click the HTML Source button to check the underlying HTML.**

   The HTML code for your page will appear. Check it, using the information about links earlier in this chapter, to make sure it's okay. Then pat yourself on the back — you've successfully created a mailto link!

Part III
Better, Stronger, Faster Pages

In this part . . .

Web graphics don't have to be hard, nor do they have to be large and slow to download. And with our help, you can place your graphics in your Web pages like a pro, with text flowing artfully around them. Once you have your page perfect, we show you how to get it onto a Web server.

Chapter 9

Creating and Adding Web-Ready Graphics

. . . .

In This Chapter

▶ Using graphics

▶ Making the most of graphics using HTML

▶ Creating advanced graphics

. . . .

*H*aving graphics as part of the Web seems like an obvious winner now — after all, magazines and newspapers wouldn't work well if you took away photographs, drawings, and the little graphical page design elements that give each publication its own "look." But in the 1980s and 90s, before the Web, the Internet was almost entirely a text-only world. E-mail, Usenet newsgroups, and online service forums were all text-only environments, running mostly on text-only computer systems like UNIX and DOS.

It was graphics that made the Web take off — and they are also the most difficult aspect of getting your Web pages right. You can use graphics to convey a thematic "look and feel," to accent certain portions of a Web page, or even to convey the main content of a Web site. Some use of graphics is necessary for any site except the blandest and most utilitarian.

In this chapter, we look at the nitty-gritty of using graphics and explain how to create the most common graphic "special effects."

To succeed in the somewhat complex task of adding graphics to your Web pages, you need to know some basics of HTML and of Web pages in general. Create your basic Web page by using the information in previous chapters before trying to add any graphics but the simplest. And if you aren't yet familiar with HTML tags, review Chapter 4 before reading this chapter.

Using Graphics in Your Web Site

Graphic images take up a lot of space on a computer's hard disk. (See the sidebar, "Text space vs. graphics space," for details about why this is so.) And when graphic images are part of a Web page, they take a long time to be sent from the Web server to your computer over the Internet.

In order to make graphics show up faster, you have to use images that have small file sizes. You have two ways to do this. The first way is to use images that are small in display size — that is, in the amount of size they take up onscreen. The second is to use images that are small in file size — that is, they have been compressed to reduce the number of bytes needed to store the image.

You can use two kinds of compressed images in your Web pages: GIF and JPEG images. The next section explains these two kinds of images and how to use them.

Using GIF and JPEG graphics formats

Each graphics program saves files in its own *proprietary graphics format* — the specific arrangement of data that the program uses to save its files. For instance, the popular graphics program Photoshop saves files in the .psd format (for Photoshop Document); Paint Shop Pro, another popular graphics program, saves its files as .psp files. (You guess what "psp" stands for!) Web browsers typically don't know how to display files stored in these formats.

Fortunately, for the purposes of using graphics in HTML, you need to concern yourself with only two formats for graphics files, GIF and JPEG — and even then you don't really need to know a lot about the gory details of these formats to use them.

✔ *GIF,* or *Graphics Interchange Format,* is the file format used by most people to exchange graphics. Originally made popular on CompuServe, GIF spread to other online services and then to the Internet and the Web. Any browser that supports graphics supports GIF.

GIF images may contain up to 256 colors, so GIF formatting works effectively for images that have anywhere from a few colors to a few hundred colors, which includes most simple images and most images created on a computer. If an image has more than 256 colors, it loses some color information when you convert the image to GIF. You have to look at the image before and after you convert it to GIF to see if the conversion noticeably affects the image's appearance.

> ✔ *JPEG*, or *Joint Photographic Experts Group* format, compresses complex images, such as photographs, with many color variations. This capability makes JPEG the image format of choice for displaying photographs and other natural-looking images on your Web page. (What makes the image look natural is the way different shades of a color appear as light falls differently on various parts of an object.) These images retain their appearance well when compressed with JPEG.

Figure 9-1 shows a Web page that uses a photo of Marc Andreesen, one of the founders of Netscape, to illustrate graphically the difference in GIF and JPEG photo file sizes. The Web page in this figure shows one complete picture of Mark Andreesen and part of a subsequent picture. On the Web page itself, you find several versions of the same picture saved using different types of compression; go to the Web page to see the comparison. Here's the URL for this Web page:

```
cgi.netscape.com/assist/net_sites/impact_docs/e-jpeg.html
```

Use this GIF/JPEG test page to test the speed of your own Internet connection. The total size of the page with graphics is about 70K.

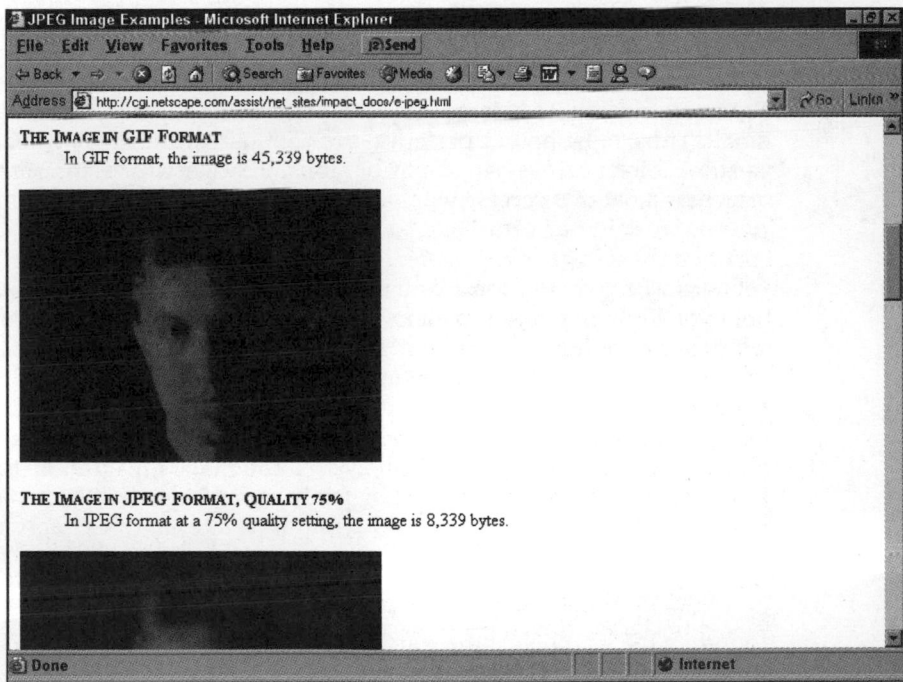

Figure 9-1:
Marc
Andreesen
served up in
a GIFfy.

Text space vs. graphics space

Text files are much more efficient for computers to store and transmit across the network than graphics files. Why? Text is very tightly coded; you can fill a typical Web page with solid text using about 2,000 characters, which can be represented in 2,000 bytes, or 2KB, of space. Graphics, on the other hand, require a lot of storage. A full-page, full-color image would take about 1.5MB of space — nearly 1,000 times as much space.

Large files take a long time to transmit over the Internet, making the Web page take a long time to download. So Web pages are made up of lots of text, fairly large areas of white space, and small, highly compressed graphics. A 2K file takes about 1 second to download over a modem, but is boring. A full-page, full-color graphic takes about 12 minutes, which is way too long.

In order to transmit quickly, Web graphics are made small in size and then compressed — mainly by using fewer colors to try to convey the same image. Graphics packages such as Photoshop allow you to save images in a compressed format, with a smaller number of colors used to convey almost all the original image. Ever notice that Web images tend to be small and have jaggy edges? Now you know why. Web images are not the prettiest to look at, but at least you're looking at them, rather than sitting and waiting for them.

For images with lots of large blocks of solid color, GIF file sizes tend to be small. Thus, most people prefer GIFs for banners or images with large areas of solid color, such as bar graphs or icons. In other words, the simple drawings that most of us create work best with GIF. Dense artistic graphics and photos work better with JPEG.

GIF files also give you some Web page display options that you don't always get with JPEG files. You can make the colors in GIF images transparent to whatever is in the background of the image, and you can save GIF images in *interlaced* format. Images saved in this way, and then downloaded by a browser, first appear in a very low resolution, and then in progressively clearer resolution, until the whole image appears. This feature makes GIF images preferable for quickly displaying a rough-looking graphic that improves with time and for creating fancy special effects. (We explain interlaced GIF images in more detail, with pictures, later in this chapter.)

Transparent images have a clear area surrounding the object of interest. For example, in a photo of a watch, you may not want any background color surrounding the watch, just the watch itself seeming to sit directly on the Web page. To achieve this effect, you use a transparent GIF, an image with a clear border area. The background color of the overall Web page shows through the transparent area, and the object of interest appears to "float" over the background. (We explain transparent GIF images in more detail, with pictures, later in this chapter.)

In some cases, the advantages of GIF outweigh the smaller file sizes that are more typical of JPEG. Use GIF if you need its special features; use JPEG the rest of the time. When you feel more confident in your design skills, you can play around with both formats and choose the one that's right for each image. Read on to find out how to obtain and create graphics for your Web pages and how to save your graphics in either format.

Newer versions of JPEG that support GIF-like features are now available. However, not as many graphics tools or as many browsers support these new JPEG features as support GIF. Stick with GIF for these features until your expertise grows.

Using "Web-safe" colors

Making your Web page look good on all the computers out there is a big issue. One of the trickiest things that you need to concern yourself with is the issue of "Web-safe" colors.

Some computer users have display systems that only allow what's called an 8-bit color display, which supports 256 colors, at a fixed resolution, such as 800 x 600. Almost all Windows and Macintosh computer systems in use today support at least this relatively low resolution and basic palette of colors.

Standards for graphics

Any up-to-date Web browser can display three types of data: text with HTML tags, GIF graphics, and JPEG graphics. (Some people pronounce GIF as "jiff," others as "giff" as in "gift." We prefer "giff" as in "gift.") A typical Web browser displays HTML-tagged text appropriately, although not all browsers understand all the same tags. A browser also displays GIF and JPEG graphics inline — that is, embedded within the Web page. A Web page with inline graphics looks like a page in a magazine, with text and images mixed seamlessly together. However, the graphics file is stored separately from the HTML-tagged text that makes up the underlying Web page. This makes the Web work better overall, but contributes to some of the problems — such as the difficulty of keeping all your Web files together for proper display — that we describe later in this chapter.

Other computers have more options. They can display thousands of colors at once, or even millions. And they can display the computer desktop in higher resolution — 1024 x 768 and, increasingly, 1280 x 1024 are fairly common. Some computers support even higher resolutions. Usually, though, going to higher resolutions means you lose the choice of displaying as many colors at once as when you use lower resolutions.

However, even these more capable systems can also run at 256 colors and 800 x 600 resolution — and they run fastest in this mode. So, many users run at 256 colors and either 800 x 600 resolution or 1024 x 768 resolution for good performance. Also, some programs, such as games, force the computer into one of these setups, and don't tell the user they're doing so. Nor do they restore the previous setting when the user goes back to Windows. So the user may be running in lower resolution, and with fewer colors, than their computer is capable of without even knowing it.

So to make sure your graphics will look good for all your users, they have to look good on a system running only 256 colors because many users will have this setup. Making matters worse, the PC and Macintosh have different 256-color palettes. Only 216 colors work in common on the low-color modes of both the Mac and the PC.

If you use a color that's not one of the 216 *Web-safe* colors, you may find that the color displays oddly on some systems. (These non-safe colors display as blends of other colors, making an odd and ugly effect.) A graphic that looks good on your computer may look awful on someone else's. If you stick to the Web-safe colors, you won't have this problem.

Several online sources allow you to mix and match different combinations of the Web-safe colors to find ones that look good. Go to this Web site to find Web-safe colors: `www.bagism.com/colormaker`.

Obtaining and creating graphics

So you want to put various graphics on your Web page. Great! But how do you create them and get them in the right format (GIF or JPEG)? Fortunately, creating the graphics you want, or finding some to use, is pretty easy.

The easiest way to obtain graphics is to get access to a clip art collection. Computer stores sell many inexpensive collections of business and recreational graphics on CD-ROM. You can also access a number of royalty-free graphics and icon collections online.

If you're doing a business or professionally focused Web page, it's important that it have a clean, professional look. To get this kind of look, you have to use attractive graphics and lay out your page carefully. Chapter 11 tells you how to design your page appropriately for various purposes.

You can spend endless hours looking for art online. In fact, just this search alone may make you glad to be creating a Web page. You may not get a lot done for a few hours while you're looking, but you'll see a lot of neat stuff!

One great site for starting your search is the Online Image Archive at

```
www.maths.tcd.ie/pub/images/images.html
```

Another good place for pointers to lots of images is the WebReference site. For a large number of different kinds of resources, go to the WebReference site; for images, go directly to the images area:

```
www.webreference.com/authoring/graphics/images.html
```

For backgrounds, visit the following area within the WebReference site:

```
www.webreference.com/authoring/graphics/backgrounds.html
```

And for photographs, try a site with preexisting stock photos, a site with all kinds of graphics, and another that converts your photographs into digital form:

```
www.weststock.com
www.eyewire.com
www.photoworks.com
```

Many more sites for images and image conversion exist. Start with the sites that we mention and expand your search until you find what you need.

The Image Search feature on the AltaVista search engine is one of the best ways to look for suitable graphics. Be careful, though: Most of the graphics you find are copyrighted, and for your Web site, you should only use images that are explicitly made freely available. Visit AltaVista at www.altavista.com.

In addition to searching online, another way to get graphics is to whip out any paint program and draw the graphics that you want. For example, Windows includes a free graphics program, Windows Paint, that you can use for your initial graphics work. Even inexpensive paint programs today enable you to create some stunning graphics; you're limited mostly by your imagination and artistic ability (which for some of us can be quite limiting!).

More on graphics

The Graphics File Formats FAQ (Frequently Asked Questions file) can answer almost any conceivable question about graphics. For the latest information, visit www.dcs.ed.ac.uk/~mxr/gfx/utils-hi.html. Links from this site lead to detailed technical information about GIF, JPEG, and other file formats. For a detailed description of how to use images well, see cgi.netscape.com/assist/net_sites/impact_docs/index.html.

For big-bucks commercial work and fine art, people regularly use high-end programs such as Adobe Photoshop and Adobe Illustrator. If you lack talent, you can always ask one of your artistically inclined friends to help you, or you can even recruit a starving art student.

Another technique is to use a scanner. You may already have one at home, or have use of a scanner in your office. If not, head to your favorite copy shop and rent some time using its scanner. Scanning is a perfect way to put photographs online. Simply scan your graphic or photo, save it in GIF (for graphics) or JPEG (for photographs) format, and slap it on your Web site. Or work with a photo developer, such as a suitably equipped local developer, a chain store such as Wal-Mart or Rite Aid, or a mail-order and Internet operation such as Seattle Filmworks (www.photoworks.com), that can develop your film right to diskette or Photo CD.

The fourth way is to take photographs with a digital camera. Most digital cameras come with cables to connect the camera to your PC to download the photographs onto your computer. They also come with software that enables you to edit the photos on your PC and save them, usually in JPEG format.

But how can you make sure that your graphics are in the proper format? That turns out to be easy, too. Many paint programs and most scanning software let you save a graphic in either GIF or JPEG formats. If your program doesn't save in these formats, it may be for one of two reasons:

- ✔ During installation, you may have chosen not to install converters for GIF and JPEG. Haul out your original install disks and see whether you can reinstall the program with the correct translators.

- ✔ If converters are not the problem, call your program's manufacturer or visit its Web site and see whether it has an update that enables the program to save to GIF and/or JPEG formats. If your software vendor can't sell you a program that handles GIF or JPEG, you can easily find one that does.

No matter what format your graphic came in originally, you can convert it to GIF or JPEG by using software that you can easily obtain from the Web. Mac users can run GIFConverter, and Windows users can run the excellent LView program to convert between multiple formats. Save your graphic as a GIF or JPEG file, and you are ready to incorporate the graphic into your Web page.

Save your image in the program's normal format as well as GIF or JPEG. When you save to GIF or JPEG, you can lose information from the image. If you reopen the GIF or JPEG image, edit the file, and then save it again, you lose even more information. So save your file in its original format to preserve the data in it for later editing, and save a separate copy in GIF or JPEG to use on the Web.

Dealing with Graphics

The most difficult aspect of including graphics in your Web pages is resolving all the design issues that accompany the use of graphics. Creating effective graphics and placing them properly in relation to your text is not as easy as boiling water. This book doesn't cover all the complexities of graphic design. However, we can tell you the additional concerns that arise when you use graphics on the Web so that you can effectively apply your own graphics skills, or those of people who work with you, to your Web pages.

Speeding up slow pages

One of the Web's ongoing problems is *download speed* — the amount of time a Web page takes to appear on the user's screen. Download times are especially slow for graphics-rich pages, which, although more interesting to view, can be more frustrating because they appear more slowly. And the trade-off is not simple; lots of variables intervene. For example:

- ✔ **Access speeds:** Different users access the Web through connections that run at different speeds. And the same server can serve up a Web page at different speeds, depending upon how busy the server is. When you test your brand-new, graphics-rich page on your local machine, everything may run fast. But when you upload that same page to a server and access the page over a 56 Kbps (kilobits per second) modem, the page loads much more slowly.

- ✔ **Good and bad graphics:** If you plan to spend your users' time on downloading big graphics, invest some of your own time and money upfront to make sure that the graphics are as high-quality as possible. People don't mind waiting for a good graphic nearly as much as they mind waiting for a bad one. A good graphic may be a product shot that shows someone exactly what they're going to get. A bad graphic may be a banner that says "HELLO!" in six Day-Glo colors.

✔ **Frustration levels:** The same users who enjoy watching your page appear in the morning while drinking a cup of coffee may be tempted to scream at their browser when they try to quickly check out your page just before heading home from work — especially if they had a bad hair day, a bad boss day, or even a bad browser day. The better the job you do with your graphics, the more your page will please people.

What on earth can you do to address all these factors, especially when they combine to make your page slow and your users grumpy? Be clever! Limit the number of colors in your graphics to make the files smaller so that they download more quickly. Get expert advice — from someone you know or a book — or look at cool sites online to help you make the graphics you do use more interesting to look at. You can also lightly sprinkle your page with small graphics, rather than burden it with several big ones.

Table 9-1 shows the time necessary to download 60K (kilobytes) of data. A text-only page is usually just 2–3K, but pages with graphics are much larger. A complex, quarter-screen GIF image, for example, may be about 50K. Compare the total size of all the elements in the page you plan to the times shown in Table 9-1 to get an idea of how quickly your page loads for the most speed-deficient user, and then design with that person in mind.

Table 9-1	Slowest Download Times	
Access Speed	*Description*	*Time to Download 60K File*
28.8 Kbps	Low-end Internet modem	35 seconds
33.6 Kbps	Mid-range Internet modem	30 seconds
56 Kbps	Fast Internet modem	20 seconds
DSL	Special phone line, modem	4 seconds
Cable modem	Special cable hookup, modem	1 second
Ethernet	Standard network	Less than 1 second

Avoiding three big mistakes

Don't make these three big mistakes relating to graphics on the Web:

✔ **No graphics:** Having no graphics on your Web pages means boring pages. Because you're reading this chapter, we assume that you're trying not to make this mistake.

✔ **Too many graphics:** Using too many large, slow-to-download graphics may be the biggest "newbie" Web author mistake. (A lot of old hands make this mistake as well.)

✔ **No text alternative:** Some users don't have graphical capability at all, and many others run around the Web with graphics turned off, only turning graphics capability on when absolutely necessary. You need to accommodate these users by creating your page in a way that supports text-only access as well as graphical access.

Try an experiment: Go into your browser, turn off the graphics display, and load your Web page. If you can't tell what is on the page or what links go where, then you need to redesign your page. (Then, just to blow off steam, or if you don't have a Web page up yet, try the same experiment on some other people's pages and send them a note if you have problems.)

The usual way to redesign your page for text-only access is to include a textual menu linking to the same places as your graphical menu. Some sites provide a whole parallel set of Web pages that are purely textual rather than graphical. Providing parallel, text-only pages lets the user choose whether to go for the attractive, bandwidth-sucking graphical pages or for the very fast text-only pages. However, because the percentage of users who choose text-only access continues to drop, providing a complete set of text-only pages may be overkill.

Here are the most important rules for supporting text and graphical access:

✔ As you design and create your page, think about how your page will look with all graphic access turned off as well as on.

✔ Test your page with graphics turned off.

✔ Test your page in different browsers.

✔ Include ALT tags in all images so that explanatory text appears whenever a graphic isn't displayed (see this chapter and Appendix C for details about HTML tags used in graphics).

✔ Provide text-only menus in addition to icon-based selections and image maps.

✔ If you want to make everyone very happy, consider creating a separate, text-only version of your site.

If you're considering creating a Web site that's accessible by portable devices such as the Palm line of handheld organizers, creating a text-only version of your site makes a great deal of sense. The text-only version of your site will make a good starting point for handhelds.

What about rights?

You can find a number of great graphics in books and magazines and on Web sites. Can you just scan or copy these graphics and use them in your own Web site? Should you?

Yes and no. Yes, you can, but no, you shouldn't. Publishers either own the images that they use or obtain a license for them. You can't legally use most images on your own Web site without either buying or licensing them.

For some images on the Web, simply sending a note to the Webmaster gets you a quick okay. But for most Web images and for nearly all images in print, permissions may be very hard to get. Creating a new image that serves the same purpose is often easier than negotiating permissions. And then maybe you can make a little money licensing your own images out to other people!

Using Graphics in HTML

The <IMG> tag is the HTML tag that causes an image to appear embedded in your Web page. (See Chapter 4 for more on HTML.) Here are the HTML tags for a page that displays the image MANUGRAPHIC.GIF by using the <IMG> tag, and then a text menu as an alternative:

```
<IMG SRC="manugraphic.gif" ALT="Menu Graphic"> [
          <AHREF="about.html">About</A> |
          <AHREF="home.html">Home page</A> |
          <AHREF="links.html">Fun Links</A> |
          <AHREF="map.html">Site Map</A> |
          <AHREF="search.html">Search Map</A> ]
```

It's good to know some HTML even if you are using a Web authoring program that allows you to drag and drop images, specify compression options, and so on. Why? Because you may need to make specific changes in options like the ALT text for the image or the directory that a file lives in. Your Web authoring program, or a text editing program, will allow you to go in and change the HTML directly, quickly, and accurately — if you know a little HTML.

With that in mind, here are three useful graphical effects for your Web pages:

- **Accents:** Small graphical images that serve as labels or highlights ("New," "Top Ten," and so on).

- **Icons:** Small graphical images that serve as links to another page. Click the icon, and you move to a different Web page.

- **Thumbnails:** Small graphical images that serve as previews of a larger image. Click the thumbnail to download the larger image.

Accents use the <IMG> tag to link to a small graphic — an inline graphic that appears as part of the page, unless graphics display is turned off.

Icons and thumbnails combine the <IMG> tag, which makes the icon or thumbnail image appear, with the <A> (or anchor) tag. (Don't start singing "Anchors Aweigh" on this one — you need anchors here!) The anchor tag establishes a link to the Web page or larger graphic that appears when you click the inline graphic. For more on the anchor tag, see Chapter 8.

The steps in the following sections describe how to use the image tag, the anchor tag, and the ALT option separately and together. With these tags, you can combine graphics and navigation to create all kinds of effects.

Review the HTML tag definitions in Appendix C to find out about other options for these tags. You may also want to check out more advanced books, such as *HTML 4 For Dummies,* 3rd Edition, by Ed Tittel et al. and *Creating Cool HTML 4 Web Pages,* 3rd Edition, by Dave Taylor (both from Hungry Minds, Inc.) for more details and how-to information on advanced HTML options.

Use the <IMG> tag for inline graphics

To use the <IMG> tag to link to an inline graphic that appears as part of your Web page, along with the ALT option to specify "alternate" text, follow these steps:

1. **Create or find a graphic that you want to use.**

   Inline graphics that are embedded in the page should be small for fast display — about the size of a business card or smaller. Use the sources we describe in the "Obtaining and creating graphics" section earlier in this chapter to find or create graphics.

2. **If you're using Netscape Composer, choose Insert⇨Image. Type the URL of the image in the text entry box, or choose a file from your hard disk with the Choose File button. If you're working directly in HTML, add the <IMG> tag with the SRC, or "source," option to specify the image's pathname.**

   For a graphic that's in the same directory as the HTML file, use the <IMG> tag and SRC option like this:

   ```
   <IMG SRC="new.gif">
   ```

   For a graphic that's at a different Web site, use the <IMG> tag and SRC option like this:

   ```
   <IMG SRC="http://www.grafixsite.com/new.gif">
   ```

3. **Add the** ALT **option to specify text that appears if the graphic can't be viewed — for example, if the user is running a text-only browser or has graphics turned off. In Netscape Composer, put the text in the Alternative Text text entry box. If you're working in HTML, add the** ALT **option and text within the** <IMG> **tag, like this:**

```
<IMG SRC="http://www.grafixsite.com/new.gif" ALT="New!">
```

Don't depend on someone else's site being up at all times and always staying unchanged. If possible, copy the graphic that you need into your own site's directory and refer to it there.

Add an A for anchor to create a graphical link

As we note in the first part of the section on graphics and HTML, one of the best ways to jazz up a Web page "cheaply" — that is, without slowing down the page a lot for everyone — is to use graphical elements as icons that link to outside information, such as a larger image or a different Web page. This technique is a great way to make your page appear graphically rich without burdening your users with long download times.

To add an anchor to create a graphical link, use the <IMG> tag within the beginning and ending anchor tags. If you also embed a word or phrase between the beginning and ending anchor tags, you give the user a choice between clicking the image or the phrase. The following steps demonstrate how to create a graphical link:

1. **In Netscape Composer, use the Insert⇨Image command to bring in an image. In a text editor, use the** <IMG> **tag to bring in the inline image that you want to use as a thumbnail image (a small image that represents a larger one) or an icon:**

```
<IMG SRC="minibud.jpg">
```

2. **In Netscape Composer, click the image and choose Insert⇨Link. In a text editor, add an anchor tag (**<A>**) to specify the link.**

To display a larger image when a user clicks the small image, specify an anchor with an HREF, or Hypertext REFerence, that points to an image file:

```
<A HREF="maxibud.jpg"> <IMG SRC="minibud.jpg"> </A>
```

Figure 9-2, from Boojum Expeditions, shows a thumbnail graphic and the larger image that appears when the user clicks the thumbnail. John Forrester's travelogue can be found at `http://boojum.com/photographs.html`.

For a link to another page, specify an anchor with an HREF that points to an HTML document:

```
<A HREF="bebakpg.htm"> <IMG SRC="bebak.jpg"> </A>
```

An HTML option not only allows you to resize an image, but also speeds up page displays. Add the `HEIGHT=` and `WIDTH=` options within the `<IMG>` tag to specify, in pixels, the height and width of your image. In Netscape Composer, use the Dimensions area within the Image Properties dialog box (which appears when you choose Insert⇨Image). Browsers use this information to fill in the rest of the page around the image first, allowing the user to scroll up and down in the page and read it before the graphic appears, and then to fill in the image itself.

Figure 9-2:
Combining
mini- and
maxi-
graphics.

The height and width options can stretch or squeeze an image to make it appear different than its actual size. However, these options don't change the actual image. You must keep the height and width options in the same proportions as the original image, or the image will be stretched in one dimension. Also, if you put a small image in a large area, it will be stretched out to fit and appear odd. If you put a large image in a small area, it will look good, but the file size will be large compared to the amount of space the image takes onscreen. To prevent these problems, use an image editing program such as Paint Shop Pro to edit the image to the correct size, rather than using the height and width options to resize the image.

One of the most important ways for intermediate and advanced Web authors to organize their pages is by using invisible tables to position text and graphics relative to one another. Chapter 11 has a brief description of tables. This method is tricky! For example, a table-structured page that looks great at one monitor size can easily look terrible on a larger or smaller screen. Find some well-laid-out Web pages and view the Web pages' HTML source to see how other Web publishers use invisible tables. To see one expert's work, visit Creating Killer Web sites at `www.killersites.com/1-design/jpeg.html`.

Experimenting with Advanced GIFfery

GIFs are widespread on the Web, and download times are important; therefore, four advanced techniques exist for doing fancy things with GIFs:

- ✔ **Transparent GIFs:** Everyone needs to know this one. All GIFs are rectangular, but many of them seem to "float" over the background with no obvious border. These GIFs are *transparent* — the images' backgrounds are invisible — so they blend seamlessly into the browser's background. Figure 9-3 shows a nontransparent and a transparent GIF from the Web 66 Web site, which is part of a cooperative effort between the University of Minnesota College of Education and Development and Hillside Elementary in Minnesota, with support from 3M.

- ✔ **Interlaced GIFs:** Not everyone needs to know about this one, but we mention it (again!) because if you use large, complex graphics, interlaced GIFs are worth knowing about. An interlaced GIF depends on an HTML feature that paints every fourth line of an image, then every second line, and so on until the image is complete. The image seems to appear in low resolution and then gradually sharpen until complete.

- ✔ **Animated GIFs:** The basic GIF specification, GIF99a, supports animation as well as static images. All you need to do is create a series of images that, when viewed in sequence, form an animation (like an old-fashioned flip book). Then you package the images together as a single GIF, using readily available tools, and include the GIF file in your Web page. Voilà! Instant animation.

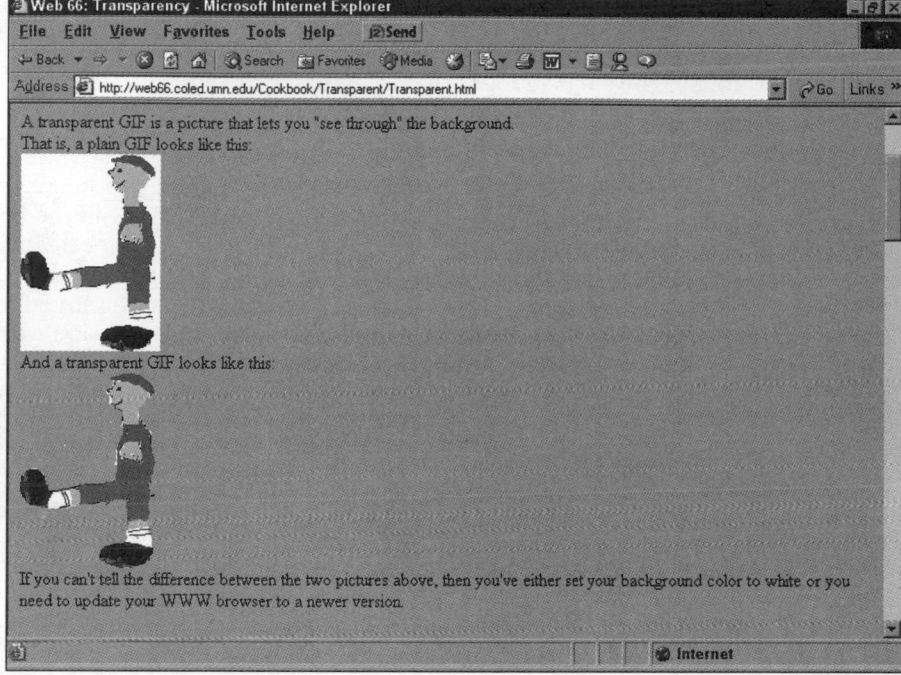

Figure 9-3:
Now you
see it (the
white
rectangle
around the
graphic),
now you
don't.

✔ **Clickable image maps:** Clickable image maps are very common in big-money sites and even in many smaller ones. A *clickable image map* is a graphic with different *hot spots* that, when clicked, take you to different Web pages or locations within a Web page. This kind of graphic is cool, but it's YABG (Yet Another Big Graphic), and you need design skills to make a good one.

Graphics can be a time sink

We spend a lot of time in this chapter discussing how much time the user can spend downloading graphics. But what about the demand that using graphics places on your time as a Web page developer?

Creating and editing graphics is fun! But creating even a simple business graphic, such as a bar graph, can consume hours of fooling around with fonts, colors, and image sizes. Getting your images Web-ready and testing them takes up even more time. Working with graphics can easily become the most time-consuming part of creating and updating your Web site.

What to do? Use small graphics and use graphics sparingly while you gain experience. After you have experience, or after you hire someone who does, you can develop and deploy those knockout graphics that distinguish the best Web sites.

Transparent GIFs

Here are the steps to create a transparent GIF:

1. **Choose a color in the image's background to make transparent.**

   Every pixel in your image that's of the selected color becomes transparent. Choose a color that's used only in the area around the image, not in the image itself, since every pixel of the selected color becomes transparent. You may need to edit the image's surrounding area — the area that you want to be transparent — so that it's a different color from the rest of the image. The usual choices for transparency are white or the light gray background color most browsers use.

   For details on the procedure for choosing an area to make transparent, see the Web 66 Web site, shown previously in Figure 9-4, at `web66.coled.umn.edu/Cookbook/Transparent/Transparent.html`.

2. **Use your graphics package or a tool to make the image transparent.**

   For the Macintosh, use Transparency, which you can find on the Web at C|NET's download.com Web site and elsewhere.

   For Windows, use Paint Shop Pro. You can find an evaluation version on the CD-ROM that comes with this book.

   For any platform, you can use a Web-based package called TransWeb on the Massachusetts Institute of Technology (MIT) site at `www.mit.edu/tweb/map.html`. This package reads the image, converts it, and displays the result. You can then right-click on the image to save it to disk.

   To use TransWeb, you have to move your image to a Web server, as we describe in Chapter 12. (You can also do this as part of the process of creating a simple GeoCities Web page, as described in Chapter 3.) Then go to the TransWeb Web and follow the instructions.

3. **Add the image to your page, as we describe in the section about the IMG tag earlier in this chapter.**

4. **Test to be sure that the image remains transparent with several different backgrounds.**

   Bring up the image in your browser and then change the browser's default background color.

Animated GIFs

Animated GIFs are also supported online. You can find out how to use them and start putting them in your Web pages by using info out on the Web. To read the true and fascinating story of how animated GIFs were invented, and to link to many supporting examples and resources, go to these two Web sites:

```
http://members.aol.com/royalef/gifmake.htm
builder.cnet.com/webbuilding/0-7330.html
```

You can find a cool tool on the Web called GIFwizard that can shrink the size of GIF graphics and animations by up to 90 percent. Try it! Go to www.optiview.com.

Clickable image maps

To create a clickable image map, you must first create the graphic. (See the SGI site at www.sgi.com for an example of an attractive, clickable image map.) Then you have to create a special file that maps regions of the image to specific URLs. A program that you can download from the Web, Mapedit (see Appendix E), maps image regions for either Macintosh or Windows. Just load the image, click and drag over it to define clickable regions, and then enter the URL you want to link to.

The complication arises during the final part of this process. The original form of image maps, called *server-side image maps,* require that the map file be in a special place where the server can find it. Unfortunately, to use this kind of image map, you may need to talk to the server administrator, because no universal standard exists about where this file should be.

Netscape 2.0 and higher, Microsoft Internet Explorer, and all other up-to-date browsers support what are known as *client-side image maps* that don't require server involvement in any processing when the user clicks an image. Browsers are now smart enough to map the image, click to a URL, and fetch the URL directly without going through the server. See the Netscape 2.0 documentation or the Netscape site at www.netscape.com for more information.

Chapter 10

Placing Graphics Right (And Left)

Chapter 9 shows you how to insert graphics into your Web page. When you start trying to get your Web page to look good, though, you start having to worry about not just the image itself, but about how it's placed on the page.

In this chapter we'll show you how to make your graphics work well within your Web page by adjusting the size of the image; by flowing text smoothly around the graphic; and by putting a border around the graphic. We'll then show you how to actually implement the changes in HTML and in Netscape Composer.

Adjusting Graphic Size

You can specify the size of an image when you insert it into your Web page. Within the IMG tag, you add two options to specify the image's size: WIDTH and HEIGHT. If you're using Netscape Composer or another WYSIWYG Web page creation tool, you enter the width and height as options within the program you're using. The program then stores these values in the WIDTH and HEIGHT options for you.

Every graphic has an actual size — a height and width in pixels. When displayed at this size, the graphic looks as good as it's going to look. However, graphics can be stretched or shrunken to fit into an available space.

There are two very different reasons for specifying the size of your graphic, one excellent and one questionable:

✔ **To tell the Web browser what size the image is:** This is the excellent reason. When you specify the height and width of your image in the Web page, the user's Web browser sets aside that amount of space, then continues displaying text while the image is loading. Because text can be transmitted so much faster than graphics, this often allows the user to see all of the text in a page and start reading it, without having to wait for the image to appear.

✔ **To stretch or squeeze the image:** This is the questionable reason. If you enter a different height or width than the image actually has, then the user's Web browser will stretch or squeeze the image to fit. This can produce some very odd-looking results.

If you are going to stretch or squeeze the image, you can set the height and width options four different ways:

✔ **Scaled smaller than the original image:** You can reduce the height and width by an equal proportion — say, one-third less, or 10 percent less — from the original image. The image will be smaller and still look good. However, it still takes up the same amount of file space as the original, while showing up as smaller onscreen. It's better to edit the original image so it actually is smaller and then display it at its new actual size — the file will be smaller and download quicker.

✔ **Scaled larger than the original image:** You can stretch the image by increasing the height and width in equal proportions. The image is stretched evenly. It doesn't look too odd, but you can usually see some "breaks" in the image as a result of its being stretched. This is a quick way to get a small image to fill a large space, but you're usually better off adjusting the image size in an editing program like Photoshop that lets you fix any problems that come up. Then use the new, edited image at actual size.

✔ **Scaled out of proportion to the original image:** The worst thing to do is to set the height and width to be different than the original image, but not to increase both height and width in proportion. Let's say you have a 50 x 50 image but you need to fill a 100 x 50 space (that's 100 pixels tall by 50 pixels wide). You can simply set the height to 100 and the width to 50, and the user's Web browser will stretch the height of the image accordingly. However, the result will look awful.

Figure 10-1 shows the results of scaling an image smaller, larger, and out of proportion. It wasn't that great a picture to begin with, but you can see that the changes have made it worse. You can use any of these options as needed, but *caveat artifex* — let the artisan beware — the results aren't likely to be great.

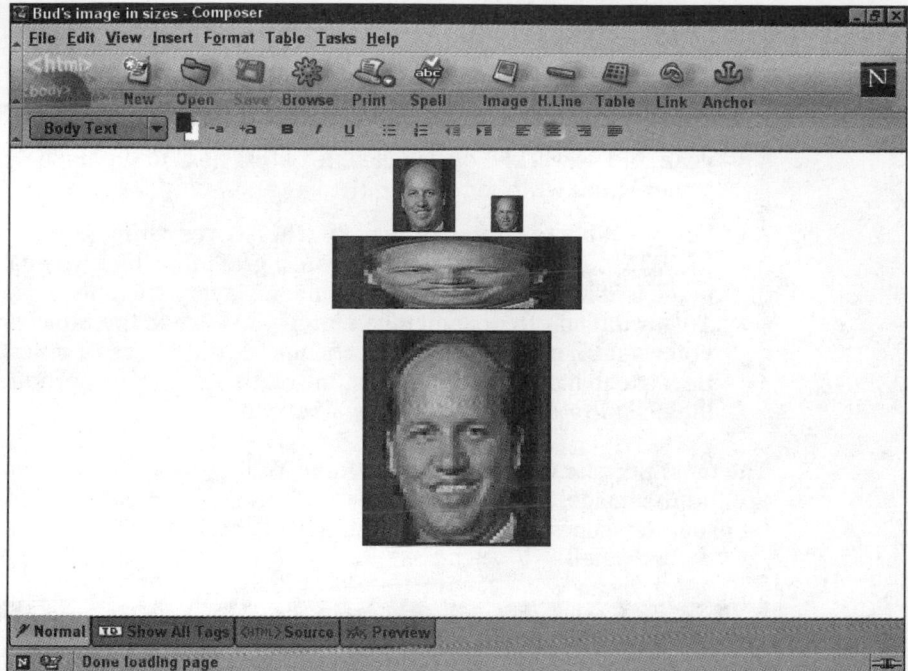

Figure 10-1:
A scaled
image can
look — well,
scaly.

Flowing Text Around Graphics

One of the trickier things to do well in your Web page is to get graphic images and text to work well together. You have several choices for placing an image, from simplest to trickiest:

✔ **Putting text above and below — but not beside — the image:** You can create a clear area in the middle of your text and put the image in the middle of it. You can also put a caption below the image. This solution wastes the area to the left and right of your image, but it's the easiest to implement in HTML and creates the simplest layout. Your readers also don't have to adjust, as they're reading, to the "bump" in the text around where the picture is.

✔ **Putting one line of text beside an image:** You can put text beside your image and align the line at the top, middle, or bottom of the image. Figure 10-2 shows an example. This used to be the only way that HTML allowed you to position an image relative to text, and it produced some ugly layouts.

✔ **Wrapping text around an image:** A command that allows text to actually wrap around an image — in the manner we're all used to from magazines — was added to HTML several years ago. By now, almost everyone
out there has a browser new enough to support this feature. When you
use this option, the few users who have a very old browser — about 7-8
years old — will see one single line of text next to the image rather than
several lines wrapped around the image.

✔ **Using a table to control precisely where everything goes:** You can use
the HTML TABLE command to create a grid into which you can then
place text and images, just like someone laying out a newspaper page.
This is difficult to do, and it can force you to redo the table every time
you want to make even a small change in your image or your text.
Because it allows such precise control, this option can produce the best-
looking — or the worst-looking — results.

The most popular approach with modern Web browsers is to wrap text
around the image. We show you how to do that, directly using HTML tags or
by using Netscape Composer, later in this chapter.

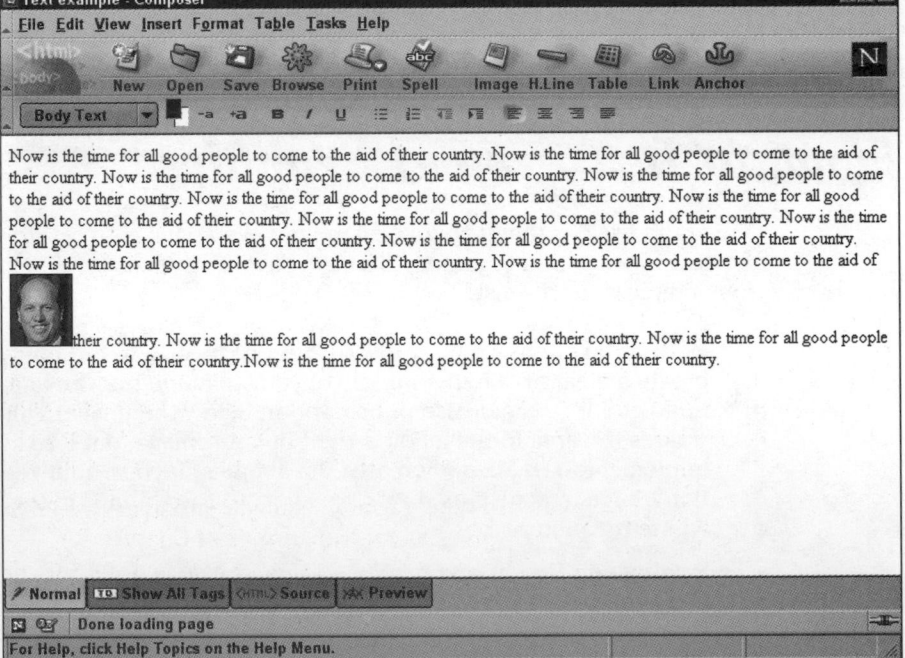

Figure 10-2:
Putting one
line of text
next to an
image looks
odd.

Putting a Border Around a Graphic

One of the more important elements in designing a page to look good is *white space* — "empty" space that separates different parts of the page from one another. If things are crowded together too closely, the page as a whole looks chaotic.

White space is especially important when you flow text around a graphic, as we described in the previous section. You can specify white space around a graphic, or a solid border to set it off, or both.

Most photos look better with a thin black border around them. We describe how to add such a border, either directly in HTML or in Netscape Composer, later in this section.

Placing a Graphic in Netscape Composer

It's good to know your HTML, but working with graphics is much easier in a WYSIWYG tool such as Composer. We recommend that you work in the tool, then look at the underlying HTML to learn about it, rather than doing all your work directly in HTML.

To place a graphic in Netscape Composer and specify the graphic size, text flow, spacing, and border, if any, follow these steps:

1. **Open Netscape Composer.**

2. **Type in some text, or copy and paste it in.**

   It's much easier to experiment with placing a graphic if you have some text in your document.

3. **Place the cursor at the start of a line of text in your document. Then use the Insert⇨Image command to insert a GIF or JPEG image, as described in Chapter 9. Click OK to close the Image Properties dialog box.**

   If you don't have an image handy, you can find instructions on how to create images and sources for free images in Chapter 9.

   An example of how your document might look at this point is shown back in Figure 10-2.

   Move the Image Properties dialog box to a spot on your screen so you can see both the image and the dialog box.

   Note that at this point the text is crowded right up against the graphic. The text doesn't all wrap around the graphic — only one line of text appears next to the graphic.

TIP

4. **Double-click on the image to open the Image Properties dialog box. If the button to the left of the Image Preview area says More Properties, click on it to show all the properties.**

Figure 10-3 shows how the dialog box appears at this point, with the image placed but with default properties chosen for the image's dimensions, alignment, spacing around the image, and border.

You don't have to specify the image's width and height in Netscape Composer. The program automatically adds the `WIDTH` and `HEIGHT` options to the `IMG` tag, using the image's actual width and height.

5. **If you want to scale the image to a larger or smaller size, click the Custom Size radio button in the Dimensions area. In most cases, you will want to leave the Constrain checkbox checked. Change the Height or Width to the value you want.**

Clicking Custom Size allows you to change the image's height and width. By leaving the Constrain checkbox checked, Composer automatically keeps the width and height scaled proportionally, in keeping with the image's actual height and width. For instance, if you change the width, the height will automatically adjust to keep the image's proportions correct.

Figure 10-3:
The Image Properties dialog box offers you many options.

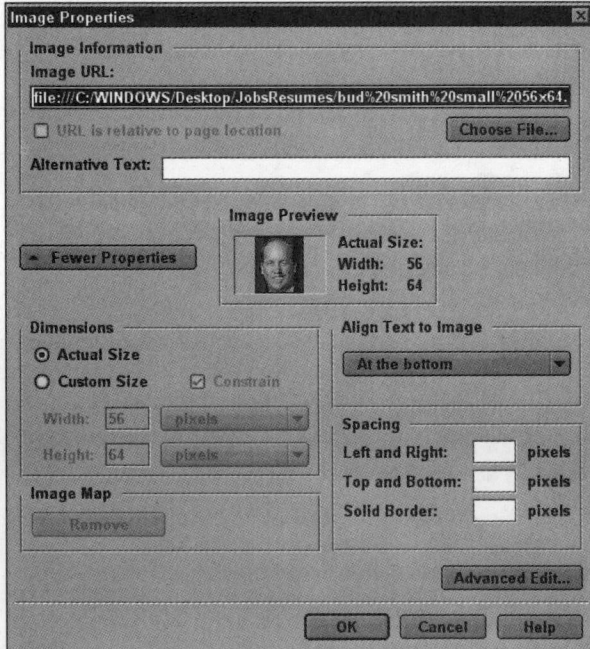

The Image Preview doesn't change to reflect the dimensions you enter. Even if you clear the Constrain checkbox and enter a height twice as large as previously, and keep the width the same, the preview will not become tall and skinny to reflect the change. The Image Preview is actually an "image view" of the underlying image, not a preview of how it will look on your Web page. To see a true preview, simply close the dialog box at any point and the current values will be reflected in the image's appearance in the document window.

After changing any of the values in the Image Properties dialog box, click OK to close the dialog box and see what your page looks like with the new values. Then double-click on the image to quickly open the Image Properties dialog box again.

6. **Change the pull-down menu in the Align Text to Image area to reflect how you want text to flow around the image: A single line of text aligned to the top, center, or bottom of the image; or all of the text flowing to the left or right of the image.**

   You probably want to use the top, center, and bottom options only, which align a single line of text beside the image, if you want to create a caption next to the image. Otherwise, choose Wrap to the right to keep the image on the left margin and wrap text to the right. Choose Wrap to the left to push the image to the right of the page and flow text down on its left.

7. **In the Spacing area, specify the number of pixels of blank area that you want around the image.**

   You usually want to start with the same amount of spacing for the Left and Right spacing and the Top and Bottom spacing. Four pixels is a good starting point. Fine-tune the numbers as needed to create the right look when you have your final text and images available.

8. **Still in the Spacing area, specify the size of the border that you want around the image.**

   A thin border around an image makes it stand out much better from the surrounding white space and text. Try a 2-pixel-wide border to start, and then adjust it from there to get the look you want.

For consistency's sake, use the same spacing and border width around each of your images. You may need to experiment to find a set of values that works well for all your images, but the effort is worth it. Even minor inconsistencies of a pixel here or there are enough to throw off the overall appearance of your page.

Figure 10-4 shows a sample Web page with various options for dimensions, alignment, spacing, and borders. Use it as a guide as you do your own experimenting.

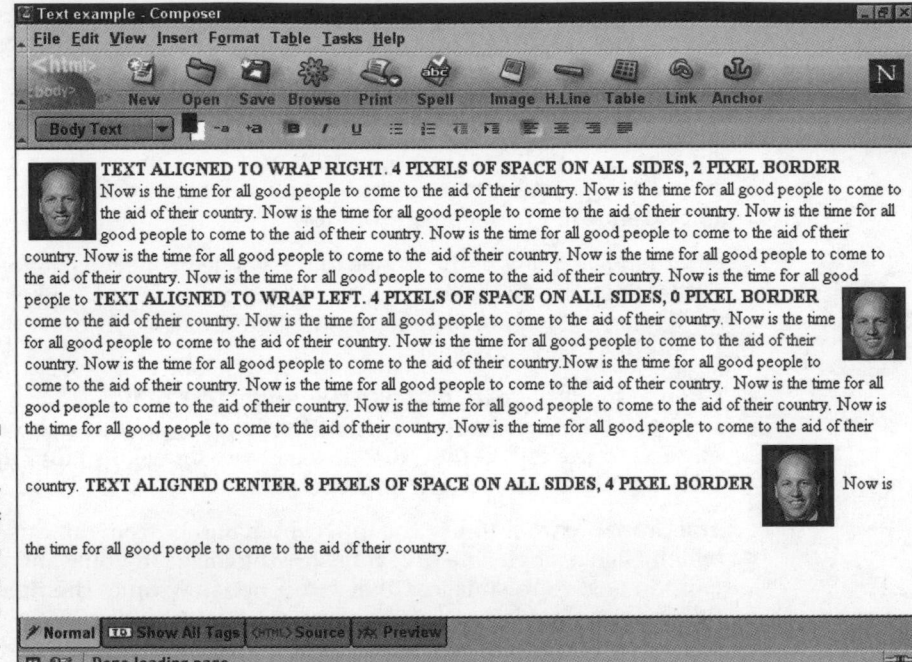

Figure 10-4:
You can try
all sorts of
options to
get the
appearance
right.

Placing a Graphic in HTML

Fine-tuning the positioning of graphics by using HTML directly is a frustrating exercise unless you're somewhat an expert in design. If you're new to design work, you need to be able to experiment, and experimenting is much easier in a tool such as Netscape Composer. So we recommend that you use Netscape Composer, as described above, to place your graphic.

However, if you prefer to work directly in HTML, use the instructions in this section. You can find figures showing how things look as you experiment with different options in the previous section.

To place a graphic in HTML and specify the graphic size, text flow, spacing, and border, if any, follow these steps:

1. **Open a document in a text editor. Save it with the extension .htm to make sure that it's treated as an HTML document.**

2. **Type in some text, or copy and paste it in.**

   It's much easier to experiment with placing a graphic if you have some text in your document.

3. **Insert an image into the middle of the text using the** IMG **tag. Add alternate text to explain what the image is.**

   The correct syntax to use is <IMG SRC=*url* ALT="*text*">, where *url* is a Web address and *text* is a brief description of the image. See Chapter 9 for details.

4. **Save your document and open it in a Web browser to see how it looks at this point.**

   Your document should look something like Figure 10-2, shown earlier in the chapter.

   Continue to save your document and look at it in your Web browser as you add tags and change options so you can see how it looks after each step.

   Click on the Refresh or Reload button in your browser to update the Web page to reflect the most recently saved version of your document.

5. **Add the** WIDTH **and** HEIGHT **options to the** IMG **tag.**

   In most cases, set them to the actual width and height of the image. If you want to change the size of the image, or to change its proportions, calculate the appropriate values for the WIDTH and HEIGHT options and enter them. Then review the result in a Web browser.

   The IMG tag now looks like this: <IMG SRC=*url* WIDTH=*xx* HEIGHT=*yy*>, where *xx* is the width, in pixels, and *yy* is the height, in pixels.

   Adding the WIDTH and HEIGHT options with the actual values of the image will not change the look of your page, but will make it easier for a Web browser to load the rest of the page quickly around the image. Using different values will change the look of your page.

   You can find the actual width and height of your image by right-clicking on the image's icon on the Windows desktop. Right-click, choose Properties, and the image's width and height will be displayed.

6. **To specify text wrapping, add the** ALIGN **option to the** IMG **tag. The most commonly used options are** RIGHT, **to wrap text to the right of the image, and** LEFT, **to wrap text left of the image and move the image over to the right.**

   Other options are TOP, CENTER, and BOTTOM. If you don't use the ALIGN option, the default value, BOTTOM, is used. With this option, the text is shoved to the right and positioned at the bottom of the image, leaving an odd gap in most of the area next to the image. This is hardly ever what you want. Start with ALIGN=RIGHT, then change it if you want a different effect.

7. **To create white space around the image, add the** HSPACE **(for horizontal spacing) and** VSPACE **(for vertical spacing) options.**

HSPACE creates an equal number of pixels of space to the left and right of the image; VSPACE creates an equal number of pixels of space above and below the image. Good settings to start with are HSPACE=4 VSPACE=4.

8. **To create a black border around the image, add the** BORDER **tag. A suitable value is** BORDER=2.

If you've specified all the possible options, your tag now looks something like this:

```
<IMG SRC=url ALT="text" WIDTH=xx HEIGHT=yy ALIGN=right
          HSPACE=4 VSPACE=4 border=2> .
```

For consistency's sake, use the same spacing and border width around each of your images. You may need to experiment to find a set of values that works well for all your images, but the effort is worth it. Even minor inconsistencies of a pixel here or there are enough to throw off the overall appearance of your page.

Figure 10-5 shows the HTML code described above and the resulting Web page. Note that the code uses double quotes around parameters such as the width and height. These quotes are optional for most parameters; they're required for text that has spaces in it, such as text used as a parameter for the ALT tag.

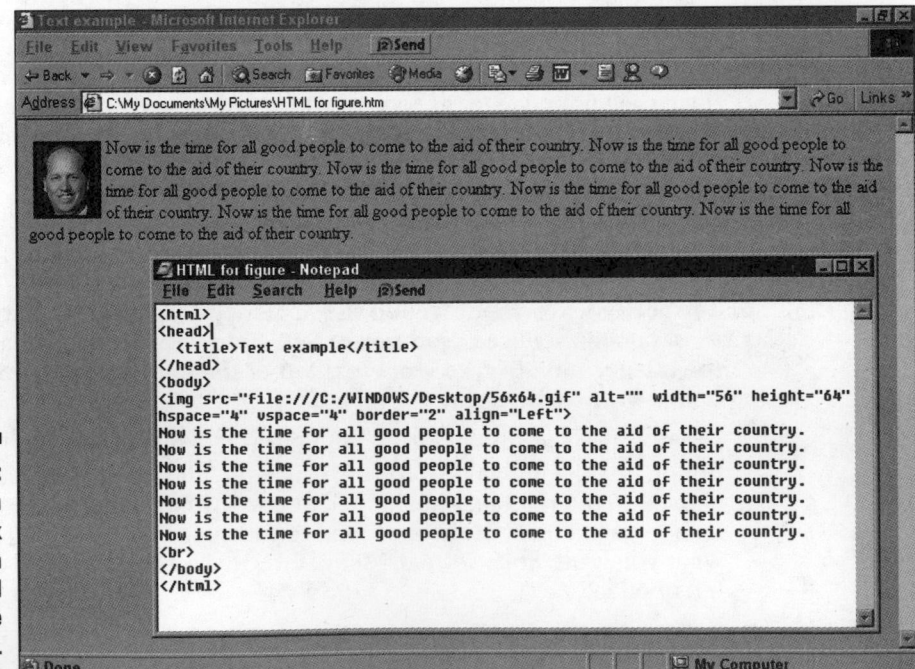

Figure 10-5:
You can work directly in HTML and see the results.

Chapter 11

Designing a Good-Looking Page

●●●

●●●

*O*ne of the trickiest issues in creating and publishing Web pages is the overall look of each Web page. Some pages look great. Others look fine. Still others look hokey and amateurish. And how good a page looks varies considerably depending on who's looking — "beauty is in the eye of the beholder." Up to a point, anyway; some pages are so bad, or so good, that everyone agrees on them.

When you create your first Web page, as described in Part 1 of this book, it really doesn't matter how your page looks. You're just trying to have fun and get a little experience. But if you're creating a Web page a lot of people will be looking at, or if you're practicing to create a Web page for business or career use, you're going to want it to look good. And explaining how to make a Web page look good is hard.

The overall impression a Web page makes depends on many different factors — the balance of white space (empty space) to text and graphics, the size of text used, the font used, appropriate use of headings versus regular text, and appropriate use of bulleted and numbered lists, hyperlinks, and other eye-catching elements. Each of these factors has to be "right," but "right" is very hard to define — you know it when you see it. And all of the choices made have to work together as a whole, and just what it means to have everything work together is even harder to define.

It takes a professional to make a Web page look really good — so at the end of this chapter, we talk about how to get professional help for the look of your Web page. But it doesn't take a professional to make your Web page look pretty good — or at least to avoid having it be out-and-out ugly. We'll show you how to make sure your Web page looks good in this chapter.

Three Key Principles of Design

The design of a Web page can be most simply described as the look of the page and how it's perceived by the user — as attractive or unattractive, and as easy to use or difficult to use. Design is artistic and aesthetic; getting it right draws on people's creativity, and judging when it's right depends on people's individual taste. So there are no hard and fast rules that will always yield a good-looking design. This fact drives some people crazy, but many of the most important things in life — like love, fine food, good wine, and good design — don't operate by specific rules.

Instead of specific rules, in design we use general principles that usually yield good results. We also depend a great deal on existing models that most people agree look good. And then, at carefully chosen times, we break the rules. Again, this process is likely to challenge one's sanity, but it's the only way to create designs that look good.

The design tips in this chapter are based on the authors' experience in designing and using many Web sites, not on formal design principles. Furthermore, our advice is just for people doing single Web pages and small Web sites of 5–10 Web pages — not large sites that have to be planned carefully from the beginning. All this means that our advice is likely to be infuriating to professionals but very helpful to people just starting out. For detailed information about Web page and Web site design, we recommend *Web Design For Dummies,* by Lisa Lopuck (Hungry Minds, Inc.).

The three most important principles for designing Web home pages and small Web sites are simplicity, predictability, and consistency. Following are a few details about how to apply these principles.

Simplicity

Simplicity is considered the hallmark of good design. The modern eye is trained to look for and appreciate simple, unornamented designs. Use the simplest design that accomplishes your task, and then figure out how to simplify it further. For Web pages, simplicity means using as few of everything — design elements, graphics, and text sizes — as reasonably possible.

Simplicity has specific advantages in Web design due to the impact of time constraints and the differences among users' computer setups. The fact that it takes time to download each element on a Web page means that a simply designed Web page usually loads faster than a complicated one, and users really like fast-loading pages. (Actually, they dislike slow-loading pages, but we'd rather describe the situation in a positive way.)

The differences among users' computer setups reward simplicity as well. One user can be looking at your Web page on a small screen with 256 colors; another can be looking at it on a large, high-resolution screen with thousands of colors. The simpler your Web page design, the more likely the page will look about the same on all the different computer setups out there.

To you as a novice Web page author, simplicity is especially important. You don't have the hard-earned experience of having tried many things that don't work. You also don't have the technical knowledge to always do things right when you're trying something new and complicated. The simpler you keep your design, the more likely you are not to mess up.

Simplicity is most important in *content pages,* Web pages where the user is reading an article or looking at a picture. The user doesn't want to be distracted from what he's doing. Figures 11-1 and 11-2 show the first and second screenfuls of content for *Web Design For Dummies,* mentioned earlier, on the For Dummies Web site. Notice how both Web pages allow you to focus on the content.

Predictability

Predictability means that the user can easily guess where things are on your Web page and how they work. Predictability could, with less efficiency but more precision, be described as "predictability of the content, layout functionality, and look of your Web page as compared to other, similar Web pages."

An important reason that the Web is so popular is that Web pages nearly all look and work alike. Web pages that go too far from the norm tend not to be very popular with users.

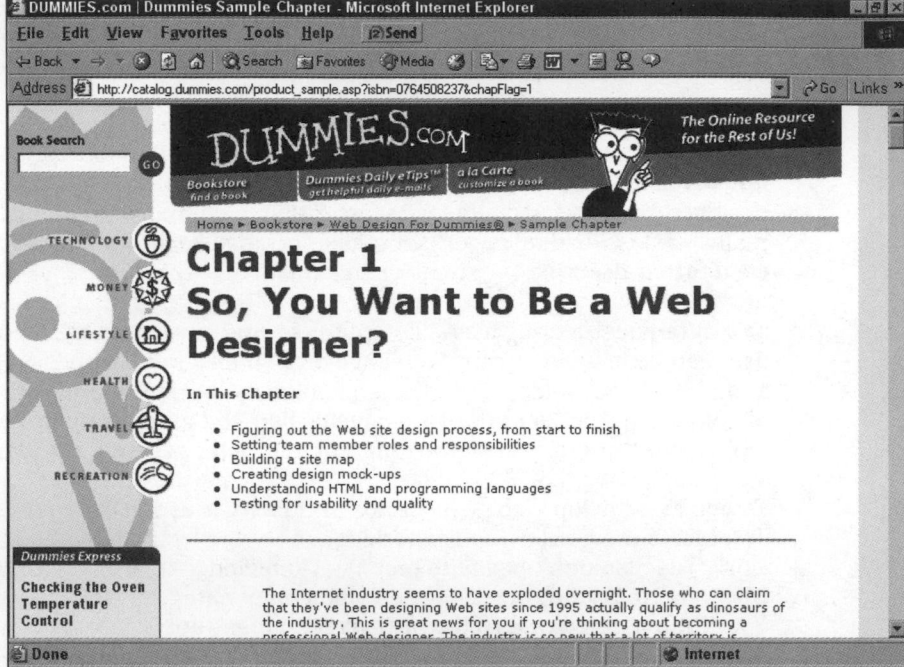

Figure 11-1:
The top of a Dummies content page is simple.

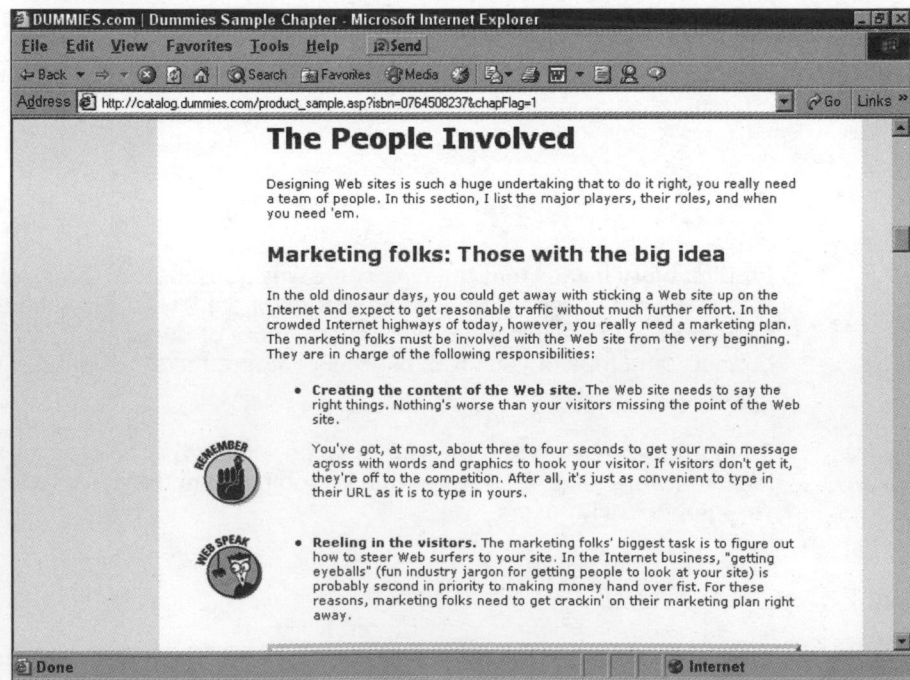

Figure 11-2:
The body of a Dummies content page is even simpler.

Part of the reason this book is called *Creating Web Pages* and not *Creating Web Sites* is that it's focused on people just starting out, who are likely to want to create a single Web page first, and then perhaps expand that page into a small site. But another reason is that users really do experience the Web as a bunch of individual Web pages. Many users aren't even aware, when they click on a link to a different site, that they've left one site and gone to a different one. People really do experience the Web one Web page at a time.

To understand the value of predictability, imagine what a Web page with a newspaper article on it should look like. The first thing to catch your eye might be a picture — almost always one picture, if any, for a typical Web news article. You'd also expect to see the headline describing the article and the reporter's byline.

You would expect to see some navigation at the top of the screen or down the left-hand side. You'd expect a banner ad across the top (but be pleasantly surprised if there wasn't one.) The left column would then be empty after the navigation was done. The right-hand column might be empty as well, or have some small ads.

On some sites you might see features, such as a button for e-mailing a copy of the article, somewhere in the first screen of the article. And you might also see a box with headlines for related articles. Figure 11-3 shows a sketch of what the major elements in an article page might look like.

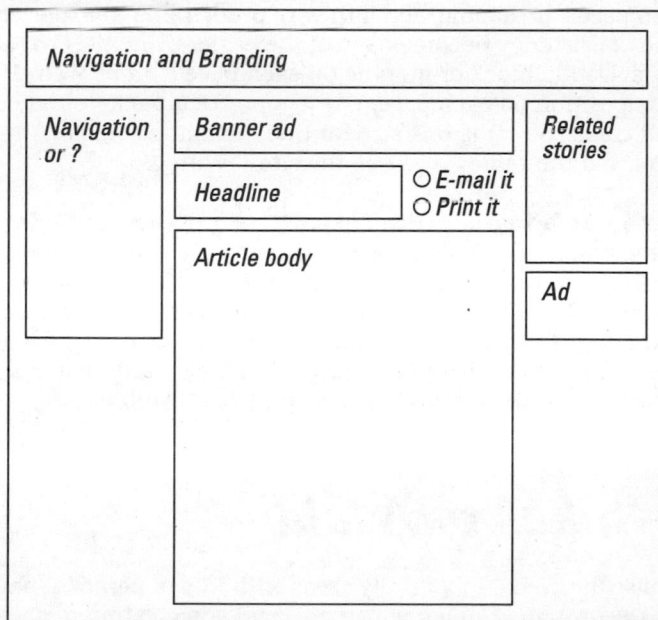

Figure 11-3:
Diagram of
a typical
article page.

Now imagine if one or more of these features was present but was implemented much differently than on other sites. For instance, imagine if the button for e-mailing the article was labeled "Send Me EZ." You'd be frustrated and confused. The clever person who wanted to put a different label on the button hasn't impressed you — they've made the page harder to understand and use.

That, in a nutshell, is what predictability is about. For any Web page you create, find a few examples of pages on the Web that basically accomplish what you're trying to do. See if your page is similar in layout, functionality, and look to the other examples. If your page is different, consider simplifying it to reduce or eliminate the differences. That's predictability.

Consistency

Whereas every Web page you create should be predictable when compared to what's out there on the Web, each page should also be internally consistent. You shouldn't dramatically change fonts, text size, or layout style within a page.

If you create a multi-page Web site (as described in Chapter 15), all the pages in the site should be consistent with each other as well. You want to do all you can to make users understand that they're on a single, unified Web site.

If your Web pages are simple, and if they're predictable to experienced Web users, then consistency becomes one of the easier principles to follow. Use a repeated navigation block or graphic on each page in your Web site — always in the same position on each page. Use a consistent background color and foreground color, the same text size for body text, the same or similar image placements, and the same "voice" in the site's writing.

If you create a large Web site (over 20 pages or so), then consistency becomes more difficult. The only way to maintain a consistent approach is to create several different templates for the different kinds of pages on your Web site: navigational pages, content pages (with and without images), forms pages, and so on. Then every page in your site uses a template, customized for the specific needs of that page. (Really large sites automatically "populate" the template with content to create individual Web pages.)

Design Mistakes to Avoid

Simply cruise the Web — especially areas with lots of personal pages, like the GeoCities site or AOL's Hometown area — and you can find many examples of badly designed pages. But what is it that makes these pages bad? Of the many design mistakes that it's possible to make, three are common among new Web page creators: slow-loading pages, ugly color combinations, and small text.

Slow-loading pages

This is the number-one bane of Web page design, whether amateur or professional. People think they're designing a magazine and throw large, uncompressed graphics around, several per page. Then they add cute little design elements, each of which has to be sent as a separate file by the Web server. As each of the different elements comes in, the page design shifts and shimmies in a manner guaranteed to cause motion sickness.

There are two main ways to make your page load slowly. One is a lack of care with one or two individual graphics. By letting these graphics files be too large, you doom the whole page to slow loading. Use the techniques described in Chapter 10 to make your graphics small in their physical size as well as in their file size.

The other is to use graphics in a profligate manner in general. Highly designed pages can have lots of little graphical elements that cause many separate file transfers as the entire page loads. Unless the page is carefully designed, it shifts a bit as each graphic comes in. The overall effect can be quite disconcerting.

Graphics not only can cause your page to load slowly, they take a long time to create, tend to have significant copyright problems, and present serious design and page layout issues. Keep the use of graphics on your page simple until you get really good at designing with graphics, or until you can get help from someone who has that talent themselves.

Ugly color combinations

Many Web page publishers don't much care if the color combinations they use are attractive or not. Others care, but can't critically appraise their own work and see how ugly and/or difficult to use the result is.

Most people understand that certain color combinations can be ugly, but why difficult to use? Because on the Web, color identifies hyperlinks, with unused links and recently used links having different colors. The standard colors for links are blue for unvisited links and purple for visited links. If you change these colors, your visitors have trouble identifying which links they've visited and which links they haven't.

Finding great home pages

Here are several places you can look to see how others have designed their home pages on the Web:

✔ **GeoCities:** As mentioned in Chapter 3, GeoCities is the top provider of home pages for the Web. From the GeoCities home page at www.geocities.com, you can access GeoCities Web pages in many different categories. However, there's no "best" or "highly rated" list to help you find the best Web pages. You're going to have to look at a lot of ugly ducklings before you find a swan.

✔ **Tripod:** Tripod is a free Web hosting company acquired by Lycos, a leading international Web portal. Visit Tripod at www.tripod.lycos.com. To see cool Lycos Web pages, look in the Member Spotlight area in the upper-left corner of the home page. The Home and Family area is particularly relevant for personal home pages.

✔ **AngelFire:** AngelFire is the other free Web hosting company acquired by Lycos.

You can find its home page at www.angelfire.lycos.com. Click the Cool Pages link on the left side of the home page to find links to top sites in various areas.

✔ **Hometown:** Hometown is AOL's free Web pages site. You can use it even if you're not an AOL member. (Though only members can use all of the AOL discussion areas and online help that make Hometown a real winner.) The Hometown home page at www.hometown.aol.com has a list of the most popular categories, but you have to search all the home pages in a category to find the best ones.

✔ **Homestead and Bigstep:** Homestead and Bigstep no longer offer free personal home pages — they only offer business pages, and you have to pay for them. But because they set the bar high, they have some great Web pages, and each prominently features some of their customers' better work. Go to www.homestead.com and www.bigstep.com to see customers' sites.

If you simply must change the link colors, try to use color combinations analogous to the standard ones — a lighter, eye-catching color for unvisited links, and a dull color for visited ones. Then test the design on a few people and see if they can quickly figure out which links are which.

Now, back to ugly. Just because the Web makes it possible to use various color combinations doesn't mean you should do so. Black text on a white or off-white background is what people are used to, and is always the safest choice. And with this combination, the standard link colors show up really well. You can use a graphical bar at some consistent location on the page to give your Web pages a colorful, graphical look without sacrificing predictability and readability.

A few other color combinations also work fairly well, but many don't. Remember also that some users run their monitors in 256-color mode and that only 216 colors out of the 256 are the same on PCs and Macs. So a color combination that looks good on your system may look poor on a system with fewer colors, or on a PC versus a Mac. Use the Web-safe colors described in Chapter 9 to choose, or find a color combination that uses Web-safe colors and that you like on an existing Web page and use the same combination for your own site. (This isn't stealing — there are only a few such useful combinations, so the person you're borrowing from didn't exactly invent the electric blender either.)

Small text

A very common mistake people make is to use small text on their Web page. Small text does look kind of cool, and it allows you to pack in a lot of information. Because of these temptations even large Web sites, such as early versions of the Microsoft site, have made this mistake. The trouble is that small text becomes very small when viewed on a high-resolution monitor. So small, in fact, that many of the people who visit your Web site may not be able to easily read the text on your page.

Less common, but equally harmful, is text that's too large. People who really need to go get glasses instead design Web pages with text that's readable from 20 feet away. (People with true vision problems switch Windows and/or their browser to display text in extra-large size, so they have a way to read text that starts out normal-size.) This looks awful, especially when viewed on a system with relatively low resolution, such as 800 x 600 resolution.

Both of these problems are made worse by the increasing tendency to embed much of a site's text in graphic images. This "text" always has a consistent look, because it is treated by the browser as a graphic image, but that look can easily be too small or large. The text can't be resized by the browser to accommodate different browser settings. So the user can't fix any problems they're having with graphically displayed text.

Match the text size in your Web page to the text size in a few Web pages you like. Then ask several people — not all younger and hawk-eyed, nor all older and less visually acute — to tell you if they can easily read the text. If not, fix the problem before it becomes a burden for all of your Web site visitors.

Breaking the rules safely

A lot of the fun in creating your own Web page is doing what you want to do and not what someone else tells you. Yet you want your Web page to look good. How can you create a design that you like that also looks good to other people?

Getting design help from the pros

If you're working on a Web site for professional or business use, you may want some help in making it look really good. The good news is, the Web has been around long enough now that experienced people are out there who will help you with your Web page design for a fairly reasonable fee. The trick to keeping the fee reasonable is in defining just what it is you want to pay for and in doing as much as possible yourself.

The best way to work with a Web graphic designer is to create your Web site yourself first. Then bring in the designer just to improve the look of the site. Improving the look of your site might take the designer a few hours and cost you a couple of hundred dollars. Money

well spent, if your Web site is going to be part of your career or your business.

The problem is that many of the people you talk to will be accustomed to doing the whole job of brainstorming your needs with you, creating content, revising it all to meet your needs, publishing the site, and then modifying it for you. This kind of project could cost you thousands of dollars — which you're going to avoid by doing nearly everything yourself for free, or for a very reasonable price, using the information in this book. The one part where you might need help is in getting the look right, so do all the other steps yourself and then bring someone in just for the graphic design piece.

We suggest you follow this five-step process:

1. **Get your Web page up.**

   First, just put up your Web page, with the content and images you want, as we describe in Part I of this book. Don't worry much about how it looks. Just do it!

2. **Find a model page or two that you like.**

   Look on the Web and find a Web page that's similar to your page in its purpose and content and that has a simple, attractive appearance. Then find another. See the sidebar, "Finding great home pages," for places to look.

3. **Create a new, basic version of your Web page.**

   Using your models as a guide, create a new version of your Web page. Get the major pieces — the main text, an image or two, and a list — in place first. Make this basic page look good.

4. **Add additional elements one at a time.**

   Now add additional elements to your Web page one at a time. By working in this piecemeal fashion, you can prevent your page from becoming a hard-to-fix mess, while still indulging your own creativity.

5. Publish the result and get comments.

Now publish your new, improved Web page and let some friends and colleagues know about it. Ask them what they think. Let the site sit for a couple of days, and then take a fresh look at it yourself. Use your own fresh perspective and the comments you get to improve your page further.

You can repeat this process again and again as you improve your Web page and add new pages to create a full Web site. Work through these steps conscientiously and you may end up with some of the best Web pages around.

Tables and Layout and Frames, Oh My

Tables were, for a long time, one of the most controversial topics in Web page design. (Not exactly an area where controversies have earthshaking consequences, but we all need some excitement in our lives.) The original purpose of tables was to allow Web designers to create tables of data (for instance, the monthly sales of a few products).

Tables are now often used to manage the layout of a Web page. Designers have found that they can make the cells of a table very large and put large graphics or whole blocks of text in them. The table can even be made to resize automatically for different sizes of the Web browser window — at least, up to a point. We only touch on this advanced use of tables in this section.

Frames are a more powerful layout device than tables, but one that's fallen into some disfavor. They allow separate parts of the Web browser window to be updated and scrolled separately. However, they produce odd effects; users seem to prefer one unified window to separate "panes" within the window. So we barely mention frames here or elsewhere in this book.

Simple tables

When used as intended, tables have rows and columns. For each spot where a row and column intersect, you have a table cell. Each cell can have its own formatting — the data in it can be aligned left, center, or right, formatted, and so on. Tables also had headers, where you put the column headings, but no predefined row descriptions. You had to create those, if needed, by adding your own formatting.

Here's the HTML code for a simple table of this type:

```
<TABLE>
<TABLE BORDER=2>
<TH><TD>Production (tons)</TD><TD>% of goal</TD></TH>
<TR><TD>North 40</TD><TD>87</TD><TD>102%</TD></TR>
<TR><TD>South 40</TD><TD>93</TD><TD>110%</TD></TR>
</TABLE>
```

Figure 11-4 shows how this simple table looks in HTML and when viewed in Internet Explorer.

Here's what each part of the HTML code does:

`<TABLE>, </TABLE>`	Begins and ends the table.
`<TABLE BORDER=2>`	Creates a 2-pixel-wide border around the table. Don't forget to include a border, so other text and graphics in your Web page don't crowd too close to the table.
`TH>, </TH>`	Begins and ends the table header. (Automatically leaves the first entry blank so rows can contain a column name.)
`<TR>, </TR>`	Begins and ends the table row.
`<TD>, </TD>`	Begins and ends the table data item.

So creating a table in HTML is fairly simple but also fairly tedious. You just create the rows and data items; if you get the data items right, the columns take care of themselves.

Getting the data items right can be a problem, though. To make your table look just right, you have to use a number of alignment and formatting options. Making mistakes becomes very easy, and updating the table's appearance becomes very hard. That's why so many people use HTML tools to create and manage tables — and then, in some cases, do final tweaking in HTML to get them just right.

Tables weren't part of the original HTML standard; they were introduced in Netscape Navigator Version 1.1. As a result, some much older browsers don't support tables at all. (Tables are the main reason why some Web pages still say "Best viewed with Netscape Navigator." For a while it was the only browser with table support.) Also, the official HTML standard and Navigator 1.1 used different versions of the same tags. Luckily, most browsers available today support both versions of table tags.

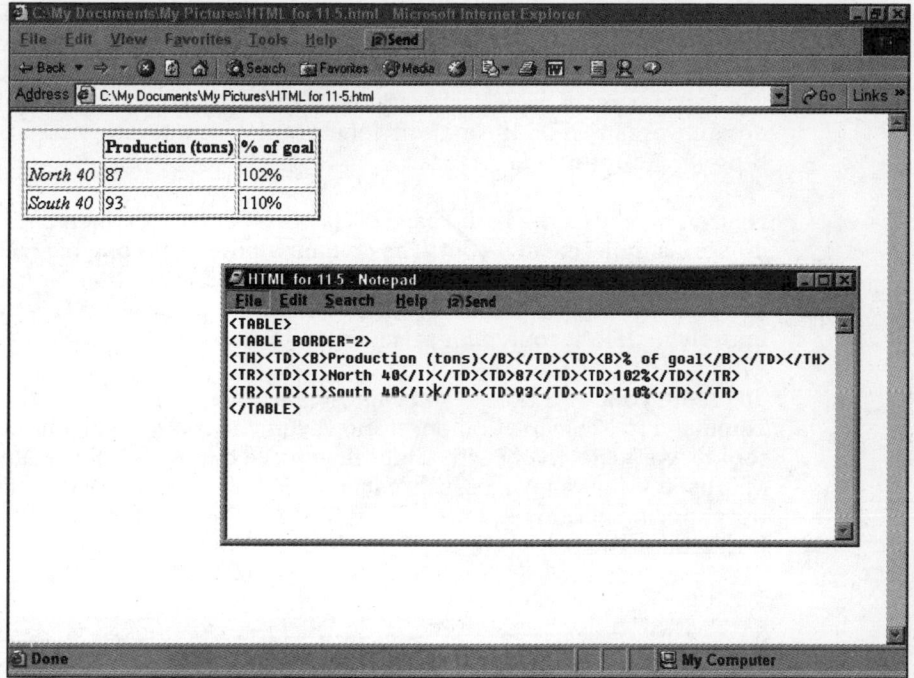

Figure 11-4:
A simple
Web table
and its
simple
HTML
source.

Tables for layout

Once tables were added to HTML, Web designers quickly figured out how to take tables to a whole other level. Imagine making all of a Web page one big table. Using HTML options, you can suppress the display of the table's cell borders. You can thus create a large, invisible grid into which you can insert chunks of text and graphics. This allows you to create a layout with columns, or to make sure that a specific block of text stays next to a specific graphic, for instance, even if the user makes his Web text large or makes the window extra narrow.

Why was this controversial? Because there were some idealistic motives behind the original design of HTML, such as having Web pages be able to display on just about any screen. Table-based layouts, by contrast, only work well on screens of at least a certain minimum size. The controversy has now largely faded because the people who pay for Web site development demand that their sites look good on most of the PCs and Macs out there, and tables are just about the only way to create a complex design that looks good.

For our purposes, though, the key word here is "complex." There are so many different elements that you have to adjust in table-based page design that you need to invest a lot of time and energy to learn how to do it well. And then a whole other set of issues arise about making sure your table-based page design works well on the majority of current computer systems and Web browser setups that are in use.

Figure 11-5 shows the home page of Netsurfer Science, which uses tables to create a simple, clean layout. The column on the left is one big cell in a table; the content in the middle and right of the page is in another large cell. Use the View⇨Source or similar command in your Web browser to view the underlying HTML source for this page to see how it's done.

To create your own tables, you can get started by using the Insert⇨Table command in Netscape Composer. However, you really need a more advanced tool to work effectively with tables in your Web pages — something like Microsoft FrontPage or Dreamweaver, which give you more direct control over specific options — or you need to start doing a lot of experimenting in HTML until you learn how to get things just how you want them.

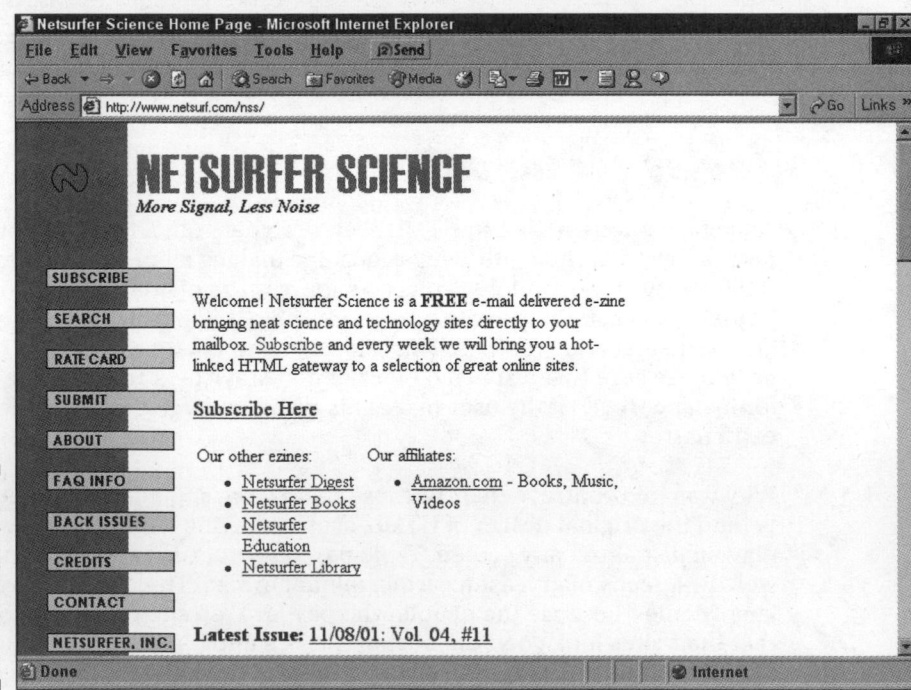

Figure 11-5:
Netsurfer Digest uses tables to organize content.

For details on how to use tables for layout, start with this article on C|NET's builder.com site, at `http://builder.cnet.com/webbuilding/pages/Authoring/AdvHtml/ss01.html`.

Friends don't let friends do frames

Frames, like tables, are a Netscape innovation. Frames separate a Web page into separate areas that can be updated individually. For example, you can click a link in a frame in the bottom half of a Web page and update it with new content while the other frame stays the same. This seems like a powerful capability. However, frames have proved to be less popular than tables.

Why are frames not as popular as tables? Well, frames are hard to create and manage, just like tables. But advanced Web authors are willing to do just about anything to make their Web pages more attractive and more useful, and tables help them do so. With frames, the trouble comes with the "useful" part; users have a hard time with framed Web pages.

When using a framed page, users have difficulty finding where the cursor is. So if they scroll, which frame scrolls? Also, going forward and backward in a frame is different from going forward and backward in the overall Web page, so users may get lost easily.

Finally, frames create a functional problem or two. When users resize a browser window, framed pages don't always resize correctly. And designing a framed page to work well for various monitor sizes is significantly harder than designing regular pages.

Usability tests have shown that users are confused by frames. There are some highly controlled framed sites (for instance, with only one window being scrollable) that give fairly good results. However, the main purpose of frames on these sites is to allow complex navigation, advertisements, or both to stay in the user's view at all times. Unless you have complicated navigational options that your users can't live without, or unless you have advertisers for your site whose dollars you can't live without, we recommend you avoid frames while creating your initial Web pages or simple Web site.

Still, framed pages can be useful to show complex sets of data and to support navigation. Because creating and managing the HTML for frames is even harder than for tables, we don't describe that process here, and Netscape Composer doesn't support frames. Use an advanced Web page tool such as Microsoft FrontPage or Macromedia Dreamweaver if you want to use frames in your pages. (Or look up the appropriate HTML tags in Appendix C and start experimenting!)

Chapter 12

Publishing Your Web Pages

• •

In This Chapter
▶ Getting Web server space
▶ Finding help for Web publishing
▶ Transferring your files to the Web server
▶ Putting your site to work

• •

*P*ublishing is the most exciting stage of creating your Web home page or Web site. After all the fooling around with tools, HTML, GIFs, and other kinds of files, and after figuring out what you want to say and how you want to say it, you can finally "go live" and let the world see your creation.

Publishing on the Web can be straightforward if you're putting up a personal or topical home page that a few friends and/or coworkers see. But if you're creating a site for a business, or just need room to grow, publishing involves several steps.

The first step in publishing your Web page is to get Web server space. You have a lot of options here. Can you get free space or must you pay for it? Do you want your own domain name, so that your site has a simple URL, or are you willing to let your site be a subdirectory in someone else's domain? You need to choose a server space provider that gives you reasonable pricing and support now and room to grow later. Then you need to transfer your files to the site and confirm that you're really online.

But you're not done yet. The whole purpose of getting your Web site online is for people to see it. With all the sites out there, you have to cut through the noise and get people to visit your site. After they see your site, you need to know that they were there, so you need some kind of reporting. You also need to receive and respond to feedback. Having all these things to think about reminds us of those U.S. Army ads — "It's not just a job, it's an adventure."

Packaged publishing

The easiest way to handle publishing your Web pages is to not handle it at all and to have it done for you. Easy-to-use Web page services such as GeoCities and AOL Homepages, described in Chapters 2 and 3, handle the publishing step for you — at least in the early stages. But as you build up your Web page, or create a multi-page Web site, you need to start worrying about things like transferring files via FTP and so on. And you may want your own domain name or other advanced features that may require you to go to a different host for your Web pages. So if publishing your Web site seems like a hassle, use a Web page service to get started and then come back to this chapter when you need to take your site to the next level.

In this chapter we cover the basic publishing steps — getting server space, transferring your files, and so on. These are the core steps that you need for either a single Web page or a multi-page Web site. In Chapter 15 we cover more advanced steps related to publishing, such as getting your own domain name and letting people know about your site.

After your site is up and publicized, you may expect to get a chance to relax. But then, while you cruise the Web, you see something neat that you want to put into your own site. Or looking back at your own pages, you suddenly see a problem in how you describe yourself, your company, or your interests. Or maybe you get a blizzard of e-mails asking a question that you thought you already answered on the site — or, worse, you get no feedback at all. Maybe it's time to fire up that HTML editor again. . . .

Sorry to plug a book cowritten by one of the authors, but if you're in a hurry to create a Web site for a business, you may want to consult *Internet Marketing For Dummies,* by Frank Catalano and Bud Smith (Hungry Minds, Inc.). *Internet Marketing For Dummies* goes into more depth about business-related issues, such as how to register the right domain name, how to present your business online, and how to use other Internet services besides the Web as part of your marketing effort.

Getting Web Server Space

A *Web server* is a computer that's connected to the World Wide Web and runs special software that enables it to provide information to Web users. Hundreds of thousands of such servers are connected to the Web. You can have a lot of fun fooling around with a Web page that you create and store on your own computer. But only by placing your Web site's files on someone else's server, or by creating your own Web server with your site's files on it, can your site really become part of the Web.

You can easily get space on a Web server. For example, the free Web-based publishing services we describe in Chapters 2 and 3 all include free Web server space. You may have a friend or an affiliation with an organization that can lend you Web server space. These are all good options for a single Web home page or a small site.

If these options aren't available to you, though, or if real money is involved, things get tricky. When you create a site for a business or another kind of organization, most of the services we mention in the preceding paragraph don't give you free space. So if you're going to start paying for server space, you want to do some comparison shopping. And to do comparison shopping, you have to know what to compare.

America Online is the one major service that continues to allow free Web server space for businesses as well as individuals. See Chapter 2 for details.

Web hosting service features

A number of businesses and organizations offer Web hosting service — that is, space on their Web server for your Web site. Most of these organizations charge for this service, and fees vary. You should look at a number of concerns when choosing a Web hosting provider for your Web pages.

Focusing only on price when you compare Web hosting service providers is understandable. But you should look at many other factors that may actually be more important than the immediate cost:

- ✔ **Pricing structure:** Instead of focusing only on the charges for your initial, bare-bones site, consider also what providers charge you when your site grows larger and attracts a moderate number of visitors, say a few hundred or a few thousand a month. Some hosting providers charge a very low rate for your initial site but sock it to you when your needs grow.

- ✔ **Support:** We all need support of one kind or another, but technical support for your Web publishing effort is one of the hardest — and most important — kinds of support. You need support for putting your pages onto the server, for answering questions about your site, and for solving problems about speedy access, uptime (how long the service is on the air trouble-free), and so on. Find out what support providers offer for each type of Web hosting option that interests you. Ask other users of each service if they're able to get support fast when a problem comes up.

- ✔ **Web-related consulting services:** Some Web hosting providers, even those that offer some services for free, also offer other Web-related services that they charge for, such as hosting business sites or managing your site for you. What do the providers charge for these services? How well do they work? Most Web-related services are billed by the hour, but some service providers get things done better and faster than others. So a less expensive hourly rate may not mean a lower total bill at the end.

- ✔ **Site services:** Some Web hosting providers offer helpful services, such as counting the number of users who visit your site. Other providers, at least, allow *you* to create and run Common Gateway Interface (CGI) scripts that perform sophisticated functions. Other Web hosting providers neither provide site services nor allow you to run CGIs. Look for a provider that does the simple stuff for you and supports you in doing the more complex functions yourself.

- ✔ **Domain name:** The *domain name* is the name of the server where your site resides, but clever providers can put multiple domain names on a single computer. So you can have your own domain name, even for a small site, but your Web hosting provider must register the name. Registering your name costs your provider anywhere from about $10 to about $30 per year. Expect your provider to pass this charge on to you, but don't let them charge you a great deal more. For more about having your own domain name, see Chapter 15.

Some Web hosting providers offer to register a domain name for you, but then retain ownership of the domain name themselves. This situation reminds us of those Peanuts cartoons in which Lucy sets up the football and then pulls it away when Charlie Brown runs up to kick it. Not owning your domain name free and clear can severely hamper your ability to move your site later.

Find out whether the Web hosting provider allows you to get your own domain name, either immediately or later. And if the provider does, ask for a clear, written statement that you own the domain name and can take your Web site to another host if you want to.

When you consider a Web hosting provider, consider in your evaluation the following factors:

- **Speed:** How fast can users access your Web site? How fast can users download files hosted on the site? You can ask, but you should also test. Try accessing some Web sites hosted by any service that you're considering and see how fast they are, especially at busy times of the day. Compare what you find to other Web sites.

- **Uptime:** Is the Web hosting service that you're considering ever "off the air"? You may think that downtime is rare but, actually, even entire online services such as America Online have downtimes. Find out the track record for uptime of the Web hosting service that you're considering and compare that service's record with competitors.

- **Switchability:** Having the ability to switch Web hosting providers is crucial. With the right to switch, you can resolve any other problems. Without the right to switch, you may be unhappy with some key element of your Web site for a long time. Two things can keep you "locked in" to a provider: contractual provisions and control of your domain name. Don't sign a contract that locks you in for more than a year, and don't let the Web hosting provider register your domain name for you unless the provider states, in writing, that you control your domain name and can take it elsewhere with you.

- **Viability:** Many Internet-related businesses have gone out of business. (Even giant firms collapse sometimes, like the energy giant Enron, but it seems that the Internet has had more than its share.) Make sure that your chosen provider has a track record and is of sufficient size to offer some assurance that they'll be around as long as you need them to be.

- **Reporting:** You really, really want your provider to offer basic reporting features, such as the number of visitors your site has each day, for free. Such features are rare but very valuable. This may be the critical factor in choosing between one provider and another.

- **Data transfer fees:** Another potential "gotcha" is *data transfer fees*. When users look at a page on your site, all the data on that page is transferred to their machines. If users download files, more data is transferred. Many Web hosting services offer some free data transfer, but your costs can rise sharply if traffic at your site increases and data transfer rises above a minimal amount. Compare data-transfer pricing carefully.

- **Price:** If all other things are equal, price is the determining factor. But all other things are rarely equal. Consider other factors first, but don't let yourself get ripped off on the price you pay.

The key factors in choosing a Web hosting provider are the freedom to switch when you need to and having control of your domain name.

What makes a Web server fast?

A Web server is usually rated by the number of *connections* — brief communication sessions between two machines — that it can handle in a given period of time. The number of connections that the server handles depends on how quickly the server establishes a connection, deciphers the request, sends the requested file, and terminates the connection. Most people assume that the most time-consuming step in this process is the speed with which files are transmitted. Surprise! When small files are transmitted, the bottleneck is usually not how fast the files are transmitted, but how quickly the server's hardware and software establish connections for each of the file transfers, and how fast the connections are terminated after the transfer is finished.

Here's a really technical tip: Engineers and various hangers-on, such as people who write computer-related books, like to call the cause of a bottleneck a *gating factor*. For example, the gating factor for completing this book on schedule is the speed at which the authors write. The gating factor in serving simple Web pages is the speed with which the server can connect and disconnect, not the speed with which data can be sent over the wire.

In addition to the speed of connecting and disconnecting to other machines, the speed of the server's connection to the Internet makes a big difference, especially for larger files such as big graphic images. If you have a direct connection to the Internet (as you find at most large companies and most universities), your client-side connection may be even faster than the server's connection: Lots of personal and small business home pages are sitting on Web servers with nothing but a 56 Kbps modem connecting them to the Internet. So don't start cussing at your own modem when that full-color JPEG photograph of the winning Weimaraner takes forever to download; the problem may be at the other end.

Options for Web server space

Now that you know what to look for in a host server, where can you find Web server space? Finding the right place for your Web site to be hosted is not an easy task. Major Web hosting options include sites that offer free server space, online service Web hosting options, Web hosting services, and a Web server of your own creation. Appendix B lists major Internet service providers; from their Web sites, you can find their current hosting options.

No matter what choice you make initially, be sure to keep your options open, because your needs may change rapidly as new Web hosting providers arise, as your own knowledge grows, and as the Web's role in business and in daily life increases.

Using free server space

You can get free server space for relatively small Web sites from several places (see Chapters 2 and 3 for details). These sites are great places to create small, initial Web sites that help you learn about Web page design and construction. However, businesses generally can't use free server space for straightforward business promotion. (But you do see lots of not-so-straightforward promotions there!) Also, to get your own domain name, you either have to move to paid server space or create your own Web server.

If you have access to free server space through a friend or work, that's also a good place to get started. Be careful, though, that you don't violate any expectations that the people providing the space to you have about the content of your Web site.

As we mentioned in the previous chapter, Bigstep.com, a Web business, will help you create a starter business Web site for low cost. Visit them at www.bigstep.com.

Get it all in a cyberstore

Online stores are a special kind of Web site that make it easy for you to sell products online. An online store operator may provide any or all of the following:

- Initial goal-setting for your Web site
- Creation of the Web page itself (expect to provide raw materials such as product or service descriptions, photographs, and price lists)
- Advertising and publicity
- Support for online sales

Yahoo!, eBay, and Amazon.com have cyberstore-type arrangements that you can use to get publicity for your online selling. Using the right cyberstore host can be a good way to get started on the Web, especially if you want to go from 0 (no Web presence or expertise) to 60 (a robust Web presence with online transaction capabilities) in a few months. Expect to pay fixed monthly fees that amount to several hundred dollars a year, plus a small share of transactions. Using a cyberstore also gives you a chance to develop Web expertise so that you can eventually do more of the work yourself. (Make sure that your contract allows you to leave the cybermall quickly if you want to take over the whole job on your own.) For popular online store providers, see the following sites:

- www.amazon.com
- www.ebay.com
- www.paypal.com
- www.yahoo.com

Is your site too cool?

What if your site is *too* successful? Believe it or not, the success of your site *can* be a problem. Many sites become overloaded when they "catch on," rise high in the search rankings, are linked with a suddenly popular subject, are mentioned in the press, or receive other similar recognition. Be ready to upgrade your Web hosting provisions if your site suddenly gets popular. In particular, if you pay extra for transferred megabytes, make sure that you have a cap on how much you must pay if usage suddenly shoots up. If you don't, set up some method to track usage frequently or to receive an alert if usage shoots up. That way, you avoid a potentially nasty surprise on your bill.

Using Internet service providers

Internet service providers (ISPs) may be best known for offering Web access, but many of them also offer a wide range of Web services, from consulting to hosting to programming and more. In fact, as larger players, such as AT&T and Earthlink, continue to establish their Web access business, the smaller ISPs that prosper will be those that move "upstream" into consulting and specialized hosting services. ISPs that are also traditional online services, like AOL and CompuServe, sometimes change their higher-level offerings as partnership opportunities change.

Some ISPs offer free Web page publishing services or free server space to customers, just like the major online services. They also offer varying levels of paid-for service. Compare major ISPs to see what they offer. If you already have Web access, don't stop checking. Many ISPs offer their paid for, add-on services even to those who get their access elsewhere, and some ISPs may offer attractive bundles for access plus other services. You still have to be a customer to get that free server space deal, though.

Using paid-for server space

Thousands of Web hosting services exist. The providers vary tremendously in service, price, and competency. Some offer hosting only and charge you per stored or transferred megabyte. Others offer additional services, which may be billed separately or bundled with the "pure" hosting services in an overall fee. This business is changing and growing so rapidly that you need to exercise great care in the selection process to protect yourself. The largest service, Verio, which acquired the former leader Best Internet, is also considered among the best (no pun intended); you may want to start your search by checking on them at www.verio.com.

As the Romans figured out, just a few years before the Internet caught on, *caveat emptor* — let the buyer beware!

Creating your own Web server

Deciding whether to create your own Web server depends, as do many other choices about the Web, on what you want to accomplish and how much experience you have. If you've set up a Web server before or have a lot of computer and communications experience, setting up your own Web server may work out very well for you. If not, setting up a Web server may turn out to be an expensive nightmare — and slow to boot! (That's "slow as well," not slow to start when you hit the On switch!)

Many proponents of doing business on the Web are quick to suggest that you set up your own Web server, but we don't share that view. Unless you're an expert, we recommend that you start with a Web hosting provider of some kind. Then consider setting up your own server after you gain some experience and get to know some people who can help if problems arise. If you want details, refer to *Setting Up an Internet Site For Dummies,* 3rd Edition, by Jason Coombs, Ted Coombs, David Crowder, and Rhonda Crowder (Hungry Minds, Inc.).

Two things to remember: If you set up your own Web server for any but the most casual purposes, use a dedicated machine that isn't doing any other work. (If you follow this very good advice, you'll spend $2,000 or so before you store or serve a megabyte!) And be ready to devote time and energy to find out about the computer you're using, its Internet connection, and associated Web technologies so that you can set up your own server to meet your needs as effectively as a Web hosting service.

Hiring help

The *dot-bomb* phenomenon — the sudden crash of so many Internet businesses in 1999 through 2001 — made a lot of talented Web pros available. In addition, ten years after the Web itself was invented, some of the amateurs are pretty good at what they do. So the odds of finding good people to help you, either on a paid basis or just because they're already a friend, is growing.

To find a good Web hosting provider — someone who can provide the Web hosting services we describe in the previous section — or get other help relating to getting your Web site up, we recommend the following steps:

✔ **Start small.** Asking the right questions to help you find a Web hosting provider or consultant is difficult if you have no Web publishing experience of your own. Start by creating a home page and then a small, special-purpose site of some kind before doing anything more robust. The experience will be valuable in finding a good hosting provider.

✔ **Figure out what services you need.** Are you going to create a simple site or a complex one? Do you want to create the site yourself and buy hosting services only, or do you want to contract out most of the work? List your needs, and then find someone who's well suited to fill them.

✔ **Investigate sites like your own.** Find Web sites that look like the kind you want to create. Ask the Webmasters how they got their sites up and running and what Web hosting providers they use. Ask others in your area about their Web sites and whether they're happy with the services they receive. When you consider a specific provider, check into a few of the sites that the provider hosts and ask customers whether they're happy. For consultants, talk to a couple of (hopefully) satisfied customers.

✔ **Go local.** For a consultant, you may want to meet with him occasionally, which means choosing someone local. (Even with all our technological aids, looking someone in the eye can contribute to better and deeper understanding. Unless meeting the person leads you to find that you really dislike them!) Although going local greatly restricts your choices, it may significantly improve your working relationship.

✔ **Be involved.** No consultant or service provider can do everything. The person or organization that pays for the site must provide content and guidance throughout the process. You need to be very much involved in the process, so plan to devote many hours to working with your consultant or service provider.

Transferring Your Files

One of the really cool things about Web publishing is the capacity to set up, test, and modify your Web site on your own machine. The problem is that, at some point, you have to transfer your files to the Web server. Until you become proficient at transferring files, you may have some anxious file-transferring moments. In this section, we try to eliminate some of the worry in getting your site online.

Arranging your files before transfer

Some of the most difficult things about creating, testing, and transferring your Web pages relate to directory structures. The problem is that a link from, say, your HTML-tagged text to a graphic has to specify what subfolder the graphics file is in. When you transfer your files to a different machine, the subfolders change, which breaks the link from your Web page to the graphics file. You can take steps, however, to keep your links from breaking when you transfer your Web files from your development machine to the Web server.

For sites with a dozen files or fewer, a simple solution exists: Just put all your files in the same subfolder. That way, your links are simple — you only need to specify the filename, not the folder name. And when you transfer files, you don't need to match up subfolder structures between machines. See Chapters 4 and 8 for details.

For sites with many files, use the simplest folder structure you can — only one level deep, if possible. Also, create your links by using relative addressing. Relative addressing doesn't specify the entire pathname from the root folder downward, just the relative path from the file with the link embedded in it to the file with the link target. Relative addressing enables you to move files from one machine to another without having to change all the links between files.

Some people prefer to use a compression program, such as PKZIP, to package files before sending them. Before you compress files, make sure that the recipient wants zipped files and that he or she can unzip them. Also realize that the largest files in a Web site are usually GIF or JPEG graphics files. Because these files are compressed already, the compression programs don't compact them much further. But the compression program does help get all the files into a single package, with relative folder locations preserved.

As you can see, the underlying theme for anyone starting out is to "keep it simple." After you have some initial successes under your belt, you can begin taking steps to organize your site better and to make it more convenient to manage and update.

Transferring your files with FTP

File Transfer Protocol (FTP) is an Internet service for transferring files between different machines. FTP helped make the Internet popular even before the World Wide Web caught on. FTP is a relatively easy way to move files from one machine to another. Most Internet users rely on FTP to download files from an FTP host to the users' own machine; however, the user often starts the file transfer from a Web page, bypassing the details of FTP. To publish your Web pages, you may be asked to send files from your own machine to a host using FTP. (You will probably be asked to "FTP the files to us.") Using FTP is a new operation for most people, but it is not all that complex.

Dozens of FTP programs exist for Macintosh, Windows, and UNIX, each with pluses and minuses. (The major online services also have facilities for uploading files, which we describe in the "Connect to an FTP site" section that follows.) You can find many free FTP clients on the Web. The steps we provide work with most popular FTP programs. However, to upload files you need a "real" FTP program. Many programs with FTP capability can download files from FTP sites but not upload files to an FTP site. So make sure that your FTP program can *put* (write) as well as *get* (read) files. For a useful program, search for FTP on CΙNET's download site at www.download.com.

Connect to an FTP site

The following steps specifically work with Fetch, the most popular Macintosh FTP program, shown in Figure 12-1. (Notice the little dog, probably a Scottie, running to fetch the file!) But the same steps generally apply to other FTP programs as well.

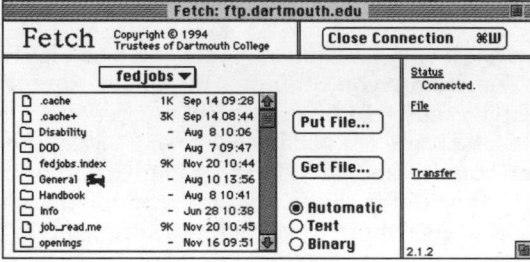

Figure 12-1:
A fetching
Mac FTP
client.

Use these steps to transfer files to a Web site:

1. **Connect to the Internet.**

2. **Start your FTP program.**

3. **Enter the host name.**

For a Web site, the FTP host name is often the same as the host name in the Web site's URL but with ftp in place of www; for example, if the Web site's URL is www.mysite.com, the host name is likely to be ftp.mysite.com.

4. **Enter the user name.**

Many sites allow you to enter anonymous as the user name and avoid having to enter a specific user name. Other sites give you a user name and password to use when uploading your Web files.

5. **Enter the password.**

   If you entered anonymous as the user name, enter nothing or your e-mail address as your password.

6. **Enter the directory that you want to put files in (that is, to write to).**

   You can also go to the correct directory after you connect, but the process is more convenient and less error-prone if you enter the correct directory first.

7. **Click OK to connect to the FTP site.**

   If you do everything right and the site is up, you connect. Refer to Figure 12-1 for the Fetch FTP dialog box that appears after you connect.

Upload your file(s) and disconnect

Getting connected is half the battle. Writing your files is usually pretty easy. Here are the steps:

1. **Click the appropriate option for the file(s) that you want to write: Automatic, Text, or Binary.**

   For HTML files, use Text. For graphics and multimedia files, use Binary. For a combination of both types, either upload the types one at a time with the proper designation, or upload them together and choose Automatic; the server tries to figure out which is which.

   Until you have experience with a specific server, transfer files one at a time and specify the correct file type before each transfer.

2. **Click Put to write your file.**

   This option may be named "Send," "Upload," or something else on some clients; to initiate the process, you may have to select the option from a menu rather than click a button.

3. **In the dialog box that appears, click the name of the file that you want to write and then click OK.**

   The file transfers. Repeat Steps 1 through 3 for each additional file that you need to transfer.

4. **Choose Quit (or Exit) from the File menu.**

Using an online service file transfer

In Chapter 2, we describe how to use the Web publishing programs on the major online services to create and publish a home page. However, the online services' Web facilities are flexible. You can create HTML-tagged text and graphics files with any tools and then upload the files to a server. The online service file transfer tools resemble FTP. Figure 12-2 shows the America Online file transfer program. Other file transfer programs are similar.

Figure 12-2:
File transfer that's not too AOL-ful.

Putting Your Site to Work

After you get your site up on the Web, you're probably too relieved and happy to worry about the site for awhile. But "going live" isn't an ending; it's really just the beginning of a whole new process. The following sections describe some initial steps to make your newly published site really stand out and accomplish your goals.

Test your site

As soon as you get your site up, log on to it as a normal user. See if the site works. Test all links to make sure that they go where they should. Make sure that you can easily move between pages. Try accessing your site from a computer with a slow modem connection to see how usable the site is at slow speeds. Also try using your site in both the Netscape and Internet Explorer browsers. You can also test it in America Online's built-in browser, if you have access to AOL.

Also note how you would react if you were a new user. What does the site look like it's for? Does this match what it's really for? Do you experience any difficulties or confusion in using it? This open-minded approach to your own site can help you quickly fix subtle problems that otherwise are hard to identify.

Testing your site is a bit frustrating because you find all sorts of things to fix, but if you follow through, you end up with a much better site. Be ready to take notes on your reactions from the moment you first log on to your site until the end of your visit — remembering first impressions later is difficult.

Use your browser's Print capability to print out the pages in the Web site, and then put your notes right on the printout. A printout enables you to easily keep track of your ideas as you go along and to make the right changes the first time.

Get feedback on your site

Ask for feedback! You can put the request for feedback right in your Web site. You can also ask friends and colleagues to try the site and give you their honest opinions. Ask them some leading questions, such as "What do you think the site is for? How does it compare to other sites you've seen? What's the one thing you'd change about the site if you could?"

Part IV
Getting Interactive

In this part . . .

Your users will enjoy seeing your Web pages, but they'll enjoy doing something with them even more. Use easily available online and offline tools to add animation, multimedia, and interactivity to your Web page. Then make your Web page into a complete, multi-page Web site.

Chapter 13

Adding Animation and Multimedia

• •

In This Chapter

▶ Using multimedia in your Web pages

▶ Adding animated GIFs to your pages

▶ Adding video to your Web pages

▶ Adding QuickTime and MP3 files

• •

Animation is a lot of fun — and it works well on the Web today. Even better, animation is easily available to beginning Web page creators. That's because there's an easy way to do simple animations, called animated GIFs. What's more, it's easy to find animated GIFs that you can put on your Web site for free and not that much harder to create your own.

Multimedia is a somewhat different beast. Audio works fairly well on the Web today. The MP3 standard has revolutionized the availability and usability of music on the Web. MP3 has also caused the greatest challenge to copyright laws in years, but that's a separate issue.

Full-motion video is a whole other issue. The Web has the potential to be the ultimate video network. There are just two little problems — the solutions to which will take several years to be realized.

The first problem is bandwidth. The Web seriously needs more bandwidth for multimedia capabilities to grow. Video clips today are limited to tiny windows — much smaller than a regular TV, let alone HDTV and other high-resolution standards. It isn't just the thin 56K connection to a typical home PC that's a problem. Corporate networks and the entire global Internet structure are not nearly ready yet for full-screen, full-motion video.

The second problem is creative capability. It takes scores of people to put on a typical TV show, or run a radio station day and night, from camera people to editors to on-air talent. When you create your own multimedia, you're taking on — or arranging for someone else to perform — many of those jobs yourself.

How TV beats PC

As an entertainment transmission system, TV beats the PC hands down. The "user experience" of watching *Why Animals Attack Scary Police Videos* far surpasses — from a technical point of view, anyway — the best of Web multimedia.

Why? Just do the math. A typical text-only Web page takes about 2KB (kilobytes, or thousands of bytes) of storage space. Let's say we're willing to make the user wait one second to see a page. So the minimum bandwidth needed for effectively transmitting text Web pages through the Internet — from the server, across the Internet backbone, and all the way down to your PC — is 2KB in a second, which is 16 Kbps (kilobits per second; 8 bits are in a byte). A 56K modem is about three times faster than this, so we're in good shape for text-only Web pages.

Now add graphics. Major Web sites try to keep their total "page weight" under 50KB for fast viewing. 50KB (kilobytes) equals 400Kb (kilobits). So to experience good response times for typical Web pages, we need a 400KB connection — about as fast as a DSL connection or a well-managed corporate network. So we're pushing the limits of the technology available to a typical user if we want to see today's typical Web pages at a reasonable speed.

Now let's look at multimedia. A typical TV displays 30 frames per second at roughly 560 x 420-pixel resolution, or over 200,000 pixels. That's 6 megabytes, or 48 megabits, per second.

(Remember, 8 bits in a byte.) And that's just the picture — no sound! Not even a cable modem, on a good day and with none of your neighbors on with you to share the cable line to your home, can hope to deliver this. Neither can most corporate networks, and the Internet backbone would get overcrowded very quickly with TV transmission added in. Displaying multimedia as good as an uncompressed TV broadcast is really beyond the capability of the worldwide Internet or of the connections to your home.

To work around these problems, we need all sorts of tricks. Compression makes sound files and short video clips using very small image sizes ready for Internet downloading and use. Streaming technology, running on a server, can dole out multimedia packets — again, for a very small image — at a rate that the user's system can handle. And creative people work hard behind the scenes to try to extract acceptable quality from the highly compressed multimedia files they have to work with.

Do-it-yourself Web authors, though, are generally the kind of people who enjoy a challenge. Multimedia on the Web is in the same early stages that the Web itself was a few years ago, when we wrote the first edition of this book. There are technical difficulties, and both authoring and using multimedia is difficult, but interest and use are exploding. Use the information in this chapter to get started now while it's still early.

Overall, however, the opportunity is tremendous. Multimedia — from the simplest animation or sound clip to a full-screen, surround-sound movie — can be much more engaging than static text and graphics. And solutions that allow you to add low-bandwidth multimedia to your Web page are becoming more and more readily available.

So expect to see and hear more and more multimedia on the Web — and to be able to include it, where appropriate, in your own Web pages right away.

Getting your page right by using the basic Web ingredients of text and graphics is a real challenge but a lot of fun. Get the Web publishing basics down before you push forward into the realm of multimedia. However, if you're adventurous, you can use the information that follows to add exciting multimedia flavorings to your Web pages.

Animating Your GIFs

Animated GIFs are the simplest, cheapest way to liven up your Web page with multimedia. It's worth trying to create animated GIFs and host them on your Web page even if your real goal is to add other multimedia files to your site — the experience you get with animated GIFs will help you with any other multimedia efforts you make.

Most people know that a movie is simply a series of still pictures. An *animated GIF* is like a short movie — anywhere from a few to a couple of dozen GIF images that, when displayed in sequence, create the illusion of motion. Think of an old-fashioned flip book; you flip through the pages, and the drawings on each page seem to come alive as a single, moving image.

The big advantage to animated GIFs is that there's no special software needed to host them on your Web server, nor to play them back on the user's machine. You don't have to have any special artistic talent, nor do you have to pay anyone a licensing fee. And if you don't want to take the time to create your own animated GIF image, there are literally thousands available for free on the Web.

There are many ways you can create GIF animations and deploy them on your site. Not all of the things you can do are obvious:

- **Buttons and icons:** Buttons and icons on your Web site are intended to get the user's attention. Animating them increase their effectiveness further. Animated buttons and icons are freely available in many places on the Web.

- **Initial letters:** A "drop cap" is a big capital letter used to add an eye-catching beginning to an article. An animated drop cap is even more eye-catching! (Or distracting, depending on how you look at it — no pun intended.)

- **Humanicons:** You can use animated images of people as human icons, or "humanicons." Images of people are very attention-getting. If the images are drawn, it's pretty compelling. However, if they're photographs, it's very compelling. See the sidebar, "Photo-animated GIFs," for details.

- ✔ **Product shots:** You can use drawn or photographic product images as a way to bring attention to your product and a way for your Web site visitors to get an experience — much like picking the product up and looking at it.

- ✔ **Advertising:** You can use any or all of these ideas to advertise on your site. You can use traditional, paid advertising, or internal "advertising" for whatever links on your site you want people to click on most.

- ✔ **Pure creativity:** You can come up with things that no one has ever thought of before. Hamster Dance, a briefly famous Web phenomenon, was a page full of animated GIFs of hamsters and other rodent-like animals doing a Macarena-type dance. (For a look at the original Hamster Dance see `accpc.com/hamsterdance.html`.) Come up with your own ideas!

It's easy to overuse animated GIFs. The same icon that looks cute the first time someone comes to your site might be annoying by the fifth time. Deploy animated GIFs anywhere on your site that they make sense, but don't hesitate to take some of them back down if the effect becomes a bit overwhelming.

Photo-animated GIFs

QuickTime VR is a technology that uses images to create things that seem like 3D objects and 3D interactive scenes on the Web. You can create a similar effect with animated GIFs.

To create an animated image of a product or other object — even a person's head — take a series of photographs of any "thing" from, say, 8 or 16 different, equally spaced angles. Use a photo-editing program like Photoshop to make each image as small as possible. Then combine the images, in order, into an animated GIF, as explained in this chapter. The resulting animation is called an *object,* or *object movie.* The effect is amazingly detailed and realistic.

Less obvious in its usefulness, but perhaps more interesting, are animated scene shots. To create one of these, stand with your camera in an open area — hopefully an interesting one — and take a series of shots at evenly spaced angles, gathering 8, 16, or some other even number of shots. As with objects, make the images as small as you can, then combine them into an animated GIF. The resulting image — called a *panorama* — gives the impression that the user is inside a scene, looking around.

Like any other creative enterprise, you can put as much time into animated GIFs in general, and photo-animated GIFs in particular, as you're willing to spend. People have even made a living at interactive photography.

Finding animated GIFs

You can find animated GIF files ready to plug into your Web page at a number of sites on the Web. This is the easiest way to get started with using animated GIF files in your Web pages.

Smaller sites with fewer files are more likely to make the files available for no obligation on your part. Larger sites with large file libraries are more likely to want something from you in exchange. You can use a search engine to look up the term "animated GIF" and find both kinds of sites.

One leading site for animated GIFs is Animation Factory, at `www.animfactory.com` (see Figure 13-1). You can use any of their 3,000 free animations on any personal Web page, as long as it's not for profit. However, you do have to include a link to the Animation Factory Web site.

You can also buy a membership to a premium site that gets you access to over 100,000 animations, with no linking requirements, but try the free ones first. Free animation categories include buttons, text, people events, computers, and many more.

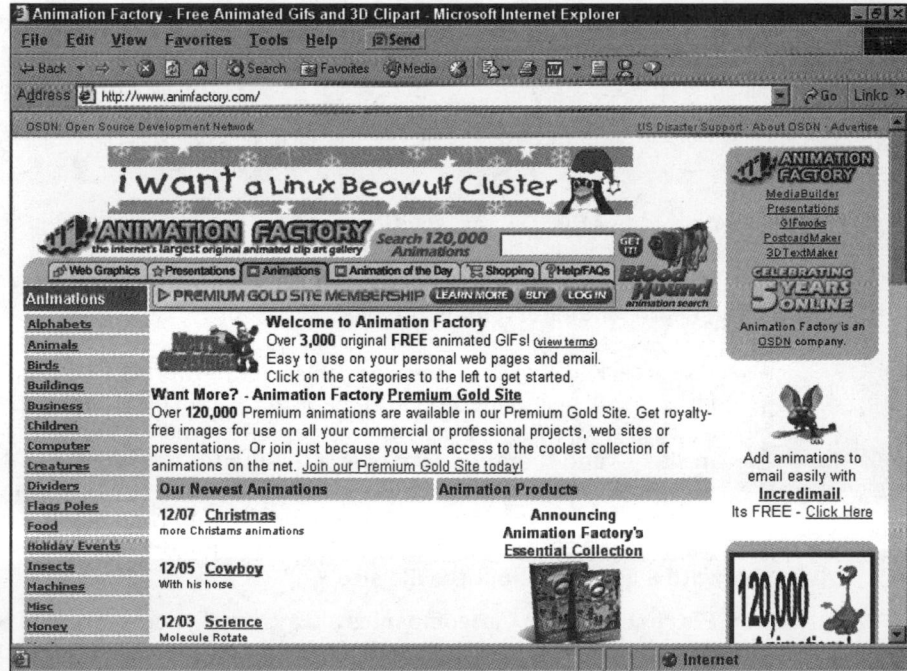

Figure 13-1: Animation Factory has thousands of free GIF animations.

Another big GIF site is 2Cool Animations at `gifanimations.com`. It's a little less polished than Animation Factory, but everything on it — including 20,000 graphics files — is free. You can't use the animations for business purposes, nor can you include animations on your Web site by linking to them.

Use these sites, and others that you find on your own, as resources for animated GIF files. And have fun!

Think before you link! It might seem tempting to link to a cool GIF animation or other illustration on the Web. By pointing directly to a GIF file on someone else's Web site, it appears on your Web page as if it belonged there. Two problems: It's bad for the owner of the Web site, and it's bad for you. The owner has to pay for all the resources needed to serve up the animated GIF file. And you have to worry about the owner moving the file and "breaking" your Web page! (A malicious site owner could even replace an image you like with one you don't like. How'd you like someone visiting your Web page to see an animated obscene gesture where they expected to see dancing hamsters?)

Adding animated GIFs to your Web page

To add an animated GIF to your Web page, use the same steps as to add any other GIF to your Web page. In straight HTML, you use the image tag (`IMG`). For instance, to show an animated GIF called `peace.gif`, the syntax would be something like this:

```
<IMG SRC="peace.gif" HEIGHT=40 WIDTH=40 ALT="Peace,
        people!">.
```

For more about the `IMG` tag, see Chapter 9.

In adding animated GIFs to your Web page, you need to keep a few things in mind, before and after adding the file:

- **File size:** File size is a concern with regular graphics files, and much more so with animated GIFs. Since every frame of the animation is a separate graphics file, it's easy to have an animated GIF be hundreds of KB in size — and therefore take over a minute for users with modems to download. In most cases, it ain't worth it! So either reduce the size of the file by editing each frame in the animation, and reducing the number of frames, or put the animation on a separate page and label the links to it with a warning about the file size.

- **Playback speed:** Car companies always say "your mileage may vary." The same is true of animated GIFs. The user's Internet connection speed affects how long it takes the animated GIF to start moving, and the speed of his or her computer and graphics subsystem may affect how quickly the animation runs. Try your animation on some different setups to make sure it runs and looks the way you want it to.

✔ **Fun factor:** Keep updating and moving your animated GIFs around on your Web page so they don't wear out their welcome with your frequent visitors. If you're getting tired of your animated GIFs, chances are your users are too.

Creating an animated GIF

You need a special program to create an animated GIF, unless you want to use a resource editor to directly edit the contents of the GIF graphics file. Luckily, we've been able to include a trial version of one of the leading GIF animation programs, Ulead GIF Animator, on the *Creating Web Pages For Dummies* CD-ROM.

Use the user manual included with the program if you need help setting it up and need details on how to use the program. But here is a set of simplified steps to help you get your first animation done:

1. **Install Ulead GIF Animator on your machine.**

   Use the instructions on the CD-ROM to get the file installed.

2. **Create a few GIF images for your animation.**

   Use the instructions in Chapter 9 to create a few GIF images in sequence. Make sure the images are all the same size and that you know the image size for use in creating the animation.

   If you're at a loss for ideas, a short series of photographs of someone turning his head produces an interesting, if somewhat spooky, effect.

3. **Start Ulead GIF Animator.**

4. **In the Startup Wizard dialog, click Close to close the dialog box. Then use the File⇨New command to open a new file.**

   You'll be asked to specify the canvas size, as shown in Figure 13-2.

5. **Enter the Width and Height of your images in the dialog box to set the canvas size to the size of your images. Click OK to accept the changes.**

6. **In the Frame Panel at the bottom of the screen, click the Add Frame button to add frames. Then click on each frame to select it. Press the Ins key to insert an image into that frame. In the Add Image dialog box that appears, select the image that appears in that frame.**

   Add each of the frames for your animation, in order.

7. **Click the Optimize tab to optimize your animation.**

   GIF Animator is able to remove duplicated information from successive frames, reducing the size of each frame and the total file size of the animation.

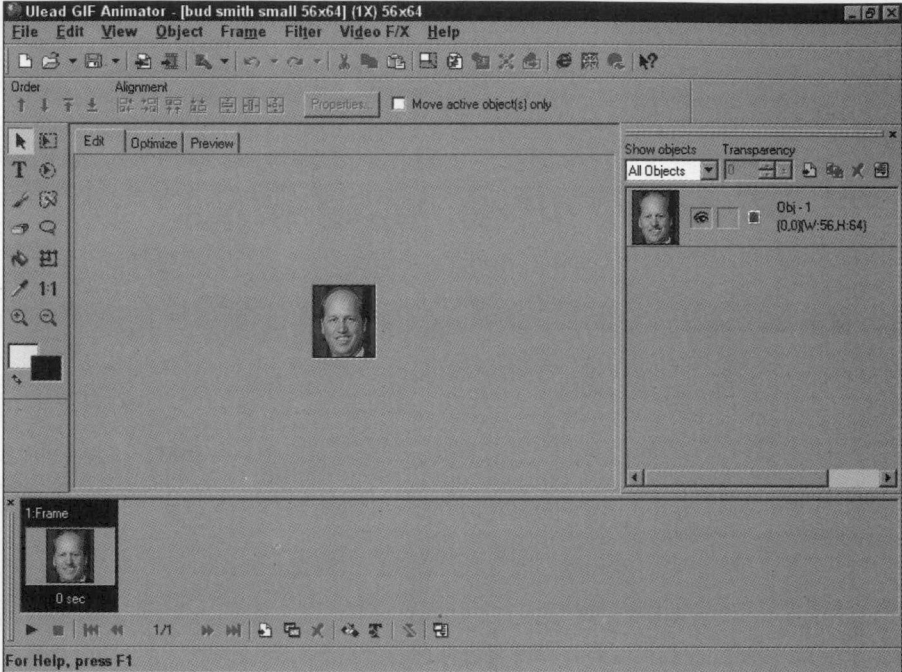

Figure 13-2:
GIF
Animator
will get you
shakin'.

8. **Click File⇨Save to save your animation. Choose GIF as the file format from the pull-down menu, and then save your file.**

9. **Insert your animation as a GIF file in a Web page on your hard disk and test it. Then publish your Web page to the Web and test again.**

GIF Animator has a vast number of options beyond those used in this example (the user manual goes into detail about each option). However, the process above is a good "quick-and-dirty" way to get your animation ready for publishing on the Web.

If you like GIF Animator, and are interested in doing more with graphics in your Web pages, Ulead has a number of other graphics-related tools that might help. Many are available in free trial versions, which is a great way to get started with new software. If you're interested, check out their offerings at

www.ulead.com.

The M- (For Multimedia) Files

Five years ago — half a person's lifespan, in Web time — people downloaded multimedia files from the Web, saved them to disk, and then started up a special player to view the files. (It's been said that Web years are like dog years — the Web changes as much in one year as other things change in seven years. So five years of regular time is like thirty-five years in Web time.) Now, people embed multimedia files in Web pages, and users are able to view them "in place," with very little waiting, by using multimedia players such as Windows Media Player and RealPlayer.

Using multimedia causes some of the same problems as using graphics files, only more so. Many users don't have the right players for viewing multimedia and don't know how to get the players and set them up when needed. The players themselves can cause annoying problems — from crashes, to frequent updates and alerts that the user has to respond to, to sending registered users all kinds of annoying promotional e-mail.

 Not having the right multimedia player, not knowing if they have the right multimedia player, or trying to download and install the right multimedia player is a tremendous source of frustration for users. If you use multimedia files on your Web site, make sure to tell users what player each file requires and provide a link to where the user can download the player.

Performance is also a problem. Waiting up to a minute for several minutes to download a small-sized, brief video clip is frustrating. And the sound quality of many video clips is poor.

However, when you get multimedia working right, it spices up a Web site like nothing else. Just look at the tremendous popularity of the MP3 format for transmitting music over the Web. Operating at nearly the level of quality of FM radio, MP3 files have spawned a whole culture of music trading and sharing on the Net. (Unfortunately, at this point much of the sharing is of MP3 song files that have copyright protection and therefore shouldn't be published for free on the Net.)

The secret to MP3 is the widespread use of compression technology that makes relatively small files with quality near what people are used to (FM radio). It will take a new generation of compression technology to create movies anywhere near as good as TV. At that point, expect an explosion of movies and TV shows on the Net that will rival the MP3 phenomenon in importance. The most important players for Web multimedia are

- ✔ **RealPlayer:** RealPlayer is a plug-in for real-time playback of audio and video files that works pretty darn well. The user of a RealAudio-enhanced Web site typically clicks a link to get an audio or a video clip. A reasonably brief pause ensues, while an initial part of the file downloads, and then sound starts playing. The sound is *streamed* in real time, meaning that no big file is stored on the user's hard disk. (Streaming also means that a faster Internet connection produces better sound quality.) See the sidebar, "I stream, you stream?" for details.

- ✔ **RealJukebox:** RealJukebox is a specialized, audio-only player from Real Networks for MP3 and other audio file types such as RealAudio and WAVE files. You can also use it to manage files to use in portable MP3 players such as Diamond Multimedia's Rio device. Other programs, such as WinAmp, are also very popular for playing back MP3 files.

- ✔ **QuickTime:** QuickTime is Apple's multimedia technology that has become the industry standard for video editing and high-quality video playback on computers. QuickTime VR is an offshoot of QuickTime that creates high-resolution virtual reality panoramas and objects. Most QuickTime content is not streamed; users have to wait until some or all of the file downloads before it will play back. This reduces immediacy but allows improved quality and greater flexibility for the user.

  The QuickTime player comes bundled with many computers and supports all kinds of multimedia formats including animation, sound, QuickTime VR, and QuickTime video clips. A large percentage of the movie files on the Web are QuickTime files. QuickTime is easy to use in your Web page, and no licensing or server fees are involved. Newer versions of QuickTime support streaming, so expect to see more streamed QuickTime content soon.

- ✔ **ShockWave/Flash:** The ShockWave plug-in allows presentations and experiences created in Macromedia Director to be played back over the Web. Figuring out Director is no mean feat, but ShockWave is a powerful tool for delivering multimedia experiences over the Web. Flash is a simple format for delivering animations in your Web page and is rapidly becoming popular. If you are a Director user, or want to become one, or if you're interested in Flash, run, don't walk, to the Macromedia Web site to get more info about ShockWave and Flash.

To find out more about how to use multimedia on the Web, start by checking out the following URLs:

```
www.apple.com/quicktime
www.real.com
www.macromedia.com
```

I stream, you stream?

Two types of video files exist (we'll just assume sound is included). The first are *streaming* video files. Streaming video is a lot like a TV/VCR combo with a very, very small screen — you click on the Go button and, after a few seconds' wait, you start seeing video. Users can pause, rewind, or fast-forward. Streaming video files are experienced by the user with minimal hassles, if they have the correct player installed. Users with the right player software simply click on a link, wait a few seconds, and watch the video clip.

Streaming video files require special software on the Web server to synchronize the transmission and reception of each frame in the video file. Usually, it costs money to either buy the software or to rent space on a server that supports streaming. For instance, the low-end version of RealNetworks' streaming server costs just under $2,000 at this writing.

Just because it's prohibitively expensive to host your own streaming video files doesn't mean you can't include video clips on your Web page. Just point to other peoples' clips! If you have a particular interest, an index of current, interesting video clips in your area is bound to be interesting and valuable to your users. Include brief summaries or reviews, and you'll save your site visitors a lot of wasted time.

Adding a QuickTime Video File

Many different multimedia formats exist, each with its own strengths and weaknesses. But no other multimedia format is as widely accepted, capable, or supported by so many different multimedia and Web page creation tools as QuickTime. Adding multimedia to your Web page is easy with QuickTime, and using QuickTime-based multimedia is likely to be easy for your users as well. Here are the necessary elements for a successful QuickTime Web publishing experience:

- **Multimedia content:** You need a QuickTime multimedia file to put in your page. Dozens of multimedia tools create QuickTime multimedia; for starters, use one someone else has created. When you're ready to create your own, look for tools at `www.apple.com/quicktime`.

- **HTML commands:** A few Web tools, notably PageMill, support embedding of QuickTime content directly. But unless you have such a tool, you need to write HTML commands to embed QuickTime content. Luckily, the commands are simple; an example follows shortly.

- **QuickTime and the QuickTime plug-in:** You and your users need the latest version of QuickTime and the QuickTime player. (New versions of QuickTime include QuickTime VR support as well, adding virtual reality to what you can do with QuickTime.) Many of your users may have the latest version of QuickTime, but many may not. To help your users get updated, provide a link to the QuickTime Web page at `www.apple.com/quicktime`.

QuickTime is big! Users who don't already have QuickTime on their machines have to download it from the Web, and several megabytes is a lot to ask your users to download. However, doing so gives them a lot of capability. Just be aware that you may get some questions and complaints about the download hassle.

You don't have to pay fees or sign special licenses before using QuickTime, as you do with competing technologies. From a business point of view, using QuickTime is as easy as putting a GIF or JPEG image in your Web page. To see some new QuickTime clips, visit `http://www.apple.com/hardware/ads/`.

For more information, visit the QuickTime VR home page and the Berkeley Macintosh User's group QuickTime authoring site at the following Web URLs:

```
www.apple.com/quicktimevr
www.bmug.org/quicktime
```

Here are the steps to add a QuickTime movie to your Web page:

1. **Install QuickTime and the QuickTime plug-in on your own machine.**

   To download these files, go to the QuickTime software page at `www.apple.com/quicktime`.

2. **Create or obtain a QuickTime movie — animation, sound, video, or VR.**

   Use a Web search engine to search for "free QuickTime" and you'll be able to find a clip you can use with minimal or no restrictions.

3. **Embed the movie in your Web page. (If you're using Netscape Composer, click the <HTML> Source tab at the bottom of the page so you can add the following HTML tag directly.)**

   Use the `EMBED` HTML command. In its basic form, for a file named `file.mov` in the same folder as the Web page, it's very simple:

   ```
   <EMBED SRC="file.mov">
   ```

   You have additional options when you use the `EMBED` command with the QuickTime plug-in; for details, see the QuickTime Web page. But try the simple command shown here first to make sure that you don't accidentally introduce a problem when you try to add options.

4. **Test it on your own machine.**

   Test the Web page by opening it in Netscape Navigator and seeing if the movie acts properly. Then test in Internet Explorer.

5. **Upload the changed Web page and the QuickTime file to the Web and test, as described in Chapter 15.**

   Congratulations — you're a multimedia Web publisher!

Adding an MP3 Audio File

MP3 audio files bring about many questions. The quality of the audio is just okay, and many of the files are illegal copies. They are, however, extremely popular, and a whole industry of sites — even new playback devices — has sprung up around MP3.

Creating MP3 files is a lot of work, and you need to search the Web for the right tools and resources to do it. Or you can search for a license-free MP3 file. Once you have an MP3 file — and even fully legal ones are easy to find — it's easy to put one on your Web page. Just follow these instructions:

1. **Get an MP3 file.**

   Just search the Web using any search engine; it won't take long.

2. **Link to the file from your Web page.**

   Use the <A> (for anchor) HTML command. In its basic form, for a file on another Web server, it's as simple as for any Web page:

   ```
   <A
   HREF="www.christcore.com/audio/feeltheburn.mp3">A
   Christian MP3 file</A>.
   ```

   The file here is just one example. Many thousands more are out on the Web.

3. **Test it on your own machine.**

   Test the MP3 file by opening it from the Web page and playing it back.

4. **Upload the changed Web page and the MP3 file to the Web, as described in the previous chapter, and test.**

   Congratulations — you're a Net DJ!

Chapter 14

Adding More Interactivity

· ·

· ·

*I*nteractivity is what distinguishes the best Web sites from the rest. In years of work creating and deploying Web sites, we have seen that the best sites are ones where users enter data, then can come back to add to it, manage it, or see if someone else has reacted to it.

E-mail is a good example of this kind of interaction. You struggle over what to say. You send your message out to one person, or two, or dozens. Then you invest countless hours into replying to the replies, checking if everyone who was meant to get your message actually did, even phoning or meeting with people to follow up. Web sites that can capture the same kind of interactivity do very well.

But interactivity is much harder to add to your Web site, and to manage, than "brochureware" — a Web site that simply puts your message, however well-written and laid out, to the world. There are real technical barriers, because it takes sophisticated databases to store and update data so it can be accessed by scores or thousands of people. The same Web hosting providers who are happy to give you a free or low-cost Web site are much less likely to want to help you create and maintain fancy databases.

Luckily, you can get started simply. In this chapter we introduce you to easy-to-add interactive features, such as site counters and guestbooks, that your hosting provider may offer you for free. If not, you can get these features for free — or at least, for the "cost" of including an ad on your site — from several independent sources. We then go on to introduce you to advanced features like CGI scripting and ActiveX programming that you may not tackle soon, but will at least want to understand for future reference.

Interactivity Made Easy

There are several forms of interactivity for your Web page that have been "canned" and made easy for you to implement. Among the interactive features you may want to add to your Web page are

- ✔ **Site counters:** A *site counter* counts the number of times a Web page has been accessed and displays the count on the Web page. Site counters let you, and your Web site visitors, know how many times the page has been accessed. You may want to add a site counter to your Web page, or, if you have a multi-page Web site, you may even want a site counter on each page.

- ✔ **Guestbooks:** A *guestbook* allows Web site visitors to leave comments. Guestbooks can be a lot of fun; they can even allow people a way to get to know each other through your site. Imagine a family site where everyone signs in and leaves a "Happy Holidays" message for each other.

- ✔ **Forms:** A *form* allows the user to enter data using entry boxes, pull-down menus, checkboxes, and so on. It's easy to create a form using HTML commands, but unfortunately you need a computer program, running on the Web server, to handle the resulting data. The computer program accesses the data using something called a CGI, or Common Gateway Interface.

A message board, or forum, is like a guestbook, but with much more flexibility. Users can post messages, reply to one anothers' messages, start new topics, and more. It's a lot of work to set up and manage a message board — after all, you don't want your friends and family to see a rude message some idiot left, do you? But having a message board can be very rewarding as well. To try using a free message board service, visit www.amazingforums.com.

Each of these forms of interactivity needs some cooperation from the Web server that's hosting your page, or from some other Web server. Why is that, you wonder? Well, think about it a bit.

When you have a site counter on your page, the counter goes up by 1 every time the page is displayed. (Actually, the counter goes up by 1 every time the *counter* is displayed. If the user visits your Web page, then clicks away before the part of the page with the counter on it is displayed, the counter doesn't go up.) How does this happen?

When the counter file is requested by some HTML code in your Web page, it reads a database to find out how many times the request has been made in the past. That's the visit count that it displays. A program notes the request. It updates a database with a request to add 1 to the number of times the file has been accessed. The next time the counter is requested, the number for it to display is 1 higher. All of this takes a bit of computer programming.

The same is true for guestbooks — data is being stored somewhere, updated with new additions, and displayed on request. Any time data is being stored and modified, some kind of computer programming is involved. Sometimes you can use a "canned," prewritten program to do the work. However, someone still had to write and test the program, and it still has to run every time the functionality is used.

Computer programs are dangerous! They can, unless carefully prevented from doing so, read and write data — which is great when it's done right, but is disastrous when done wrong. (Just think of computer viruses for an example of a computer program doing the wrong thing.) The same people who will happily host your Web page on their server for free, or at a small price, will suddenly become very unhappy if you try to run your program on their server. So interactive features, even simple ones like site counters and guestbooks, are carefully managed by the administrators of Web servers. Ordinary people aren't allowed to put their own programs to support these features on other people's Web servers.

Site counters

A site counter is a graphic that goes on your Web page, just like any other GIF image, but it has a rather magical property: It displays the current count of the number of pages your Web page has been displayed. (Of course, if you want a lot of visitors and you're only getting a few, that property might not seem so magical.)

How does the site counter do this? As described earlier, a very simple bit of database programming is involved. Every time your counter graphic is *served* — requested by your Web page, then sent to the user's machine — a request is made to get the current number of times the graphic has been served in the past, and a command is sent to add one more to the count. The counter is then updated to the correct number and sent as a graphic file to your computer.

Your access to site counters depends on where your Web page is hosted:

- ✔ **AOL Member pages:** If you create your Web page at members.aol.com, as described in Chapter 2, you can use the built-in Web counters there. The same people who host your Web page run the program and database that support the counter, so you don't have to do anything tricky. Just follow AOL's instructions.

- ✔ **Yahoo! GeoCities pages:** As on AOL's Member pages, Yahoo! hosts your Web pages and the counter software. Start by creating your Web page on Yahoo! GeoCities, as described in Chapter 3. Then follow the instructions at geocities.yahoo.com to add a site counter to your site. Figure 14-1 shows counter styles for GeoCities.

Figure 14-1:
GeoCities
makes
your pages
count.

✔ **Other hosts:** If you have your site hosted by another free or paid Web pages service, or by an ISP other than AOL, you may have access to a free Web site counter feature. If so, use it, as described by your Web page's host. Otherwise, see the next bullet.

✔ **Free Web-based service:** Several "free" Web-based services will provide a counter for you. (We say "free" in quotes because many of them require that you include an ad or link to their server, though they don't charge money.) One good one is at `www.bcentral.com/products/fc`. Check it out, or search for other free Web-based counter services on the Web.

✔ **Run your own server:** You can run your own Web server software on your own computer over your own Internet connection. Then you can create and run any computer program on the server that you want! This is a much more difficult approach than we recommend in this book, but if you want to do a lot with your site, having this degree of control may be worth it. The book *Building a Web Site For Dummies,* by David A. Crowder and Rhonda Crowder (Hungry Minds, Inc.) has the instructions and software — including CGIs — that you need to get started.

Guestbooks

A guestbook is a place where visitors to your site can leave comments. If you get a lot of activity in your guestbook, users will return to your site more often to see what's in it and then leave additional comments themselves, which means other users will return more often. As you can see, a guestbook can be great for making your site more interesting and increasing traffic to it.

As with site counters, a guestbook requires that a program run on a Web server somewhere, store the data that users enter in it, and display the data when needed. Also as with site counters, your access to guest counter functionality depends on where your Web page is hosted:

- **AOL Member pages and Yahoo! GeoCities pages:** If you create your Web page at members.aol.com, as described in Chapter 2, you can use the built-in guestbook there. Same thing if you create your Web page at Yahoo! GeoCities at geocities.yahoo.com, as described in Chapter 3. With the same people supporting your Web page and your guestbook, you just need to follow the on-site instructions and everything will work.

- **Other hosts:** For other hosts, check to see if you have access to a free guestbook feature. If not, use a free Web-based service, as described in the next bullet.

- **Free Web-based service:** There are a few Web-based services that support a guestbook. They may be truly free, free with an ad or link, or paid. You can use an ad-based or paid guestbook at guestbook.mycomputer.com.

- **Run your own server:** You can run guestbooks all day and all night if you take on the challenge of running your own Web server. *Building a Web Site For Dummies,* by David A. Crowder and Rhonda Crowder (Hungry Minds, Inc.), will help you get started.

A chat room can be even more fun than a guestbook. To learn about a good one that you can try, go to www.icq.com/ircqnet.

Forms and CGIs

A *form* is just what the name implies: a place where a user can enter data, such as name, address, and telephone number. Figure 14-2 shows a simple form used by Netsurfer Digest for signing up subscribers. On the part of the form shown in the figure, you enter data by clicking your choice from a scrolling list.

Figure 14-2:
Netsurfer
Digest is
informative.

Since forms are part of HTML 2.0, a very early version of HTML, they've been around for years, and most HTML books describe them. Getting data from users via forms is pretty easy. What's more complicated is figuring out what to do with the information after you have it.

Processing the data from a form requires one or more computer programs. A common way to handle data is to use a CGI script and an application. A *CGI script,* sometimes simply called "a CGI," is a Common Gateway Interface script — a program that sends the data to an application that you create. The CGI script runs on the server that hosts your Web page. CGI scripts are different on NT, UNIX, and Macintosh. Many CGI scripts are written in C language or PERL, a cross-platform scripting language.

To run a CGI script, you need the permission of the *sysop* (system operator) responsible for the server that hosts your Web page. Sysops are paid to protect their systems from harm, so getting your sysop to run an unknown program on his or her precious server may not be possible. Many Web hosts, including AOL (see Chapter 2) and Yahoo! GeoCities (see Chapter 3), have prepackaged forms or CGI packages that handle common tasks such as counting visitors, allowing users to register, and more. Finding and using one of these prewritten packages is a good intermediate step toward creating your own CGI scripts and applications.

For basic information about CGI scripting, check out this Web site
`www.comvista.com/lessons/CGI.html`.

For more about using JavaScript to process form data, visit About.com's
JavaScript Web site at `http://javascript.about.com`.

Programming Your Pages

You can do an awful lot on the Web with only text and graphics, and adding
interactive features such as a counter or guestbook extends your powers
even further. However, to really "do business on the Web" and support interactivity, you need to consider doing some programming.

Web programming is a complicated topic that is beyond the scope of this
book. However, you may want to experiment with programming on your own.
JavaScript, for example, is a scripting language that gives you increased control over your Web pages without true programming. To go further requires
more books, more training, and more work. Want to read *JavaScript For
Dummies,* 3rd Edition, by Emily A. Vander Veer (Hungry Minds Inc.), anyone?
Check out Web sites that you like to see how they achieve certain effects, and
then search your bookstore and the Web to see the different techniques that
are available.

For a long time, a big advantage of living in certain areas was the improved
access some places have to large and specialty bookstores. For example,
both authors of this book live in Silicon Valley, home of the excellent
Computer Literacy bookstores, which used to give the authors a leg up over
people living elsewhere. Now, through the Web, most people can find whatever books they need. And recently, the Computer Literacy bookstores have
gone out of business!

To find computer books, you can start by looking at the following URLs:

```
www.amazon.com
www.barnesandnoble.com
www.fatbrain.com
```

Java

Java is the Sun Microsystems programming language that makes the creation
of interactive Internet applications easier and more flexible. Java promises
much more spectacular Web pages, incorporating animation, smart updating,
and collaboration applications. However, Java has been bedeviled by security
problems and by the sheer size of the software needed to run Java programs.

Java is a variant of the overly complex computer programming language C++ and so requires considerable experience and skill to use. (At least, that's what our well-paid programmer friends tell us.) Java is now widely used by professional programmers writing software applications that run on large computer systems, but not by Web page authors. Widespread use of Java on Web pages has been held up recently by the fact that Microsoft, in a legal dispute over rights to Java, has stopped distributing Java with its market-leading Internet Explorer browser. Netscape has also stopped including Java in the basic installation for its browser software. For more about Java, see the Sun Java Web site at java.sun.com and Earthweb's Java directory site at softwaredev. earthweb.com/java.

ActiveX

ActiveX is technology from Microsoft that allows Microsoft Visual Basic programs to work with the Web. The good news is that ActiveX enables you to do some pretty amazing things. The bad news is that it has had serious security problems, doesn't work well on the Macintosh, and doesn't work at all on 16-bit Windows (Windows 3.1 and before) or on UNIX. However, if you are willing to do Windows-only Web work and want more information on ActiveX, you can start at Microsoft's .NET site at www.microsoft.com/net.

Also, see Appendix D and the *resource.htm* file on the CD-ROM that comes with this book for pointers to more information about ActiveX.

Database interactivity

Tying your Web site to a database is a way to supercharge it beyond anything we demonstrate in this book. Technologies whose names you may have heard or seen within a URL, such as Active Server Pages (ASP) and PHP (PHP: Hypertext Preprocessor), are used for this purpose. Some free hosting services will let you set up your own database and tie it to your Web site. One of them, from a Web hosting company called Brinkster, Inc., is at www.brinkster.com.

Many, many resources

There are many resources on the Web for learning advanced topics such as those described here. However, if you're trying to get a good overview, it can be worthwhile to go to one or two major resources, where the different pieces tie together in an understandable way. Try these resources to get started:

```
www.about.com
builder.cnet.com
www.webmonkey.com
```

Going Beyond HTML

While the simplicity and flexibility of HTML has been key to the success of the Web, HTML does, of course, have limitations. Two major languages, Dynamic HTML and XML (eXtensible Markup Language), address many of the limitations.

Although you should be aware of upcoming technologies, you're better off waiting to implement them in your own Web pages until most users have browsers that support the new capabilities. In the case of Dynamic HTML and XML, even an optimist would agree that it will be a couple of years before most users are equipped with browsers that support either of them.

HTML gets Dynamic

Dynamic HTML, or DHTML for short, is an extension of HTML that allows multiple layers of information to be sent to the user during a server connection. The user only sees part of the information at first. Additional information can be unveiled as time passes or as the user undertakes different actions, all without having to reconnect to the server.

At this writing, Netscape and Microsoft offer somewhat different implementations of Dynamic HTML. Netscape uses its own LAYER tag to allow some layering to be defined fairly simply. Both browsers support Style Sheets, a more complex and more capable way of supporting Dynamic HTML being defined through the official Web standards process. But Microsoft, which always followed Netscape's lead on new tags in the past, refuses to support the LAYER tag.

Only the 4.0 and later versions of Netscape Navigator and Microsoft Internet Explorer support any of these Dynamic HTML features, which leaves out users of other browsers. If Netscape and Microsoft can agree, and if the majority of users upgrade their browsers to gain access to Dynamic HTML extensions, many Web authors may take the time and trouble to support these new features in their Web pages. Until then, however, DHTML won't be used by most Web page authors.

XML x-es out HTML

HTML is a subset of an overall standard called *Standard Generalized Markup Language,* or SGML. (We bet the people who created SGML didn't know what would happen with their invention!) *XML,* or *eXtensible Markup Language,* is a superset of HTML, which has been created within the overall SGML standard. XML allows complex data structures to be built into a Web page. With XML, authors can create database applications and deliver them across the Web. Our guess is that XML will be deployed on intranets first because companies will want to develop such applications for internal use and will be able to ensure that all Web authors and users in the company use the same version of XML. If you're responsible for intranet-related activity, keep an eye on this one.

The Web enters the twenty-first century

Because of its flexible nature, the Web has the theoretical capability to support almost anything that can be done or imagined on a computer. As the connection speed available to the average user improves, as more technology is used in advanced Web pages, and as users move up to more capable browsers, more and more will be possible. The trick is not to chase down any of the new pathways before they settle into widely used standards. Develop your skills in the key areas that make the Web useful and productive today. Using the capabilities of today's mainstream Web is the best way to prepare yourself to take advantage of the advanced Web that will be here the day after tomorrow.

Chapter 15

Creating a Full Web Site

So far, this book has focused on creating individual, separate Web home pages. In this chapter we'll tell you how to tie several different Web pages together into a multi-page Web site. However, it's good to keep your focus on each individual Web page even as you combine them all together.

Users of your site are always able to leave for any other site or page on the Web. If you make sure every Web page you put up is interesting, fun, and attractive, as described throughout this book, you'll end up with a strong Web site.

The terms Web page and Web site are used very similarly. In this book we use the term *Web page* to refer to a single Web page consisting of an HTML document and the graphics that go with it. We use the term *Web site* to refer to an area on the Web consisting of multiple Web pages tied together by shared navigation.

Creating Your Web Pages

It's typical, when designing a Web site, to use a top-down approach to start thinking a lot about navigation, organization, navigation, and so on. (We mention "navigation" twice because it's such a big concern when you're creating a large Web site.) But for a small Web site, go bottom up — building the site from carefully crafted individual pages — rather than top down.

Your approach to creating Web pages for a small Web site should be similar to your approach to creating a single Web home page. Each page should stand alone as a worthwhile place for your Web visitors to spend time, learn something, or have some fun.

Getting your pages right

Think of each Web page as a separate "information asset." Why would people want to come to your Web page? What would they take away from having seen it? Is there anything about your page that might make people come back, or want to encourage someone else to visit? Most of us have enough to say to easily create a Web home page that our friends, family, and colleagues find interesting. But it takes extra work to make each Web page in a multi-page site valuable to people.

One of the best ways to create a strong Web site is to first create each Web page separately. Make sure each page has the information you want, that it downloads in a reasonable amount of time, that all the links work, and that the page looks good. Then use the information in this chapter to add navigation and make your Web pages into a unified Web site.

What about consistency? Consistency is important within a Web site, but not that difficult to achieve if your site is only a few pages to perhaps a dozen pages in size. Use the same background color, text color, font, and text size throughout your pages. If you use standard HTML headers, bulleted and numbered lists, and small images to break up your text, your pages will have a consistent appearance.

Figures 15-1 and 15-2 show two Web pages from within the Netsurfer Web site created and managed by one of the coauthors (Bebak). Note how the pages use a similar design, making it clear they're from the same Web site, yet are clearly individual as well. The Netsurfer pages are a good example of the effectiveness of simple, clean design across a Web site.

In addition to a standardized design across pages, the other elements that make a site consistent are predictable, understandable Web page addresses and repeated navigational elements throughout the site. The next section explains how to achieve these qualities in your site.

You may want to take the design consistency of your Web site to another level by adding repeated graphical elements and a strong, consistent approach to layout across all your Web pages. This is the approach taken by the pros. We suggest that, unless you have some design experience, you first create the site's pages and navigation. Then work on improving the overall design after the site is up and working. (This is also the approach taken by the pros!)

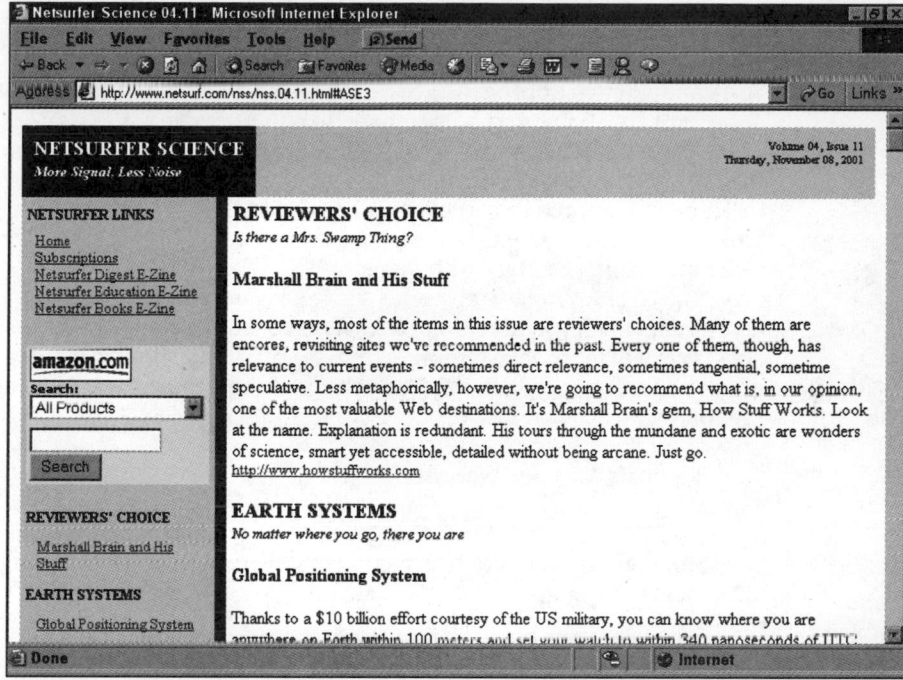

Figure 15-1:
Netsurfer
has a clean,
simple
design...

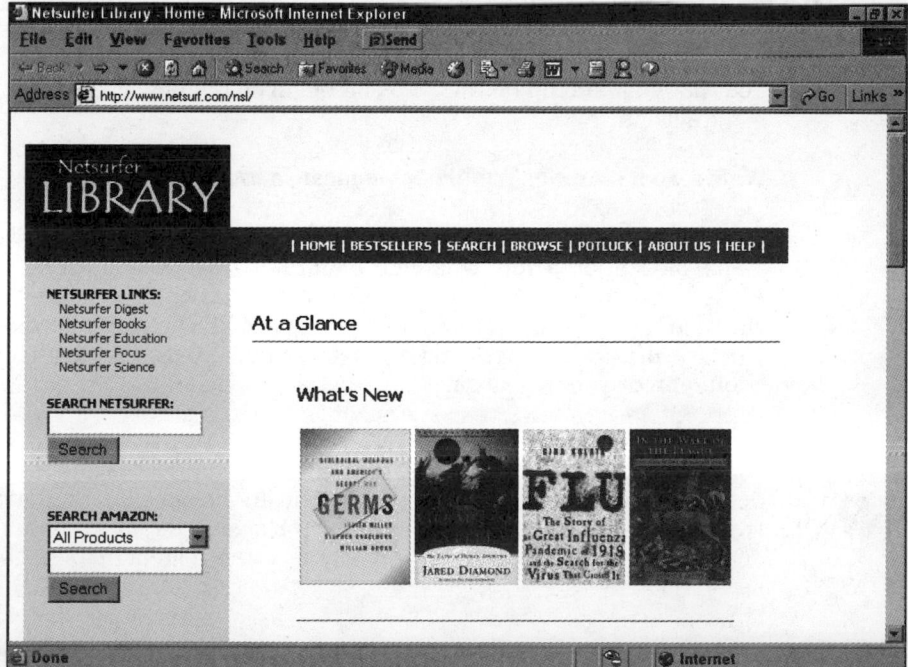

Figure 15-2:
...that varies
subtly from
one section
to the next.

Planning versus pushing ahead

You can take two approaches to your role as a Web site publisher: the spontaneous approach favored by someone like Captain Kirk, the risk-taking leader of the Starship *Enterprise* in the original Star Trek TV series and movies, or the careful approach favored by the more logical Mr. Spock. The spontaneous Captain Kirk approach can be summarized in the well-known Nike slogan "Just Do It." You can get a simple site up on the Web with just a little more work than doing a single Web page.

If you're trying for a more complex Web site, such as a Web site for your business, you'll want to take a more careful approach. In contrast to Captain Kirk's quick-and-dirty approach, Mr. Spock's more logical method requires you to do the following:

- ✔ Set goals for your Web site.
- ✔ Plan the contents of your site to meet those goals.
- ✔ Storyboard your site to specify what's on each Web page and how the pages fit together.
- ✔ Compare your planned site to similar or competing sites and revise your plans accordingly.
- ✔ Create your site on your own machine first and test it thoroughly.
- ✔ Carefully choose a Web service provider that will do the best job of hosting your site.
- ✔ Get your site up on the Web and begin an ongoing cycle of testing and revision.

Whew! That's a lot of Tribble — we mean, a lot of trouble!

Either the spontaneous or the careful approach is just fine, but you should match your approach to what you want to do on the Web. We recommend that you try the spontaneous approach first. Don't put out a great deal of effort, and don't use your initial page to try to start a Web-based business empire. Just create a personal or business home page that says something about you or your organization.

If you don't own or run your organization, make sure that you have the permission you need before putting up a Web site that represents the organization. Otherwise, you could find yourself on an unexpected, rapid transition off your current career path. (The Monster job search database at www.monster. com is a good example of a fun Web site — and is a great help in looking for a new job!)

If that one page is all you ever publish on the Web, that's fine. A lot of the fun of being on the Web is seeing the Web pages created by individuals who are just trying to have fun and share their interests. Whether you go on to create a Web presence for a business or even create a Web-based business of your own, the experience that you get when you "just do it" may prove invaluable. Table 1-1 suggests when to use the careful versus the spontaneous approach to Web publishing.

Table 15-1	The Kirk (Spontaneous) and Spock (Careful) Approaches to Web Publishing				
	Have Fun	Learn Now for Advanced Work Later	Small Business Web Presence	Larger Business Web Presence	Web-Based Business
Spon-taneous	X	X	X		
Careful			X	X	X

Planning your Web site

The only tools you need for this part of the Web publishing process are Web access, for doing research, and either a word processing and drawing program, or a pencil and paper — whichever is more comfortable — for sketching your plans and taking notes. A few extra hours upfront can save you a great deal of time later and help you produce a better Web page. Yet the planning step is the most frequently overlooked part of the Web publishing process. To plan your Web site, follow these steps:

1. **Determine the purpose of your site.**

   Decide which type of site you want to create: personal, topical, commercial, or comical. (We could also call the last two "business" and "entertainment," but those don't rhyme.)

   Once you decide what type of site you want, research existing sites, and then research other media that serve the same purpose (magazines, brochures — even television). Ask what it is about your material, or about the Web, that makes the Web a good way to get your material out. Think some more about your own needs and interests. Then write a few goals for your initial site and for later versions of it.

2. **Decide on the structure of your site and the layout of your pages.**

   The structure of your site can help guide readers to the parts that interest them most. The layout of your site's Web pages can make them more useful, more interesting, or more entertaining, whichever is their purpose. Here are a few general rules:

   - Decide how many pages to have and how they link to each other.

   - Put the purpose of your site near the top of your home page.

   - Indicate the purpose of each additional page near the top of that page.

   - Use headers, bullets, icons, and other graphical or emphasis elements to highlight key points.

   - Think about what graphics you need. Start the process of generating or obtaining them.

   - Use summary elements, such as a site map and a Frequently Asked Questions (FAQ) page.

   - Put navigational elements — links from your home page to other pages in your site, and from other pages back to the home page — in a consistent spot at the top or bottom of each page.

3. **Decide which links to include.**

   A Web page that has no links is generally pretty boring. You already decided in Step 2 which links to include between the pages in your site. Now think about what links to include from your pages out to other sites. What links make sense? What links are fun? Use Web search engines such as Google (www.google.com) to search the Web and find suitable links (see Figure 15-3). Then check the links and cut the list down to the personally significant ones, not just a laundry list. (Unless you're making a list of laundries!) Create a place to save links that you run into while using the Web so that they're available for you to use in future versions of your pages.

   Now think some more. Do the links that you're including fit the purpose of your page? How can you organize them? Should you group sets of key links together? Are some of the links repetitive or superfluous? Getting your links right makes your site more useful. And although no one likes to be left behind, which is what happens to you when people click an outbound link in one of your pages, a good set of links can, paradoxically, make users more likely to return to your site in the future.

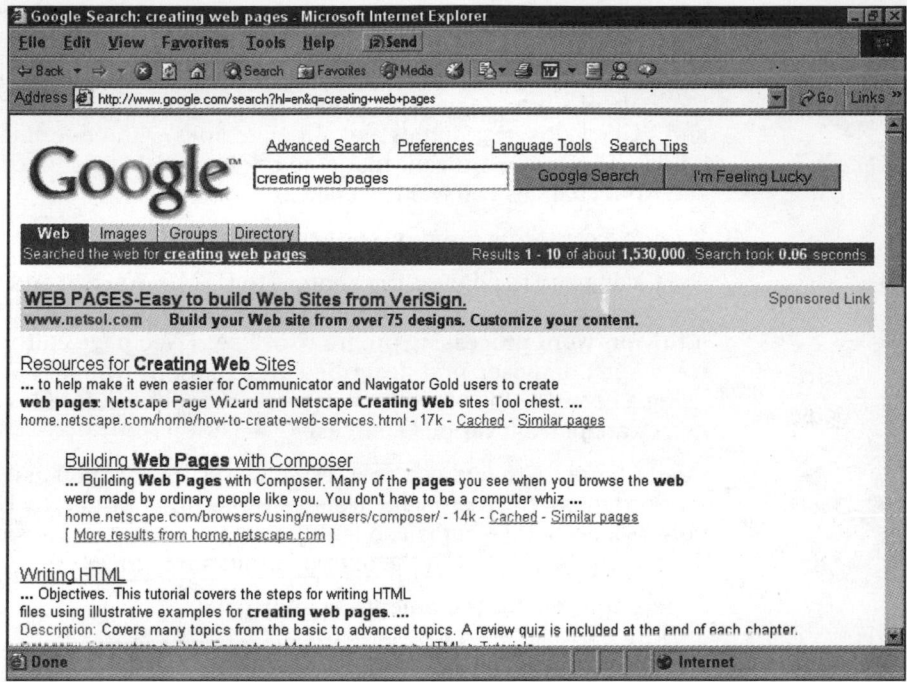

Figure 15-3:
Don't get all
Google-
eyed while
searching.

Creating the content

Creating content is the part of the Web publishing process where tools come in. You need tools to create HTML-tagged text (or a word processing program or text editor if you want to work in HTML directly) and graphics tools to create graphics and convert them to one of the common Web formats, GIF or JPEG. (Yes, you can use other file formats for Web graphics, but, as we say in Chapter 9, GIF and JPEG are the only formats that are widely supported by all browsers.) For simple sites, one person can do all the work (but it will be a lot of work); for creating and maintaining larger sites, you need a team of people, often including consultants who have HTML expertise or other skills.

1. **Create the text for your pages.**

   The best thing to do here, if you're new to Web publishing, is to work in a word processing program without putting in HTML tags, at least at first. That way you can use a familiar tool to get the text right and to spell check it. Just remember that you can achieve much more precise formatting in a word processing program than you can in a Web page.

   If you've already created a Web home page in HTML or a Web editing tool such as Netscape Composer, as we describe throughout the book, then you can use the same techniques for your Web site.

You may want to consider going an extra step and creating a "dummy" of your Web site — pun intended — in your word processing program before you commit to HTML. Making a *dummy* (a printer's term for a mock-up of a printed page) is a good way to plan what's on each page, and you can insert graphics and simulate links with underlines and colors. Then compare your model to relevant Web sites you admire and see what changes you want to make.

2. **If you've created a dummy, convert the content to HTML.**

   Next, you need to convert the content to HTML. You can add the HTML tags yourself (see Chapter 4), use HTML conversion capabilities built into your word processing program, or use a Web page editor (like Netscape Composer, first described in Chapter 5). You may well end up using a combination of methods for new content and for files that you use or adapt from various sources.

Read Chapter 4 to find out how HTML works. Even if you use a Web authoring tool to create your Web page and don't put in the HTML tags yourself, knowing what is and isn't possible in basic HTML saves a great deal of time and effort in the overall publishing process.

3. **Create the graphical elements in your pages.**

   Graphical elements often take a long time to create, so start early. They include not only photos and computer-generated images but also mastheads, separator bars, and icons. This is also the time to create multimedia elements, such as sounds or video clips, if you really want to push the envelope. We cover these elements in Chapter 13.

4. **Add navigation and test it.**

   As described later in this chapter, you have to add navigation to make your separate Web pages into a site. Then you'll be ready for the next step — publishing your site!

Publishing your Web site

Putting your site on the Web — either on an intranet or on the open World Wide Web — is the most exciting part of the Web publishing process. (But watch out! Your excitement may quickly turn to anxiety as you think of people actually looking at your carefully crafted baby.) For this part of the process, you don't need any tools, except possibly an FTP (File Transfer Protocol) program to move your files to the Web server. Usually, whoever is providing your Web hosting service supports this process.

First, bring the elements of your site together, then test it on your local machine, and finally publish it! Here are the steps for publishing (or republishing) your site:

1. **Put it all together and test it.**

   Check that you have all the content and links in the places that you want them and then test each Web page and the entire site. On your own machine, you can use a Web browser not only to see what your pages look like but also to follow links from your site to other sites. Then you can use the Back button on your browser to return. (The only thing missing is that the people who eventually surf your site can't get to it until it's actually published on a Web server.)

2. **Put your content on a Web server.**

   This is when it gets real. After you get your pages on the server, as described in Chapter 12, test them again. Especially, test all the links to make sure that they really go somewhere; remember, nothing is more frustrating than clicking on a broken link.

3. **Publicize your site.**

   Get some users onto your site. Tell your friends, use Web resources, and, especially, get related Web sites to put in links to your site. Offer some kind of reward for feedback on your site — even if it's just taking that person's site off your "bad HTML examples" list! (For more detail on this part of the process, see the section "Getting the Word Out" later in this chapter.)

4. **Bask in the glory of being a Web publisher.**

   Having a Web site up and running is something to be proud of. Sit and enjoy it for awhile.

After you get your site on the Web, you'll experience a brief moment of elation, and then feel concern as you think of all the things you wanted to do with the site before you ran out of time. Then you'll click around your site and realize that something doesn't look quite as good as you wanted. You may compare your site with others and decide to add new features. Back to square one!

Stumbling blocks on the Web

For all its great characteristics, the Web has some problems that you're more likely to run into when you're creating a full Web site than when you're just publishing a single Web page. Among these issues:

✔ **Differences in browsers:** Different browsers, such as different versions of Internet Explorer or Netscape Navigator, display the same HTML tags differently. And some browsers support newer or nonstandard tags, so pages displayed in them look better — or at least different — than they look on other browsers. This inconsistency can drive you to distraction. Use basic tools and keep your site simple until you learn your way around some of these concerns.

✔ **Faster and slower connections:** Some users have fast network connections to the Web, whereas many home users dawdle along at 28.8 Kbps — ten times slower than a typical corporate connection. So a graphics-rich page that comes up fast on one machine downloads *very s-l-o-w-l-y* on another. See Chapter 9 for information on how to keep your graphic file sizes small and Chapter 11 for information on how to keep your overall page size small.

✔ **Those darn users:** Users have different screen sizes, and they can reconfigure their browsers to use different fonts, different window sizes, and so on. So even users who connect to the Web through the same network and run the same browser can see the same Web page quite differently. Chapter 11 has details.

✔ **Getting on a server:** For your Web pages to show up on the Web, they have to be on a Web server. This means that you have to find either a volunteer or a vendor with a Web server and some hard disk space to spare. Luckily, space for a small Web site is usually either free or cheap, but finding server space and getting your files to the server can be a big hassle. You can find out more in Chapter 12.

Consider using non-English Web pages

One of the most limiting factors to the spread of the World Wide Web is that it's largely in English. This situation is changing; already many larger sites, such as the Yahoo! Web directory, offer their services in several other languages. But the amount of non-English content is small compared to the size of the Web.

To create Web pages, you need to know enough English to figure out and use HTML and Web tools. But what about your audience?

First, find out how many people in your target audience speak a specific language and how many of them have access to the Web. Then consider the cost of translating your content into each language that you're interested in. Compare that cost to the size of the potential audience.

Be optimistic; having native-language content distinguishes your site. At this point in the Web's development, you're better off having the Web's best list of movies in Farsi (Iran's predominant language) than yet another list of movies in English.

At the least, if you have printed materials already translated into other languages, either put those materials on the Web or publicize them there. In some languages and some areas of information needs, using non-English languages on the Web offers the same kind of ground-floor opportunity that the Web as a whole offered when its popularity started about ten years ago.

The first three problems are related to inconsistencies in the Web, and you may have run into them as a user looking at different Web pages. Now that you're a beginning Web publisher, the answer to all these problems is the same: Keep it simple! In this book, we use simple Web page layouts and stick almost completely to the basic HTML features available in all browsers to help you avoid these problems.

The problem of getting your Web page on the server is a little different — the kind of hurdle that can stop neophytes cold, but one that experienced users clear with ease. In Part I of this book and in Chapter 12, we show you enough varied server solutions to meet any needs — and some of the solutions are even free!

Page description languages

HTML is not a *page description language* — that is, a specification for exactly how your text and graphics should look when they're displayed or printed. But Adobe Acrobat *is* a page description language, and so are Envoy from Novell, Inc., and the MiniViewer that's part of Common Ground from Hummingbird Communications, Ltd. (**Note:** Even though you may overhear at the supermarket: "Give me a pound of premium Java and half a pound of that common ground," Common Ground is not a cheap version of Java, the programming language we describe later in this chapter.) Adobe Acrobat is the only page description language that has gained widespread acceptance on the Web.

So if you want to put up a formatted page that keeps its look, feel, fonts, and more, use Acrobat. You can put the page up on the Web so that it looks exactly like a printed version. The problem: Users have to download a special viewer for your information, which they're unlikely to bother with unless you have something they really, really want to see. (And expect a few technical support calls from users who can't figure out what to do.) *The New York Times* is the biggest "name" to adopt Acrobat so far, and many organizations use PDF files internally.

To bypass this viewing problem, Acrobat is now supported by a plug-in for Microsoft Internet Explorer and Netscape Navigator. Many computers ship with a version of Acrobat Reader already installed. For more information and for a look at *The New York Times* daily online edition that uses Acrobat, see the following URLs:

```
www.adobe.com/prodindex/acrobat
nytimesfax.com/sample/sample.pdf
```

Creating Navigation

Navigation is what helps users find their way around your Web site. If you have previously put up a single Web home page and are now expanding to a multi-page site, creating navigation is a new challenge for you. But using navigation isn't. Every time you visit a major Web site, you encounter carefully designed navigation. Luckily, for a small site, consistent navigation is easy to achieve.

Arranging your pages

Arranging your Web pages in your Web site is most like creating a very small newspaper. You divide your Web pages up into a few sections, perhaps three to seven. Each section of your Web site is like a section of a newspaper. It can include one or several Web pages that fit within the theme of that section.

The home page of your site is kind of like the front page of a newspaper, and somewhat like the table of contents in a magazine. The home page grabs people's attention with one or a few elements that are interesting in and of themselves, and also serves as a guide to what's inside the rest of the site.

Take your Web pages — you may want to print them out for this exercise — and arrange them into sections. Be a little creative. If you have two pages in a section, you may want to combine them into a single page (to eliminate the need for navigation in that section), or rearrange them into three pages (to have more than one other page within the section to navigate to).

The original Web site for Zanzara, a Web usability company, can be found at www.zanzara.com/old. It's a good example of simple, consistent navigation for a small site. Most of the sections have a single page. A few have a front page to the section that links to one or two additional pages that give further details. Figure 15-4 is a chart showing the layout of the site.

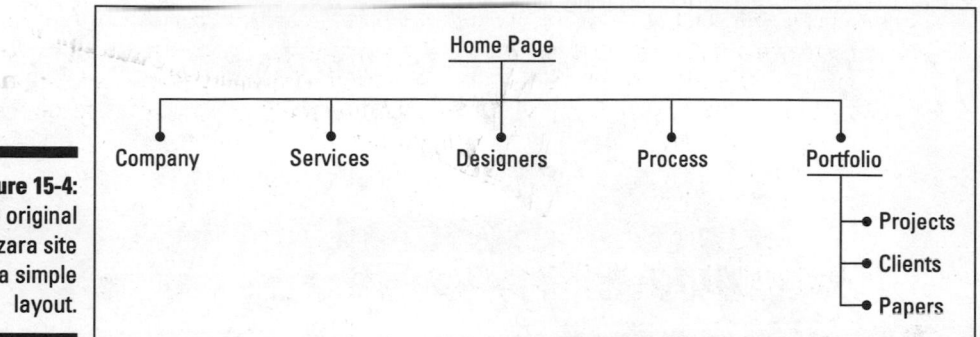

Figure 15-4:
The original
Zanzara site
has a simple
layout.

Getting the addresses right

One major navigational element is easy to achieve: consistent Web addresses for your Web pages. For a small Web site, you want to have an understandable URL for the site, a few major sections, and then one or a few Web pages within each section.

Let's say your Web site is within the Yahoo! GeoCities site and is mainly focused on rotifers, a small creature made up of a few hundred cells. You've cleverly created the user ID "rotifers" in GeoCities, so the home page of your site is at www.geocities.com/rotifers.

Now you're going to create a multi-page Web site. You decide to redo your home page to make it a site home page, and have four sections to your site: About Rotifers, Roti-Photos, Web Resources, and About Me. This way you've isolated the bulk of your photos, which will tend to download slowly, onto pages where people might reasonably expect a slow download. They can get the basic information about rotifers and you from text-intensive pages, without a long wait, then go to the photo-intensive pages when they're ready to take their time.

Further, you decide that About Rotifers will be a single page of text, Roti-Photos will be several pages with one photo each, Web Resources will be a single page of Web links, and About Me will be two pages: a text-intensive page with a small photo of you, and a copy of your résumé on its own page.

Given these decisions, a list of possible choices for the Web addresses for your photos might be:

```
www.geocities.com/rotifers/index.htm
```

```
www.geocities.com/rotifers/aboutrotifers/index.htm
```

```
www.geocities.com/rotifers/photos/index.htm
```

```
www.geocities.com/rotifers/photos/photo1.htm
```

```
www.geocities.com/rotifers/photos/photo2.htm
```

```
www.geocities.com/rotifers/photos/photo3.htm
```

```
www.geocities.com/rotifers/photos/photo4.htm
```

```
www.geocities.com/rotifers/resources/index.htm
```

```
www.geocities.com/rotifers/aboutme/index.htm
```

```
www.geocities.com/rotifers/aboutme/resume.htm
```

To make these URLs work, you'll need to put the files in folders that match the hierarchy that you want to have appear in the URLs, so you'll need a main folder enclosing all the other files and folders. Within the main folder you should have the `index.htm` file for the site's home page, plus any photos that will display on that Web page, plus folders for the other pages. The folders at that level will be `aboutrotifers`, `photos`, `resources`, and `aboutme`. Each folder will then contain the `index.htm` file for that part of the site, plus any HTML files for additional pages in that section, and the photos needed for that section of your Web site.

If you want to keep all your files in a single folder, just use filenames to achieve the same effect. For instance, call the HTML file that displays the first photograph `photos-photo1.htm`, and so on.

Having your site organized well, with understandable URLs, makes life easier for users. Many users look at URLs to see where they are in a site. And users frequently write down or e-mail URLs to bring a page to the attention of others.

Many large Web sites have abandoned the convenience (for users) of having easy-to-understand URLs, in favor of the convenience (for them) of using a database to store all the content in their site. Each new Web page is displayed as a result of a database call, with the parameters for the database call placed in the URL. For instance, here's a (slightly disguised) URL from a search engine:

```
http://dir.saltavista.com/search?pg=dir&tp=Entertainment/
        Music&crid=317855
```

Users would be happier with something like:

```
http://dir.saltavista.com/Entertainment/Music
```

Some companies do cover up the database call with an understandable URL like the one immediately above, but most don't. If you provide a sensible set of URLs for your Web pages, you'll be ahead of most of the big fish.

Creating a navigation bar

Consistent navigation is key to a good-looking Web site. Follow these steps to create consistent navigation:

1. **Type in some text, or copy and paste it in.**

   It's much easier to experiment with placing a graphic if you have some text in your document.

2. **Decide on the sections of your site.**

   Decide on the major sections of your site, as described in the previous section of this book.

3. **Create a set of navigation links.**

   Navigation links are a set of words, linked to the major sections of your site, and usually separated by the horizontal bar character (|) on your keyboard. (You may not know about this character now, but you will after you create your navigation links!) A typical set of navigation links looks something like this:

   ```
   Home | About Rotifers | Roti-Photos | Web Resources |
        About Me
   ```

   You can create a set of navigation links in Netscape Communicator or other Web page creation tools by typing in text and then assigning a link to the name of each section. In HTML, use code something like the following:

   ```
   <A HREF="index.htm">Home</A> |
        <AHREF="aboutroti.htm">About Rotifers</A> |
        <A HREF="photos.htm">Roti-Photos</A> |
        <A HREF="resources.htm">Web Resources</A> |
        <A HREF="aboutme.htm">About Me</A>
   ```

4. **Add the set of navigation links to the same spot — usually centered, at the bottom of the page — on each page in your Web site.**

Testing navigation

Always carefully test the navigation on your site. Test every link, on every page, at least twice: Once after you create the site on your own computer, and again after you publish your site to the Web. It's very common for links to stop working — to "break" — right after you publish your site to the Web, so be ready to quickly fix any problems.

If you want to have a graphical navigation bar, use a graphics program to create the image you want to use. Then use Netscape Composer or another Web page creation program to create the image map that goes with it. Alternatively, you can use a group of small graphics in a table. Use the navigation bar at the top of each page; keep the navigation links at the bottom, so users have a choice.

Getting the Word Out

Getting people to come to your site can be very easy, or very difficult. The main thing that makes it seem hard to get traffic is your own expectations. If you expect huge numbers of visitors — or even more difficult, huge volumes of online sales — without doing a lot of work, you're bound to be disappointed. But if you set your expectations at a reasonable level and use several different techniques to get people to come to your site, you're likely to meet your own goals.

Publicize your site

After your site is up and tested, publicize it. The amount and type of publicity you need depends upon your goals for the site. If you are trying to impress press and analysts, issue a press release. If you are publicizing a personal site, you may find that telling friends and family about it is sufficient. If you are trying to give customers another avenue for communicating with you, put your URL on stationery, business cards, and advertisements. If you are trying to sell on the Web, put ads on other Web sites that attract your prospective customers. Tailor your publicity strategy to your goals.

There's an old saying that "you have to spend money to make money." Contrary to popular belief, this saying is just as true on the Web as it is anywhere else. You can do a tremendous amount with a personal, hobby, or group Web site while spending little or no money and only a moderate amount of time. But don't expect to make money from your Web site unless you're willing to spend money — or enormous amounts of time, remembering that "time is money" — creating, marketing, and updating it.

Playing the name game

One of the best ways to get people to remember your site is to get your own *domain name*. A domain name is the first part of a Web address, usually not including the `www.` at the start. For example, `yahoo.com` and `whitehouse.gov` are domain names. What people use to reach you is the *Web address* or *URL* (Uniform Resource Locator), which is just a standardized, or uniform, way of finding resources such as Web servers and files on the Internet.

`www.smithtires.com` is much easier to remember — and much more impressive — than `www.geocities.com/smithtires`. In the first case, the domain name is `smithtires.com`; in the second case, it's `geocities.com`. Clearly, an individual might plausibly own the first domain name; the second is owned by Yahoo!, one of the busiest sites on the Web.

There are a lot of ways to get a domain name, but the most popular way is to go to the Network Solutions Web site at `www.networksolutions.com`. Network Solutions charges $60–$70 for a two-year license for a name. The Network Solutions Web site makes it easy to try different domain names to see what's available. (It also gives you the ability to build a Web site hosted by Network Solutions for a reasonable, but not insignificant, fee.) You can also purchase your domain name, often for a higher fee, through a Web hosting company such as GeoCities or AOL.

We recommend that you follow a little bit of a process for deciding on your domain name. Come up with a list of desired domain names. Then check on the Network Solutions Web site to see which ones are available. When a domain name is not available, the Network Solutions Web site will suggest similar names that are available — and, the whole process might give you new ideas. Write down the best of those as well. Then check your top three to five names with a few friends or colleagues for their reactions and ideas.

Go through this process a couple of times, and give yourself a day or so to think about your final candidate before finally purchasing a domain name. Getting a name is so easy that it's all to easy to end up buying three names before you finally end up with the one you really want.

The first and most important place to publicize your site is on the Web itself. Your basic goal is to get as many links as possible to your site from What's New lists, What's Cool lists, and especially directories or pages that are specific to the interests your site addresses. Find pages with a similar purpose and trade pointers from their site to yours and from your site to theirs.

The Web publicity picture changes all the time, so the best place to go for information is any of several Web sites with publicity info and pointers:

```
webmagnet.com/howtodoit.html
www.cyberwave.com/ppoint2.html
www.netbusiness.com
www.bcentral.com
```

These sites give you information on how to get your pages publicized on popular sites such as the Yahoo! What's New page. (See Figure 15-5 for an example.) You can find this page at `www.yahoo.com/new`.

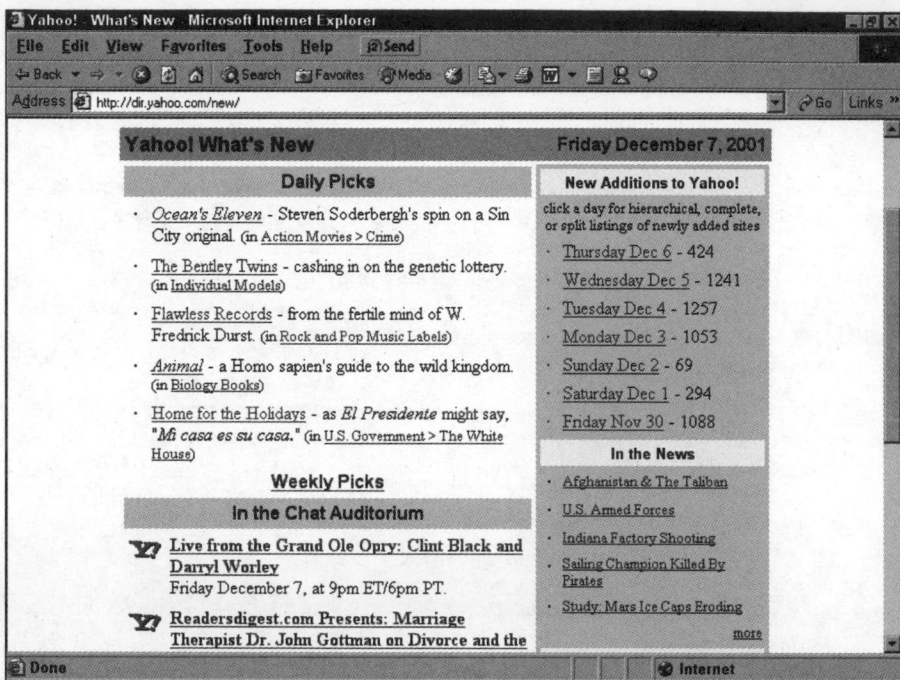

Figure 15-5:
Yahoo! for
new stuff.

You should also use non-Web means of publicizing your site. Put out a press release — but be sure to wait until your site's really ready, not full of Under Construction signs. Many companies proudly include their Web site URLs on business cards, stationery, print ads, and even television ads. You've invested a lot in your Web site — now's the time to benefit from your efforts.

Count your blessings — and your users

For Web pages in general, and for business Web pages in particular, knowing how many users visit your site is important. For a business site you need to establish goals for the number of users who visit your site and for the number who take specified actions, such as downloading software, visiting certain parts of the site, or buying products. Set goals and then measure against them. Microsoft's Bcentral site at www.bcentral.com includes many useful tools for Web traffic measurement.

Among the things you can track are the number of e-mails you receive from users and the number of people who register on your site (if you support that option). But the most widely accepted measurement of success is *page views*, or the number of pages that users have visited on your site. Obtain the server log for your site from your Internet service provider and pore over it, or obtain any reports that are available. Many Web hosting providers give you a monthly report, or at least let you access the log files from your site for your own review and analysis.

Keep people coming to your site

The missing link for many Web sites is *return visitors* — people who have visited your Web site before, then come back again and again. Given how busy people are, it's hard to get them to build visits to your site into their habits.

One of the best ways to get people to come back to your Web site is through e-mail. For a personal site, send your friends and family e-mail when you put something new on the site. For a business site, plan on adding something new at least once a month. Then tell people about it using your customer and partner e-mail list — a list that, as a businessperson, you'll put time and money into expanding and maintaining.

Be sure to give users a place to see the progress of your Web site and find out about your plans for it. Some sites have a "What's New" page to describe recent additions; such a page would also be a good place to describe your plans for expansion. Avoid giving specific dates unless you're very sure of them. Be sure to convey excitement about what you already have up and what you're planning to add, not embarrassment about what's missing.

What about hiring out your Web work?

Getting help in creating your Web site is often a good idea. Use this book to learn enough about Web publishing so you can communicate effectively with a consultant, and so you can do some of the work yourself. Then find someone to help. Bigstep, at www.bigstep.com, is a service that will help you very inexpensively. For a more customized approach, hire your own consultant. eLance, at www.elance.com, is a good place to start looking.

If you work in a large organization, you or your boss may consider hiring out all the Web work for your company. This is a bad idea. Although using consultants to help introduce and use new technology is a good idea, developing a reasonable amount of expertise in-house is also a good idea. So don't hire out the entire process; have a mix of employees and contractors working on your company's Web site. A good way for you to get the necessary experience to be a useful member of such a team is to create one or two small Web sites yourself, as described in this book.

Part V
The Part of Tens

"OK, I think I forgot to mention this, but we now have a Web management function that automatically alerts us when there's a broken link on The Aquarium's Web site."

In this part . . .

Our Top Tens tell you the do's and don'ts of creating Web pages so you can look like a pro your first time out on the Web.

Chapter 16

Ten Web Publishing DO's

Anyone else remember Mr. Do-Bee from the *Romper Room* TV show of the 1960s? He was famous for words of wisdom that always began, "Mr. Do-Bee says . . ." Well, if Mr. Do-Bee were a Web author, here are ten things he would definitely do.

DO Think about Your Target Audience

Who is your Web site targeting? A little thought along these lines can make your pages much more appealing to your visitors. Before you begin creating your Web site, choose the right look and feel and a style of presentation that is appropriate for your audience. Include links that your visitors find interesting, not just the ones that you find interesting — unless that's the point of your page, of course. In addition to using good sites as models (see the next "DO"), research other media, such as newspapers and magazines — the articles and the ads — that have an audience similar to yours, to find good and bad examples.

DO Use Good Sites as Models

Many good sites are out there. Ignoring those good examples when designing your own site is not the best idea. Take a look around and find the designs that work. (Many top-rated sites have settled on relatively simple designs.) Think about why each design you like works well for you. Is it the use of color and the layout of the Web page? The fact that the site loads quickly? Well-organized content? Note what works and why, and then strive to duplicate that effect in your own Web pages. Look for conventions in presenting information that Web users have grown accustomed to, neat design ideas, and various types of content. You'll be surprised by how many ideas you get from this huge reservoir of Web expertise — the Web itself.

DO Get Permissions for Content

You can easily peek at the HTML source of any Web page, and that's a good way to figure out new design techniques. But you can also easily grab any content that exists on the Web, even privately owned content that belongs to others. However, the fact that you can easily grab others' content does *not* make doing so right or legal. It's also not necessary.

A great deal of public domain content is out there, and getting permission to use some private content is not all that hard to do. If a Web page doesn't explicitly say that its content can be freely borrowed, assume that it's copyrighted or otherwise protected, which means you should ask before borrowing any of it. Many people are happy to let you use their content in order to gain exposure on your pages, as long as you provide proper attribution and reciprocal links. In the process, you may just gain new friends or business contacts, as well as avoid legal problems down the road. (And in case you get tempted to borrow quietly, keep in mind that word of unethical practices gets around quickly on this amazing global network.)

DO Use Links to Outside Sites

No matter how great your content is, you're wasting the most important feature of the Web if you don't include links to sites outside your own. No matter what your topic, you can find complementary sites out there. Giving your visitors links to those sites is only courteous. If you research your links carefully and organize them well, your links can be a valuable resource to others. In your own Web surfing, you've probably found that one of the best experiences on the Web is the serendipity of stumbling upon some cool site that you had no idea existed. Give your visitors that same experience. Point them to the outside world. That's why it's the Web and not the Cave.

DO Use Graphics and Multimedia

A prime attraction of the Web is that it's designed to present graphical information; yet there are still many beginning Web authors who are intimidated by graphics and shy away from using them. Include pictures, icons, bars, and graphical menus in your Web page. Go ahead, try out transparent GIFs. Multimedia is a great addition, too; one or two sound files, a QuickTime movie, even a simple animated GIF can really liven up a site. The bottom line is that sites that carefully use graphics and multimedia are much more interesting than purely text-oriented ones. Give it a go. (But be prudent; see Chapter 17 for a complementary DON'T.)

DO Think Before You Create

A surprising number of people just jump in and start throwing around text and HTML tags with no clue about where they're going or what they want to accomplish. That approach is fine if you just want to play around; in fact, that approach can be a lot of fun. But if you want to make a good impression on the Web, sitting down and thinking about a few things ahead of time really pays off. Sketch your ideas on paper. Then describe them to someone else and ask for feedback. This prep work forces you to consider things that you may not think about otherwise: Page layout, graphic design, relationship between pages, target audience, content structure, link grouping, and other issues that, when properly integrated, can make your site a first-class Net surfing experience.

DO Ask for Feedback

You'll be amazed by what people say about your pages. (Some of the comments may even be complimentary!) Put your e-mail address on your home page and ask for comments. People who have never before seen your site can offer a good, fresh perspective and give you feedback on things that you may not have thought about. Everyone can benefit from outside input. Criticism by your prospective audience is not only useful, it's also educational. You can learn a lot about what people expect and want. Criticism can't hurt anything but your pride, and listening to it almost always improves your site.

DO Test Your Pages

Testing your pages is easy. You probably don't write a memo without spell checking it. Similarly, you should not put up your Web pages without testing them. That means looking at your pages on your own machine before testing them on the Web — follow links, see how graphics and text fit together, and so on. Also, looking at your pages in different browsers doesn't hurt. If you can't do it, ask a friend or even a stranger to help. Oh, again, don't forget to spell check your pages.

DO Publicize Your Site

Nothing is more frustrating than putting up a site that no one visits. Fortunately, publicizing your site is not hard. Add your site to the popular indexes, for example, through the excellent Submit-It site at www.submit-it.com.

You can also post to appropriate Usenet newsgroups, put out a press release, send e-mail to friends and business contacts, or shout from the rooftops. Just building a site doesn't necessarily mean people will come to it. You still have to get the word out.

DO Update Your Site

A static site is a boring site. True, it works for some purposes, but in general, if you want people to continually revisit your site, you must keep it updated. The best sites are those that continually provide new and interesting content. Include pointers to information that's frequently updated, like "Thought for the day" or "Links to new, cool sites." Let users know how often to expect updates and be sure to showcase new content. A "New" icon next to recently added or updated content can work wonders.

Chapter 17

Ten Web Publishing DON'Ts

*T*hose of us who remember Mr. Do-Bee, who we mentioned at the start of Chapter 16, probably also remember Bozo the Clown, another TV character. (When you hear someone say, "What a bozo," they're memorializing our friend Bozo.) When someone did something wrong it was a "Bozo no-no." Don't-don't do these no-no's.

Don't Limit Your Audience

Be careful when designing your pages not to inadvertently limit your audience by using some oddball feature that can't be read by large numbers of people who use different Web browsers. Stick to basic HTML through HTML Version 4.0. Think twice before using HTML frames, Java programs, or ActiveX programs — some people won't be able to access Web pages with these features. Warn people if you use nonstandard features. Often, providing alternative pages, such as text-only versions of your pages, is worthwhile. And including links to the software that works with your pages often pays off — a link to the QuickTime site if you host QuickTime movies or a link to the RealAudio site if you include RealAudio sound are two good examples.

Many features of Microsoft FrontPage only work if hosted on servers that support FrontPage extensions. Other FrontPage features only work if the user is running Microsoft's Internet Explorer browser. Test your pages extra widely if you are using FrontPage to create your pages.

Don't Abuse Netiquette

Abusing *Netiquette* — the etiquette, or "Miss Manners" rule book, of the Internet — is easy to do and can bring you a lot of negative attention. If you make any serious offenses against good Internet practices, your Web service provider's server may remove your pages. And you can even get into legal problems. Avoid dubious practices such as *spamming,* sending unwanted e-mail to publicize your site or sell things; *flaming,* being fervently disparaging of other people or other Web pages; or putting up offensive material without some kind of warning label. Netiquette is an amorphous and evolving area of online behavior, so you may want to join a Web-oriented newsgroup where you can ask questions before publishing. Also, check out this site for in-depth info:

```
http://www.albion.com/netiquette/corerules.html
```

Don't "Borrow" Content Without Asking

Make sure that content you get from the Web to use on your own Web page is labeled as being freely available for reuse, or else get permission to reuse it. Many people are quite happy to help if you ask nicely and credit their work. The best part is that you make some good contacts with other interesting people. You also keep the law on your side.

Don't Abuse Graphics and Multimedia

The biggest mistake that beginning Web authors — and some experts — make is overusing graphics on a page. Keep in mind that not everyone has a cable modem or DSL connection wired directly to his or her home PC; the majority of folks receive your Web pages via a more limited 56K or slower modem. Keep your page size, including both text and graphics, under 50K. Here are ways that you can keep down your page size without sacrificing design flexibility:

✔ Convert photos to JPEG format.

✔ Use simple icons and banners — images without very many colors or complex textures — in GIF format.

✔ Lay out your site to limit the amount of graphics on any one page; add pages if you need to display more graphics.

✔ Use thumbnail icons to give access to larger images.

All these strategies make your pages smaller and faster for others to download. Your Net surfers will thank you.

Don't Forget ALT Tags and Text Versions of Menus

Another basic mistake is not offering text versions of menus needed because some people turn off graphics when surfing the Net. Who would turn off graphics, you ask?

Many home users turn off graphics to speed things along, downloading only the graphics that they really need. Some people pay a high hourly rate for their Internet access, especially in much of the non-Western world, and turn off graphics to save money on their connection time. Others may be looking at your Web page through a palmtop computer or Web-enabled cell phone with no graphics capability. And some people who are visually impaired use the Web with software that translates text — but not graphics — into spoken words. If your navigation bar or other menu-type items are in graphical form, provide a text version as well, as shown in Chapter 15, Always use the ALT tag to provide text equivalents to your graphics, as we describe in Chapter 9. Using the ALT tag is easy to do and makes it easier for all these people to access your content.

Don't Forget the Basics

Your site may be the greatest thing since sliced bread, but if you forget to include contact information for yourself in the site, how will you find out that you misspelled "bureaucracy" all over the place? Similarly, you won't get many orders for your spiffy new widget if you put the ordering information five levels down in a Web page called "Fruitbat guano statistics — 1776." More basics:

✔ Include your e-mail address on your Web page.

✔ Include a copyright notice.

✔ If you create a Web site of more than 5–7 pages, add a site map.

✔ Give credit where credit is due.

✔ Make the important info prominent.

✔ Be ready to revise, based on user feedback.

Don't Start by Setting Up Your Own Web Server

Several "easy-to-use" Web server packages exist on the market, and Web server capability is even being built into Macs and PCs. But even with these efforts, buying, setting up, and maintaining a Web server can become the most expensive, most complicated, and most frustrating part of Web publishing. Luckily, you can use the free services we describe in this book, or inexpensive paid services, to put your content on someone else's Web server while you figure out the other tricks of the trade. Then, as your knowledge and experience grow, consider setting up your own Web server.

Don't Make Your Site Hard to Navigate

Beginners often organize their pages so that their sites are hard to navigate. If your site has more than 5–7 pages, you should give some thought as to how your visitors navigate it. Nobody likes wandering from link to link with no idea what is where or having to follow ten links to find one piece of information. Keep the relationship between your pages simple. Make clear which links are internal to your own site and which go out to other sites. Provide a site map or a common menu. And make navigation work consistently throughout the site.

Don't Forget the "World" in World Wide Web

Remember that your Web pages are available and accessible to the whole world. Think a bit about the foreign audience. Is including some foreign language content worthwhile? Do you use colloquialisms that may not be understood by your foreign Net surfers? How do your pages look to your overseas colleagues who view them through a slow transoceanic Net link? Will your humorous or risqué content offend someone in another country or culture?

When you become a Web publisher, you also become a global citizen, and your Web pages play on a global stage. Think through the accessibility and meaning of your pages in advance.

Don't Be Afraid to Find Out More

Web publishing is not rocket science. It is computer science, but it's relatively easy computer science. You're not trying to land the space shuttle here — and chances are, lives are not at stake. After you have your site working the way you want it to using the basics that we describe in this book, experiment. Try weird things. Ask for feedback. Never be afraid to figure out complex and hard stuff. (It's only complex and hard because you don't understand it yet!)

Neat stuff is out there that can make your Web publishing even more exciting — JavaScript, multimedia, new browsers and publishing tools, Net-based games, and online business infrastructure. All this new stuff is understandable and usable by normal folks like you. Don't be intimidated. You can use all of it. (If you've come this far, you've got what it takes!)

Part VI

Appendixes

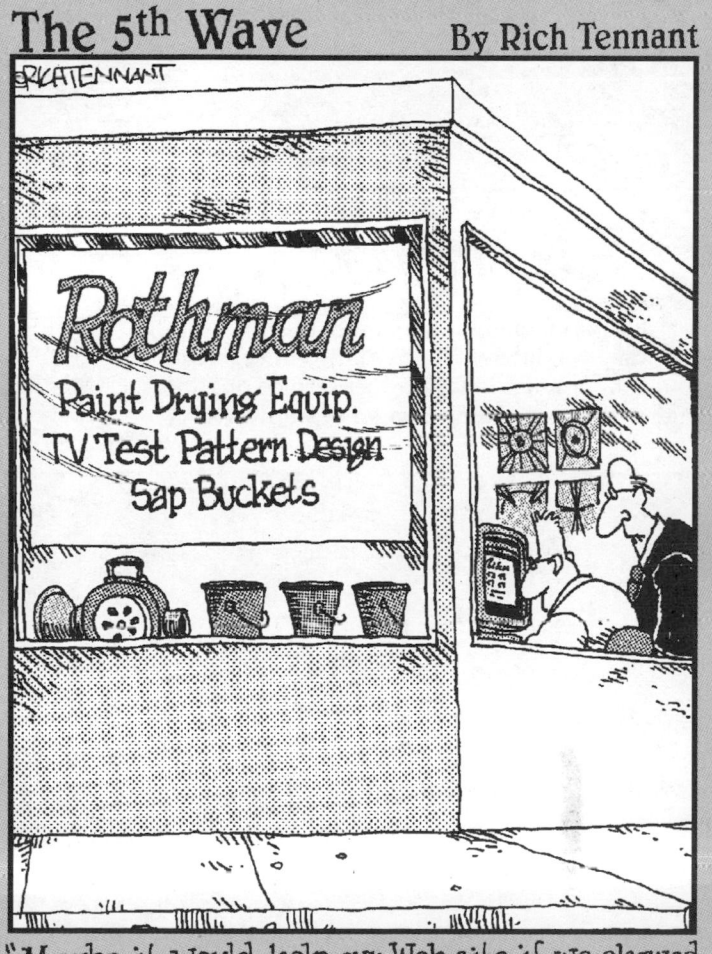

"Maybe it would help our Web site if we showed our products in action."

In this part . . .

This part includes appendixes that are a bridge to a wide range of different kinds of resources, including Web publishing definitions, Internet service providers, HTML tag definitions, and online developer resources.

Appendix A

Web Words Worth Knowing

• •

*T*his glossary defines important terms used in this book. To see where a term is used in the book, check the index.

56K. The name of a faster standard for Internet access that is now used by most new modems. 56K is nearly twice as fast as the previous standards, 28.8 Kbps and 33.6 Kbps. However, online access speeds are actually limited by U.S. government regulation to a top speed of about 53 Kbps, and your 56K modem may not even achieve that speed reliably, depending on the quality of the connection you get when you dial in.

absolute address. A description of a file's location that starts with the machine name or disk name on which the file is located. See also *pathname* and *relative address*.

anchor. One end of a link between two files. When you look at a Web page, the underlined, colored text that you see is an anchor at one end of a hypertext link. Clicking the text brings up another Web page, which is the anchor at the other end of the link.

animated GIF. A GIF graphic that includes several slightly different images in sequence. Browsers that support animated GIFs display the graphics one at a time to create an animation.

attribute. In HTML, an attribute is a qualifier added within an HTML tag. The attribute modifies the tag's purpose. For example, in the tag `<IMG SRC="budpic.jpg">`, the attribute is `SRC` (short for "source"). See also *tag*.

broadband. A newly popular term for any kind of fast Internet access, whether by cable modem, DSL, or other connection significantly faster than the 56K top speed of a modem.

browser. A program used to look at World Wide Web documents. Mosaic was the first popular browser, and Netscape Navigator and Microsoft Internet Explorer are the current market leaders.

bulleted list. See *unordered list*.

cable modem. A form of fast access to the Internet through a cable TV connection. If the local cable company that serves your house offers this service, it's worth a look.

clickable image map. A graphic that includes areas called "hot spots," which, when clicked, take you to different Web pages or locations within a Web page. Many large Web sites use clickable image maps on their home pages to entice the user to move farther into the site.

Common Gateway Interface script (CGI script). A kind of program often used to transfer data from an HTML form to an application. The CGI script runs on the server that hosts the Web page with the form. See also *form*.

definition list. A type of HTML list in which terms occupy a column on the left side of the screen and definitions occupy a wider column on the right side.

domain name. A domain name represents a Web site to the outside world. In the United States, the domain name can end in .com (for businesses), .edu (for educational institutions), .org (for nonprofit organizations), or the prestigious .net (for organizations that are part of the structure of the Web itself). Newly added suffixes, which haven't necessarily caught on yet, include .biz and .firm. Other countries can use different suffixes such as .uk, for United Kingdom, can be added to represent a country or region. The part before the suffix, such as stanford in stanford.edu, is either the name of the group that puts up the Web site, or something that attracts people to the site. Domain names can start with www if desired, but it's not necessary.

DSL. Digital Subscriber Line, a form of fast Internet access through a phone line. Only available in limited areas, but worth serious consideration if it's available to you.

electronic mail (e-mail). A message sent over a network from one computer user to another computer user. The most popular service on the Internet. Used as a noun ("I just got an e-mail") and a verb ("E-mail me on that, will you?"). Also used as singular ("I just deleted an e-mail") and plural ("I just deleted all my e-mail.").

File Transfer Protocol (FTP). An Internet service for transferring files between different machines, including those that run different operating systems.

firewall. Hardware, software, or a combination that protects a network from unauthorized access while allowing authorized access.

form. An HTML-defined way to specify text boxes and pull-down menus to enable users of a Web page to enter data. The data from the form must be processed on the Web server by a program such as a *CGI script*.

freeware. Software that can be used for free, though often with a license that contains some restrictions on its use. See also *shareware*.

Graphic Interchange Format (GIF). Can be pronounced "jiff" or (our preference) "giff." A format for encoding images, including computer-generated art and photographs, for transfer among machines. GIF format is the most popular means for storing images for transfer over the Internet and is supported by all graphical Web browsers. An image stored in GIF format is often referred to as "a GIF." See also *transparent GIF.*

Graphical User Interface (GUI). Software that enables you to interact with a computer by using a mouse and keyboard to manipulate images and menus on the computer's screen. The Windows and Macintosh user interfaces are both examples of GUIs.

hexadecimal. What the witch did to her accountant so that her tax bill would be more favorable. More commonly, a way of counting that uses 16 "digits," 0–9 plus A–F, instead of the 10 digits that common decimal numbering uses. Hexadecimal numbers are often used to describe values stored inside a computer.

In hexadecimal numbering, 0–9 have their normal values, but A represents 10, B represents 11, and so on through F, which represents 15. Place values are also different; each successive place represents the next greater power of 16. For example, 2F in hexadecimal translates to 47 in decimal; the 2 represents two 16s, and the F represents fifteen 1s.

hit. This is what you hope your Web site will become. Also, a successful connection, file transfer, and disconnection between a Web client and a Web server. Accessing a single, text-only page generates one hit; accessing a single page with three graphics on it generates four hits. Hits can be counted fairly easily and are a crude measure of the popularity of a Web site. When you see a site that advertises "a million hits a week," remember that the number of hits may be many times greater than the number of different people who visited. See also *Web client* and *Web server*.

home page. A Web page that you intend users to come to directly. If a Web site has multiple pages, the home page usually serves as a guide to all the pages.

HTML 4.0. Currently the most broadly used version of Hypertext Markup Language. All browsers available today support this version of HTML, though different browsers may interpret some tags differently.

Hypertext Markup Language (HTML). The language used to annotate or "mark up" text documents so that they can be formatted appropriately and linked to other documents for use on the World Wide Web.

Hypertext Transfer Protocol (HTTP). The agreed-upon format for exchanging messages among World Wide Web servers and between Web servers and clients.

image map. See *clickable image map.*

Integrated Services Digital Network (ISDN). A special type of phone line available to many businesses and homes. ISDN supports faster transmission of data than standard phone lines.

Internet. The hardware and software that together support the interconnection of most existing computer networks, allowing a computer anywhere in the world to communicate with any other computer that's also connected to the Internet. The Internet supports a variety of services including the World Wide Web.

Internet Protocol (IP). The networking specification that underlies the Internet. IP's most important feature is its support for routing of the packets — small chunks of information that make up a communication — across multiple connections to the final destination.

Internet service provider (ISP). An Internet service provider offers connections to the Internet and support for Internet services such as the World Wide Web.

intranet. An internal network used for distributing information broadly within an organization but not to the general public. Many intranets work just like the Internet and World Wide Web, only on a smaller scale.

Java. A programming language that supports the creation of distributed programs, called *applets,* whose functionality can be easily and flexibly split between a client computer and the server that it's connected to. Java provides a way for the Web to support easy sharing of programs as well as data. Java has become less widely used within Web pages, but it is widely used on Web servers and corporate networks.

Joint Photographic Experts Group (JPEG). A format for storing compressed images. JPEG images were once supported by helper applications but are now directly supported by nearly all browsers. JPEG is the best format for most photographs.

link. A connection between two documents on the Web, usually specified by an anchor in an HTML document.

mirroring. Keeping a copy of data on additional servers to make data available more quickly and to a greater number of simultaneous users.

multimedia. Literally means "many media," and in this sense, a Web page with graphics is multimedia. However, multimedia is usually understood to mean either more than two types of media or, alternatively, time-based media such as animation, sound, or video and space-based media such as 3-D and virtual reality. On the Web, multimedia is also used to mean any extension of the Web beyond the basics of text, hyperlinks, GIF graphics, and JPEG graphics.

newsgroup. An ongoing exchange of electronic messages about a specific topic, such as pets, restaurants, or Web authoring. To access newsgroups, use news reader software, which you can find on the Web or included as a feature of current browsers.

numbered list. See *ordered list.*

online service. Also referred to as a "traditional" or "proprietary" online service to differentiate from the Internet, which is seen as an "open" online service. Traditional online services, such as America Online, CompuServe, and The Microsoft Network (MSN), package access and content into a single branded product. The Internet and the Web have eroded the boundaries between online services by allowing cross-service functionality, such as e-mail between subscribers of different online services. The online service providers are further eroding these boundaries by offering Internet access, Web access, and Web authoring support.

ordered list. A type of HTML list in which each item is given a number, in sequence, when the list displays. The author of the list can rearrange the items as needed, and the numbers adjust accordingly because the numbers are assigned only when the list appears on-screen.

page description language. A defined format for specifying the appearance of a document when displayed or printed. Adobe's PostScript, used by many programs and in many laser printers, is a page description language, not a structural markup language such as HTML or SGML.

pathname. A description of the location of a file. Pathnames can be specified by absolute addressing or relative addressing.

plug-in. A small program that works with a Web browser to allow multimedia files to be displayed in a Web page, or that otherwise extends the capabilities of the browser.

protocol. A format for exchanging data.

QuickTime. A multiplatform standard from Apple Computer, Inc., for multimedia. See also *multimedia, QuickTime plug-in,* and *QuickTime VR.*

QuickTime plug-in. A plug-in for Netscape Navigator and Microsoft Internet Explorer that supports user interaction with QuickTime and QuickTime VR content embedded in a Web page. See also *QuickTime* and *QuickTime VR.*

QuickTime VR. A multiplatform standard for image-based virtual reality. See also *QuickTime* and *QuickTime plug-in.*

relative address. The path from a base document, such as an HTML document, to another document on the same computer, such as another Web page on the same site. See also *pathname* and *absolute address.*

shareware. Software that can be used for free for a limited period of time, after which the user is requested (though usually not forced) to pay a fee for continued use. See *freeware.*

shrink-wrapped software. No, this is not software developed and packaged by psychiatrists. Actually, shrink-wrapped software is just software that is sold as a product and packaged in a box, with the user paying upfront before taking possession of the software. See also *freeware* and *shareware.*

site management. Capabilities in a Web authoring package that help authors work on characteristics of an entire Web site, instead of just one page at a time. Site-management capabilities include the ability to easily manage links between Web pages, the capacity to spell check and search and replace across an entire site, and notification when links are no longer functional.

standard. An agreed-upon way to do something, such as building a computer system (for example, the IBM-compatible standard) or exchanging data (for example, the ASCII standard). Many different standards exist, ranging from those created by a single manufacturer for its own purposes (the DOS standard) to those created by internationally recognized standards bodies such as ISO (the International Standards Organization). In other words, in computing, the definition of standard is not very standard.

Standard Generalized Markup Language (SGML). A full-featured specification for describing the content and structure of documents but not their exact appearance when displayed. HTML is a subset of SGML.

syntax. A fee paid for moral or legal violations — no, wait, that's a "sin tax." A syntax is the ordering of the elements in a language or protocol.

system operator (sysop). A person responsible for some part of the operations of a computer system, including online services. A sysop's responsibilities can vary from the technical, such as backing up a computer hard drive, to the nontechnical, such as monitoring a newsgroup for inappropriate or irrelevant content and removing it if found.

tag. Part of an HTML document that contains information besides the actual document content, such as formatting information or an anchor. For example, the `<B>` tag starts bolding the characters that follow it, and the `</B>` tag ends bolding. So to make a word or phrase bold, surround it with the `<B>` and `</B>` tags.

text editor. A program that allows text to be entered and edited but not formatted for display. Text editors save their files without proprietary formatting information, so the files are portable across different application programs and different computer systems. Examples are Notepad (Windows), BBEdit (Macintosh), and vi (UNIX).

thumbnail. A small graphical image that serves as a preview of a larger image.

Transmission Control Protocol/Internet Protocol (TCP/IP). A communications protocol developed under contract from the U.S. Department of Defense in the 1970s to connect different systems and different networks. TCP/IP is the protocol on which the Internet is based.

transparent GIF. A file stored in Graphic Interchange Format and modified so that the area around the objects of interest is assigned the color "transparent." This capability makes the rectangular frame around the objects seem to disappear so that the graphic appears to "float" over the page on which it appears.

Uniform Resource Locator (URL). A specification for identifying any file on the Internet. The URL is made up of the name of the protocol by which the file should be accessed, the name of the server that the file is stored on, and the pathname of the file on the server. Here is a sample URL for an HTML file named `MyCruise`, to be accessed by using the Web protocol `http`, which is stored on a server called `www.bigweb.com` in the `Travel` directory:

```
http://www.bigweb.com/Travel/MyCruise.html
```

If no filename is given at the end of the path, a default file, typically `index.html`, is returned.

unordered list. A type of HTML list in which each item is displayed next to a symbol such as a bullet.

Web authoring. Creating documents for use on the World Wide Web. Web authoring includes creating text documents with HTML tags, as well as creating or obtaining suitable graphics and, in many cases, multimedia files.

Web browser. See *browser.*

Web client. A computer that connects to the World Wide Web and downloads Web pages and other data from it.

Web page. A text document with HTML tags to specify formatting and links from the document to other documents and to graphics and multimedia files.

Web publishing. The entire process of creating and maintaining a Web site, from creating text documents with HTML tags and graphics, to putting the documents on a server, to revising the documents over time.

Web server. A computer that connects to the World Wide Web and hosts HTML-tagged text documents, graphics, and multimedia files to be down-loaded by Web clients.

Web site. One or more linked Web pages accessed through a home page. The URL of the home page is made available to users on other Web sites, and often through other advertising and marketing means as well.

word processor. A program for creating and editing text files with formatting. Files created by a word processor contain formatting codes and cannot be used on the Web unless specifically saved in "text-only" or "plain-text" format, without the proprietary codes that word processors embed in the file to indicate formatting.

World Wide Web (also known as the Web). An Internet service that provides files from servers linked by Hypertext Transfer Protocol. The Web specification allows formatted text and graphics to be viewed directly by a Web browser and allows other kinds of files to be opened separately by helper applications specified in the Web browser's setup. The Web is the most popular Internet service, partly because it can also be used to access other Internet services, such as newsgroups and FTP.

Appendix B

Internet Service Providers

· ·

*O*ne of the best resources for Internet service providers is on the Web itself at

```
www.ispworld.com
```

You can log on to ISPWorld to get a directory of local Internet service providers (ISPs) in any part of the United States or Canada. Local providers sometimes offer the best access, but, of course, the level of service you get varies from one provider to another. ISPWorld also offers a list of national service providers; click the "Find an ISP" link to see it.

Another great source for Internet access providers is Yahoo!; check out

```
www.yahoo.com>Business_and_Economy>Business_to_Business>
Communications_and_Networking>Internet_and_World_Wide_Web>
Network_Service_Providers>Internet_Service_Providers_(ISPs)
```

Typing out the long URL is worth it; Yahoo! provides links to regional, national, and international ISPs, as well as links to other ISP directories online.

For your browsing pleasure — in the old-fashioned, analog sense of the word "browsing" — here's a brief list of some of the top national Web service providers. This list is U.S.-centric; if you live elsewhere or travel, check online sources, or check with the providers listed in this appendix to see which can meet your needs.

America Online

Tyson's Corner, VA

800-827-6364

```
www.aol.com
```

AT&T WorldNet
Basking Ridge, NJ

800-967-5363

```
www.att.net
```

CompuServe
(owned by America Online)
Columbus, OH

800-848-8990

```
www.compuserve.com
```

Earthlink
Atlanta, GA

800-890-6356

```
www.earthlink.com
```

The Microsoft Network
Redmond, WA

800-635-7019

```
www.msn.com
```

Prodigy
White Plains, NY

800-776-3449

```
myhome.prodigy.net
```

WorldCom
Clinton, MS

800-967-5326

```
www.worldcom.com
```

Appendix C

A Quick Guide to HTML Tags

O ne of the best resources on the Web is *The Bare Bones Guide to HTML.* At this writing, this excellent reference lists nearly all the tags in the most widely supported version of HTML, Version 4.0, plus Netscape extensions. Unless otherwise noted, HTML tags are compatible with later HTML versions. This site was developed and is maintained by Kevin Werbach, a Harvard Law graduate and former FCC attorney in Washington who has invested a lot of time and thought into Web authoring. You can find out an awful lot about Web authoring from the thoughts, resources, and examples on Kevin's home page at www.werbach.com.

The Bare Bones Guide lists tags from the different versions of HTML with notes describing which version of HTML a given tag supports. We thought splitting out the HTML tags into separate tables by the version of HTML they support would help you.

In the version of *The Bare Bones Guide* in this book, we include only HTML tags from HTML versions up through Version 4.0. For frames only, we use HTML 4.0 tags; see Table C-26 at the end of this chapter. We do this because these tags are the most commonly used by the broad range of Web pages and Web browsers out there. The online version of *The Bare Bones Guide to HTML* lists tags up to the current version of the HTML standard at the time that you access the site.

The original *The Bare Bones Guide to HTML,* from which we adapted this version, is copyrighted ©1995-2001) to Kevin Werbach. You can reproduce the original, as long as you include this statement:

Copyright ©1995-2001 Kevin Werbach. Distribution is permitted, so long as there is no charge and this document is included without alteration in its entirety. This Guide is not a product of Bare Bones Software. More information is available at http://werbach.com/barebones.

Note: The Bare Bones Guide to HTML is not affiliated with Bare Bones Software, makers of the BBEdit text editor for the Macintosh (www.barebones.com).

Twenty-two world languages in *The Bare Bones Guide*

Online, you find versions of *The Bare Bones Guide* in English in plain text, formatted text, and table versions, as well as translations into 21 additional languages: Chinese (two versions), Danish, Dutch, Estonian, Finnish, French, German, Hebrew, Icelandic, Indonesian, Italian, Japanese, Korean, Norwegian, Portuguese, Romanian, Russian (three versions), Slovenian, Spanish, Swedish, and Turkish.

Versions of HTML

The tags in this table are part of the HTML 4.0 standard and are supported by all up-to-date browsers. So if you aren't worried about ancient history — in Web terms, that's anything that happened more than a year ago — and aren't worried about the stubborn few users of your Web pages who may still have old browsers, you can ignore this section and go straight to the tables. But if you really want to know the details, read on.

The versions of HTML we describe in this appendix are

- **HTML 2.0:** All browsers available today support this basic version of HTML. However, some tags are interpreted differently by different browsers. For example, a top-level heading, marked by an <H1> tag, may be formatted somewhat differently in different browsers.

- **Netscape Navigator 1.0, 1.1:** These early versions of Netscape Navigator fueled the first huge surge in the growth of the Web. These were the first browsers to provide support for centered text, floating graphics, and colored text and backgrounds by using new "extensions" to HTML 2.0. Other browsers and HTML 3.2 have adopted many of the features and new tags introduced by Netscape in Netscape Navigator 1.0 and 1.1.

- **HTML 3.2:** This is a widely supported version of the HTML standard. Many of the ideas originally included in the HTML 3.0 proposal, such as tables and paragraph alignment, were first supported by Netscape Navigator 1.0 and 1.1.

- **Netscape Navigator 2.0:** This years-old used version of Netscape Navigator implements a few minor features, plus a major one: frames, which are specific areas within the browser window that contain different content and can be updated separately.

> ✓ **HTML 4.0 and later browser versions:** HTML 4.0 is the latest standard-
> ized version of HTML. It includes some features that were introduced by
> Microsoft and Netscape in their own browsers. However, HTML 4.0
> includes some complex features that are not consistently implemented
> in current browser versions.

Over time, browsers are updated and improved to support a wider range of
tags. However, some users still have the old version of their browser. So don't
assume that just because a new version of a browser supports specific tags,
all users of that browser will upgrade and gain the ability to view those tags
correctly.

How to Use This Appendix

To use this appendix when creating your own pages, start with the first table,
a basic list of HTML 2.0– and HTML 3.2–compliant tags that work with almost
any browser. If you use only the tags in this list, your pages will be as widely
usable as possible. Then you can selectively spice up your pages by using tags
from the different sets of HTML extensions listed in the later tables. You can
also use this list to create separate versions of your pages: one version for all
browsers and another for browsers that support the specific extensions that
you use.

This appendix includes HTML tags that we did not discuss in the text of this
book. To find out more about a specific tag, experiment with it in your Web
text and your browser. If you need more information than you can get by
experimenting, buy a more advanced book on HTML, such as *HTML 4 For
Dummies,* 3rd Edition, by Ed Tittel et al (Hungry Minds, Inc.).

Reading the Tables

Within the tables you may see some tags that are not preceded by a dash,
followed by tags preceded by a dash, such as

Tag Name	Tag	Notes
Preformatted	`<PRE></PRE>`	Display text spacing as is
- Width	`<PRE WIDTH=?></PRE>`	Width in characters

The tags with descriptions that start with a dash are actually options within
other tags. These optional tags modify the effect of the tag that they appear
with. You will always see the option listed with the tag that it modifies, so
that you can see how to use it in your own HTML-tagged text.

The use of the dash symbol to indicate optional tags and other symbols in the tables are described in Table C-1.

Note: In order to align columns correctly, some tags are broken. At the points that these tags break, we placed a downward, left-curving arrow (↵) to indicate the break.

Table C-1	Symbols Used in the Tables
Symbol	**Meaning**
URL	URL of an external file (or just filename if in the same directory)
?	Arbitrary number (for example, `<H?>` means `<H1>`, `<H2>`, `<H3>`, and so on)
%	Arbitrary percentage (for example, `<HR WIDTH=%>` means `<HR WIDTH=50%>`, and so on)
***	Arbitrary text (for example, `ALT="***"` means fill in with text)
$$$$$$	Arbitrary hexadecimal number* (for example, `BGCOLOR="#$$$$$$"` means `BGCOLOR="#00FF1C"`, and so on)
|	Alternatives (for example, `ALIGN=LEFT|RIGHT|CENTER` means pick one of these)
- Option	An option within a tag

For an explanation of hexadecimal numbering, see Appendix A.

HTML 2.0– and 3.2–Compliant Tags

The following tags are in the HTML 2.0 or 3.2 specification and should work in all browsers.

Table C-2	Generally All HTML Documents Should Have These Tags	
Tag Name	**Tag**	**Notes**
Document Type	`<HTML></HTML>`	Beginning and end of file
Title	`<TITLE></TITLE>`	Must be in header
Header	`<HEAD></HEAD>`	Descriptive info, such as title
Body	`<BODY></BODY>`	Bulk of the page

Table C-3 **Structural Definition: Appearance Controlled by the Browser's Preferences**

Tag Name	Tag	Notes
Heading defines six levels	`<H?></H?>`	The HTML 2.0 specification
Block Quote	`<BLOCKQUOTE>↵ </BLOCKQUOTE>`	Usually indented
Emphasis	`<EM></EM>`	Usually displayed as italic
Strong Emphasis	`<STRONG></STRONG>`	Usually displayed as bold
Citation	`<CITE></CITE>`	Usually italics
Code	`<CODE></CODE>`	For source code listings
Sample Output	`<SAMP></SAMP>`	
Keyboard Input	`<KBD></KBD>`	
Variable	`<VAR></VAR>`	
Author's Address	`<ADDRESS></ADDRESS>`	

Table C-4 **Presentation Formatting: Author Specifies Text Appearance**

Tag Name	Tag	Notes
Bold	`<B></B>`	
Italic	`<I></I>`	
Typewriter	`<TT></TT>`	Displayed in a monospaced font
Preformatted	`<PRE></PRE>`	Displays text spacing as is
- Width	`<PRE WIDTH=?>↵ /PRE>`	Width in characters

Table C-5 **Links and Graphics**

Tag Name	Tag	Notes
Link	`<A HREF="URL"></A>`	
Link to Target	`<A HREF="URL#***"></A>`	If in another document

(continued)

Table C-5 *(continued)*

Tag Name	Tag	Notes
	`<A HREF="#***"></A>`	If in current document
Define Target	`<A NAME="***"></A>`	
Display Image	`<IMG SRC="URL">`	

- Alignment	`<IMG SRC="URL" ALIGN↵`
	`=TOP|BOTTOM|↵`
	`MIDDLE|RIGHT| LEFT>`
		HTML 3.2 only

- Alternate	`<IMG SRC="URL" ALT="***">`	
- Imagemap	`<IMG SRC="URL" ISMAP>`	Requires a script

Table C-6   Dividers

Tag Name	Tag	Notes
Paragraph	`<P>`	See Table C-14 for more info
Line Break	` `	A single carriage return
Horizontal Rule	`<HR>`	HTML 3.2 only

Table C-7   Lists: Can Be Nested

Tag Name	Tag	Notes
Unordered List	`<UL><LI></UL>`	`<LI>` before each list item
Ordered List	`<OL><LI></OL>`	`<LI>` before each list item
Definition List	`<DL><DT><DD></DL>`	`<DT>` = term, `<DD>` = definition

Table C-8   Special Characters: Must All Be Lowercase

Tag Name	Tag	Notes
Special Character	`&#?;`	Where ? is the ISO 8859-1 code for the character
<	`&lt;`	
>	`&gt;`	

Tag Name	Tag	Notes
&	&amp;	
"	&quot;	
Registered TM	&reg;	
Copyright	&copy;	

See a complete list of special characters at www.bbsinc.com/symbol.html.

Table C-9	Forms: Generally Require a Script on Your Server	
Tag Name	**Tag**	**Notes**
Define Form	<FORM ACTION= "URL" METHOD=GET| POST></FORM>	
Input Field	<INPUT TYPE="TEXT| PASSWORD|CHECKBOX| RADIO|IMAGE|HIDDEN| SUBMIT|RESET">	
- Field Name	<INPUT NAME-"***">	
- Field Value	<INPUT VALUE-"***">	
- Checked?	<INPUT CHECKED>	Check boxes and radio buttons
- Field Size	<INPUT SIZE=?>	In characters
- Max Length	<INPUT MAXLENGTH=?>	In characters
Selection List	<SELECT></SELECT>	
- Name of List	<SELECT NAME="***"> </SELECT>	
- # of Options	<SELECT SIZE=?> </SELECT>	
- Multiple Choice	<SELECT MULTIPLE>	Can select more than one
Option	<OPTION>	Items that can be selected
- Default Option	<OPTION SELECTED>	

Table C-9 *(continued)*

Tag Name	Tag	Notes
Input Box Size	`<TEXTAREA ROWS=? COLS=?>↵` `</TEXTAREA>`	
- Name of Box	`<TEXTAREA NAME="***">ccc↵` `</TEXTAREA>`	

Table C-10   **Miscellaneous**

Tag Name	Tag	Notes
Comment	`<!-- *** -->`	Not displayed by the browser
Prologue	`<!DOCTYPE HTML↵` `PUBLIC " ↵` `//IETF//DTD HTML ↵` `2.0//EN">`	
URL of This File	`<BASE HREF="URL">`	Must be in header
Relationship	`<LINK REV="***"↵` `REL= "***"↵` `HREF="URL">`	In header
Meta Information	`<META>`	Must be in header

Other Widely Used Tags

These tags work with nearly all the browsers currently in use. For a frequently updated list of widely used tags, see *The Bare Bones Guide to HTML* at the URL listed at the beginning of this chapter.

Table C-11   **Structural Definition: Appearance Controlled by the Browser's Preferences**

Tag Name	Tag	Notes
- Align Heading	`<H? ALIGN=LEFT|↵` `CENTER| RIGHT></H?>`	HTML 3.2 Option within the HTML 2.0–compliant Heading tag
Division	`<DIV></DIV>`	HTML 3.2

Tag Name	Tag	Notes
- Align Division	`<DIV ALIGN=LEFT|↵ RIGHT| CENTER|↵ JUSTIFY></DIV>`	HTML 3.2
Large Font Size	`<BIG></BIG>`	HTML 3.2
Small Font Size	`<SMALL></SMALL>`	HTML 3.2

Table C-12	Presentation Formatting: Author Specifies Text Appearance	
Tag Name	**Tag**	**Notes**
Subscript	`<SUB></SUB>`	HTML 2.0
Superscript	`<SUP></SUP>`	HTML 2.0
Center	`<CENTER></CENTER>`	Netscape 1.0. widely implemented; for both text and images

Table C-13	Links and Graphics	
Tag Name	**Tag**	**Notes**
Dimensions	`<IMG SRC="URL"↵ WIDTH= "?"↵ HEIGHT-"?">`	HTML 3.2. Image width and height in pixels

Table C-14	Dividers	
Tag Name	**Tag**	**Notes**
Paragraph	`<P></P>`	HTML 3.2. Paragraph tag, `<P>`, redefined as a container tag, `</P>` is optional
- Align Text	`<P ALIGN=LEFT|↵ CENTER|RIGHT|↵ JUSTIFY></P>`	HTML 3.2
- No Line Breaks	`<P NOWRAP></P>`	Internet Explorer only

Table C-15	Backgrounds and Colors	
Tag Name	*Tag*	*Notes*
Tiled Background	`<BODY BACKGROUND=↵ "URL">`	HTML 3.2
Background Color	`<BODY BGCOLOR=↵ "#$$$$$$">`	HTML 3.2. Color order, red/green/blue
Text Color	`<BODY TEXT=↵ "#$$$$$$">`	HTML 3.2. Color order, red/green/blue
Link Color	`<BODY LINK=↵ "#$$$$$$">`	HTML 3.2. Color order, red/green/blue
Active Link	`<BODY ALINK=↵ "#$$$$$$">`	HTML 3.2. Color order, red/green/blue
Visited Link	`<BODY VLINK=↵ "#$$$$$$">`	HTML 3.2. Color order, red/green/blue

You can find more info at www.werbach.com/web/wwwhelp.html.

Table C-16	Tables	
Tag Name	*Tag*	*Notes*
Define Table	`<TABLE></TABLE>`	HTML 3.2
- Table Border	`<TABLE BORDER>↵ </TABLE>`	HTML 3.2. Either on or off
- Table Border	`<TABLE BORDER=?> </TABLE>↵`	HTML 3.2. Can set the border width in pixels
- Cell Spacing	`<TABLE CELLSPACING=?>`	HTML 3.2
- Cell Padding	`<TABLE CELLPADDING=?>`	HTML 3.2
- Desired Width	`<TABLE WIDTH=?>`	HTML 3.2. In pixels
- Width Percent	`<TABLE WIDTH=%>`	HTML 3.2 Percentage of page
Table Row	`<TR></TR>`	HTML 3.2
- Alignment	`<TR ALIGN=LEFT|RIGHT|↵ CENTER|JUSTIFY VALIGN=↵ TOP|MIDDLE|BOTTOM>`	HTML 3.2

Tag Name	Tag	Notes
Table Cell	`<TD></TD>`	HTML 3.2. Must appear within table rows
- Alignment	`<TD ALIGN=LEFT|RIGHT|`↵ `CENTER VALIGN=TOP|MIDDLE|`↵ `BOTTOM>`	HTML 3.2
- No Line Breaks	`<TD NOWRAP>`	HTML 3.2
- Columns to Span	`<TD COLSPAN=?>`	HTML 3.2
- Rows to Span	`<TD ROWSPAN=?>`	HTML 3.2
- Desired Width	`<TD WIDTH=?>`	HTML 3.2. In pixels
- Width Percent	`<TD WIDTH=%>`	HTML 3.2 Percentage of table
- Desired Height	`<TD HEIGHT=?>`	HTML 3.2. In pixels
- Height Percent	`<TD HEIGHT=%>`	HTML 3.2 Percentage of page
Table Header	`<TH></TH>`	HTML 3.2. Same as data, except bold centered
- Alignment	`<TH ALIGN=LEFT|RIGHT|`↵ `CENTER|JUSTIFY|CHAR.`↵ `VALIGN=TOP|MIDDLE|BOTTOM>`	HTML 3.2
- No Line Breaks	`<TH NOWRAP>`	HTML 3.2
- Columns to Span	`<TH COLSPAN=?>`	HTML 3.2
- Rows to Span	`<TH ROWSPAN=?>`	HTML 3.2
- Desired Width	`<TH WIDTH=?>`	HTML 3.2. In pixels
- Width Percent	`<TH WIDTH=%>`	HTML 3.2. Percentage of table
- Desired Height	`<TH HEIGHT=?>`	HTML 3.2. In pixels
- Height Percent	`<TH HEIGHT=%>`	HTML 3.2. Percentage of page
Table Caption	`<CAPTION></CAPTION>`	HTML 3.2
- Alignment	`<CAPTION ALIGN=TOP|`↵ `BOTTOM>`	HTML 3.2. Above/ below table

Table C-17	Miscellaneous	
Tag Name	*Tag*	*Notes*
Script	`<SCRIPT></SCRIPT>`	
Location	`<SCRIPT SRC="URL"></SCRIPT>`	
Type	`<SCRIPT TYPE="***"></SCRIPT>`	
Language	`<SCRIPT LANGUAGE="***"></SCRIPT>`	
Java Applet	`<APPLET>`	HTML 3.2
- Applet Name	`<APPLET NAME="***">`	HTML 3.2
- Alternate Text	`<APPLET ALT="***">`	HTML 3.2
- Applet Code Location	`<APPLET CODE="URL">`	HTML 3.2
- Code Base Directory	`<APPLET CODEBASE="URL">`	HTML 3.2
- Applet Window Height	`<APPLET HEIGHT=?>`	HTML 3.2. In pixels
- Width	`<APPLET WIDTH=?>`	HTML 3.2. In pixels
- Horizontal Offset	`<APPLET HSPACE=?>`	HTML 3.2. In pixels
- Vertical Offset	`<APPLET VSPACE=?>`	HTML 3.2. In pixels
- Alignment	`<APPLETALIGN=[left|right↵ |top|middle|bottom]>`	HTML 3.2
Applet Parameter	`<PARAM>`	HTML 3.2
Parameter Name, Value	`<PARAM NAME="appletname",↵ VALUE="parameter value">`	HTML 3.2
3.2 Prologue	`<!DOCTYPE HTML PUBLIC"-↵ //W3C//DTD HTML3.2 FINAL//EN">`	HTML 3.2

Less Frequently Used Tags

Some Netscape Navigator-only tags were slow to be adopted by non-Netscape browsers. However, most of these tags can be used with up-to-date browsers. HTML 4.0-specific tags are only supported by relatively recent browsers.

Table C-18	Structural Definition: Appearance Controlled by the Browser's Preferences	
Tag Name	**Tag**	**Notes**
Defined Content	`<SPAN></SPAN>`	HTML 4.0
Quote	`<Q></Q>`	HTML 4.0. For short quotations
- Citation	`<Q CITE="URL"></Q>`	HTML 4.0
Insert	`<INS></INS>`	HTML 4.0. Marks additions in a new version
- Time of Change	`<INS DATETIME=":::"></INS>`	HTML 4.0
- Comments	`<INS CITE="URL"></INS>`	HTML 4.0
Delete	`<DEL></DEL>`	HTML 4.0. Marks deletions in a new version
- Time of Change	`<DEL DATETIME=":::"></DEL>`	HTML 4.0
- Comments	`<DEL CITE="URL"></DEL>`	HTML 4.0
Acronym	`<ACRONYM></ACRONYM>`	HTML 4.0
Abbreviation	`<ABBR></ABBR>`	HTML 4.0

Table C-19	Presentation Formatting: Author Specifies Text Appearance	
Tag Name	**Tag**	**Notes**
Blinking	`<BLINK></BLINK>`	Navigator 1.0. Most derided tag ever
Font Size	`<FONT SIZE=?></FONT>`	HTML 3.2. Ranges from 1–7
Change Font Size	`<FONT SIZE=+|-?></FONT>`	HTML 3.2
Base Font Size	`<BASEFONT SIZE=?>`	HTML 3.2. From 1-7; default is 3
Font Color	`<FONT COLOR="#$$$$$$"></FONT>`	HTML 3.2
Underline	`<U></U>`	HTML 2.0
Strikeout	`<S></S>`	HTML 2.0
Select Font	`<FONT FACE="***"></FONT>`	HTML 4.0

Table C-20	Links, Graphics, and Sounds	
Tag Name	*Tag*	*Notes*
- Target Window	`<A HREF="URL"TARGET=↵ "***"></A>`	HTML 4.0
Action on Click	`<A HREF="URL"ONCLICK=↵ "***"></A>`	HTML 4.0
Mouseover Action	`<A HREF="URL"ONMOUSEOVER= "***"></A>`	HTML 4.0
Mouseover Action	`<A HREF="URL"↵ ONMOUSEOUT="***"></A>`	HTML 4.0
- Alignment	`<IMG SRC="URL"ALIGN= LEFT|↵ RIGHT|TEXTTOP|ABSMIDDLE|↵ BASELINE| ABSBOTTOM>`	Navigator 1.0. Option within the HTML 2.0-compliant Display Image tag
- Image Map	`<IMG SRC="URL"USEMAP="URL">`	HTML 3.2. Option within the HTML 2.0–compliant Display Image tag
- Map	`<MAP NAME="***"></MAP>`	HTML 3.2. Describes the map. Option within the HTML 2.0–compliant Display Image tag
- Section	`<AREA SHAPE="RECT"COORDS="↵ #,#,#,"HREF="URL"|NOHREF>`	HTML 3.2. Option within the HTML 2.0–compliant Display Image tag
- Border	`<IMG SRC="URL"BORDER=?>`	HTML 3.2
Runaround Space	`<IMG SRC="URL"HSPACE= ?↵ VSPACE=?>`	HTML 3.2. In pixels
Low-Res Proxy	`<IMG SRC="URL"LOWSRC= "URL">`	
N1.1 Client Pull	`<META HTTP-EQUIV="Refresh"↵ CONTENT= "?; URL=URL">`	HTML 2.0
Embed Object insert	`<EMBED SRC="URL">`	Navigator 2.0. Insert object into page

Tag Name	Tag	Notes
- Object Size	`<EMBED SRC="URL"↵` `WIDTH ="?"HEIGHT="?">`	Navigator 2.0, Internet Explorer
Object	`<OBJECT></OBJECT>`	Navigator 4.0
Parameters	`<PARAM>`	Navigator 4.0

Table C-21	Dividers	
Tag Name	**Tag**	**Notes**
- Clear Text Wrap	`<BR CLEAR=LEFT|RIGHT|ALL>`	HTML 3.2. Option within the HTML 2.0–compliant Line Break tag
- Alignment	`<HR ALIGN=LEFT|RIGHT|CENTER>`	HTML 3.2. Option within the HTML 2.0–compliant Horizontal Rule tag
- Thickness	`<HR SIZE=?>`	HTML 3.2. In pixels. Option within the HTML 2.0–compliant Horizontal Rule tag
- Width	`<HR WIDTH=?%>`	HTML 3.2. In pixels. Option within the HTML 2.0–compliant Horizontal Rule ta
- Width Percent	`<HR WIDTH=?%>`	HTML 3.2. As a percentage of page width. Option within the HTML 2.0–compliant Horizontal Rule tag
- Solid Line	`<HR NOSHADE>`	HTML 3.2. Without the 3-D cutout look. Option within the HTML 2.0–compliant Horizontal Rule tag

(continued)

Table C-21 *(continued)*

Tag Name	Tag	Notes
No Break	`<NOBR></NOBR>`	Navigator 1.0. Prevents line breaks
Word Break	`<WBR>`	Navigator 1.0. Where to break a line if needed

Table C-22   **Lists: Can Be Nested**

Tag Name	Tag	Notes
- Bullet Type	`<UL TYPE=DISC|↵ CIRCLE|SQUARE>`	HTML 3.2. For the whole list. Option within the HTML 2.0–compliant Unordered List tag
	`<LI TYPE=DISC|↵ CIRCLE|SQUARE>`	HTML 3.2. This and subsequent list items. Option within the HTML 2.0–compliant Unordered List tag
- Numbering Type	`<OL TYPE=A|a|I|i|1>`	HTML 3.2. This and subsequent list items. Option within the HTML 2.0–compliant Unordered List tag
	`<LI TYPE=A|a|I|i|1>`	HTML 3.2. This and subsequent list items. Option within the HTML 2.0–compliant Unordered List tag
- Starting Number	`<OL START=?>`	HTML 3.2
- Count	`<OL VALUE=?>`	HTML 3.2 For the whole list. Option within the HTML 2.0–compliant Ordered List tag

Table C-23   **Backgrounds and Colors**

Tag Name	Tag	Notes
N1.1 Active Link	`<BODY ALINK="#$$$$$$">`	HTML 3.2

You can find more info at werbach.com/web/wwwhelp.html#color.

Table C-24	Forms: Generally Require a CGI Script on Your Server	
Tag Name	**Tag**	**Notes**
- File Upload	`<FORM ENCTYPE="multi part/` `form-data"></FORM>`	HTML 4.0
- Wrap Text	`<TEXTAREA WRAP=OFF|VIRTUAL|` `PHYSICAL></TEXTAREA>`	HTML 2.0
Button	`<BUTTON></BUTTON>`	HTML 4.0
- Button Name	`<BUTTON NAME="****"></BUTTON>`	HTML 4.0
- Button Type	`<BUTTON TYPE="SUBMIT|RESET|` `BUTTON"></BUTTON>`	HTML 4.0
- Default Value	`<BUTTON VALUE="****"></BUTTON>`	HTML 4.0
Label	`<LABEL></LABEL>`	HTML 4.0
- Item Labelled	`<LABEL FOR="****"></LABEL>`	HTML 4.0
Option Group	`<OPTGROUP LABEL="****">` `</OPTGROUP>`	HTML 4.0
Group Elements	`<FIELDSET></FIELDSET>`	HTML 4.0
Legend	`<LEGEND></LEGEND>`	HTML 4.0. Caption for fieldsets
- Alignment	`<LEGEND ALIGN="TOP|` `BOTTOM|LEFT|RIGHT"></LEGEND>`	HTML 4.0

Table C-25	Tables	
Tag Name	**Tag**	**Notes**
- Table Alignment	`<TABLE ALIGN=LEFT| RIGHT|` `CENTER>`	HTML 4.0
- Table Color	`<TABLE BGCOLOR="$$$$$$"></TABLE>`	HTML 4.0
- Table Frame	`<TABLE FRAME=VOID|ABOVE|BELOW|` `HSIDES|LHS|RHS|VSIDES|BOX|` `BORDER></TABLE>`	HTML 4.0

(continued)

Table C-25 *(continued)*

Tag Name	*Tag*	*Notes*
- Table Rules	`<TABLE RULES=NONE|GROUPS|ROWS|`↵`COLS|ALL></TABLE>`	HTML 4.0
- Desired Width	`<TD WIDTH=?>`	HTML 4.0. In pixels
- Cell Color	`<TD BGCOLOR="#$$$$$$">`	HTML 4.0
- Desired Width	`<TH WIDTH=?>`	HTML 4.0. In pixels
- Cell Color	`<TH BGCOLOR="#$$$$$$">`	HTML 4.0
Table Body	`<TBODY>`	HTML 4.0
Table Footer	`<TFOOT></TFOOT>`	HTML 4.0. Must come before `<THEAD>`
Table Header	`<THEAD></THEAD>`	HTML 4.0
Column	`<COL></COL>`	HTML 4.0. Groups column attributes
- Columns Spanned	`<COL SPAN=?></COL>`	HTML 4.0
- Column Width	`<COL WIDTH=?></COL>`	HTML 4.0
- Width Percent	`<COL WIDTH="%"></COL>`	HTML 4.0
Group columns	`<COLGROUP></COLGROUP>`	HTML 4.0. Groups column structure
- Columns Spanned	`<COLGROUP SPAN=?></COLGROUP>`	HTML 4.0
- Group Width	`<COLGROUP WIDTH=?></COLGROUP>`	HTML 4.0
- Width Percent	`<COLGROUP WIDTH="%"></COLGROUP>`	HTML 4.0

Table C-26	Frames: Define and Manipulate Specific Regions of the Screen	
Tag Name	**Tag**	**Notes**
Frame Document	`<FRAMESET></FRAMESET>`	HTML 4.0. Instead of `<BODY>`
- Row Heights	`<FRAMESET ROWS=#,#,#,>`↵ `</FRAMESET>`	HTML 4.0. Pixels or- percent
- Row Heights	`<FRAMESET ROWS=*></FRAMESET>`	HTML 4.0. * = relative size
- Column Widths	`<FRAMESET COLS=#,#,#,>`↵ `</FRAMESET>`	HTML 4.0. Pixels or percent
- Column Widths	`<FRAMESET COLS=*></FRAMESET>`	HTML 4.0. * = relative size
- Borders	`<FRAMESET FRAMEBORDER="yes|no"`↵ `</FRAMESET>`	HTML 4.0
- Border Width	`<FRAMESET BORDER=?</FRAMESET>`	HTML 4.0
- Border Color	`<FRAMESET BORDERCOLOR="******"`↵ `</FRAMESET>`	HTML 4.0
Define Frame	`<FRAME>`	HTML 4.0. Contents of an individual frame
- Display Document	`<FRAME SRC="URL">`	HTML 4.0
- Frame Name	`<FRAME NAME="***"|_blank`↵ `|_self|_parent|_top>`	HTML 4.0
- Margin Width	`<FRAME MARGINWIDTH=?>`	HTML 4.0. Left and right right margins
- Margin Height	`<FRAME MARGINHEIGHT=?>`	HTML 4.0. Top and bottom margins
- Scroll bar?	`<FRAME SCROLLING="YES |NO|`↵ `AUTO">`	HTML 4.0

(continued)

Table C-26 *(continued)*

Tag Name	Tag	Notes
- Not Resizable	`<FRAME NORESIZE>`	HTML 4.0
Borders	`<FRAME FRAMEBORDER="yes|no">`	HTML 4.0
Border Color	`<FRAME BORDERCOLOR="#$$$$$$">`	HTML 4.0
Inline Frame	`<IFRAME></IFRAME>`	HTML 4.0. Takes same attributes as FRAME
Dimensions	`<IFRAME WIDTH=? HEIGHT=?>↵` `</IFRAME>`	HTML 4.0
Dimensions	`<IFRAME WIDTH="%" HEIGHT="%">↵` `</IFRAME>`	HTML 4.0
Unframed Content	`<NOFRAMES></NOFRAMES>`	HTML 4.0 For non-frames browsers

Note: Frame tags introduced prior to HTML 4.0 are not supported by all browsers.

Table C-27   **Miscellaneous**

Tag Name	Tag	Notes
- Prompt	`<ISINDEX PROMPT="***">`	HTML 2.0. Text to prompt input
Base Window Name	`<BASE TARGET="***">`	HTML 2.0. Must be in header
Other Content	`<NOSCRIPT></NOSCRIPT>`	HTML 4.0. If scripts not supported
Base Window Name	`<BASE TARGET="***">`	HTML 4.0. Must be in header
Bidirect Off	`<BDO DIR=LTR|RTL></BDO>`	HTML 4.0. For certain character sets

Appendix D

Using Resource.htm

······································

A great many resources are available online for Web developers of all skill levels. On the CD-ROM enclosed with this book, you will find a file called Resource.htm. To use this file, start your browser and then use the Open command from the File menu to open the Resource.htm Web page. You can find it on the CD-ROM.

In Resource.htm, you will find links to numerous sources of Web authoring information and links to sites that support some of the more popular Web software packages. The CD-ROM includes some of those packages, but it's always a good idea to check the support sites for the latest upgrades and bug fixes. The following is a short description of the key sites and software packages that you can access via this resource page. Note that some of the resources will lead you to more advanced Web page creation topics not covered in this book, such as XML, Java, and VRML.

General Web Developer Resources

Probably the most useful sources of Web information are the excellent World Wide Web FAQ files by Thomas Boutell. The files are brimming with answers to many questions about the Web and contain numerous links to a variety of sites that provide further information or support for Web and Internet-related software. We're giving you the URLs for both his new and old FAQ documents, since both are still wonderfully useful. These files are an excellent starting point for any would-be Web author and netsurfer.

✔ World Wide Web FAQs:
   `http://www.boutell.com/faq/oldfaq/index.html` and
   `http://www.boutell.com/faq/`

The indispensable Yahoo! Index has a superb collection of links to just about every Web- and Internet-related topic under the sun. We saved you the trouble of searching by providing a link to the Yahoo! World Wide Web section directly. The topic selection is vast and comprehensive.

✔ Yahoo! World Wide Web Resources:
   `http://yahoo.com/Computers_and_Internet/Internet/World_Wide_Web/`

For more advanced topics and resources specifically related to Web authoring, check out the following sites:

- ✓ ZDNet Developer's Resources: `http://www.zdnet.com/devhead/`
- ✓ The Web Developer's Virtual Library: `http://www.wdvl.com/`
- ✓ Webdeveloper.com: `http://www.webdeveloper.com/`

Some special topic resources are always in high demand. A great basic HTML tutorial can be found at the NCSA Beginner's Guide to HTML site. The WWW Security FAQ covers various aspects of maintaining secure Web sites and writing secure Web scripts. Finally, the GIF-related sites teach you all you need to know about creating transparent, interlaced, and animated GIFs.

- ✓ NCSA Beginner's Guide to HTML:
  `http://www.ncsa.uiuc.edu/General/Internet/WWW/`
- ✓ The World Wide Web Security FAQ:
  `http://www.w3.org/Security/Faq/`
- ✓ Web Diner's Get Animated!:
  `http://www.webdiner.com/annexe/gif89/snowstp1.htm`

Microsoft Windows Web Resources

In this section, you'll find a number of sites that deal specifically with Microsoft Windows Internet and Web software. You will find browsers, Web page creation tools, file viewers, specialized network clients, helper applications, and even various system administration utilities. If you're looking for just the right Windows netsurfing tool, these sites are the place to start:

- ✓ C|NET Download.com: `http://download.cnet.com/downloads/`
- ✓ ZDNet Downloads: `http://www.zdnet.com/downloads/`
- ✓ Tucows Software Library: `http://www.tucows.com/`
- ✓ CWSApps — Stroud's Consummate Winsock Apps List:
  `http://cws.internet.com/`

Microsoft Windows Software

The Resource.htm Web page on your CD-ROM contains links to support sites for a variety of software programs that make life easier for the Web developer. You can find some of these programs on the enclosed CD-ROM (see Appendix E for a list). Others are freely available online either as shareware, freeware, or demo versions.

Your Resource.htm Web page offers links to no less then three browsers (Netscape Communicator, Microsoft Explorer, Opera) and seven HTML editors. Other goodies include Mapedit the elegant image map editor, several image editing programs including the excellent Paint Shop Pro paint program, image animation programs, an HTML syntax checker, software to add special effects to your Web pages, as well as several other generally useful Web page utilities. If you need support or updates to any of the packages on the CD-ROM, the Resource.htm file will link you directly to the software Web sites.

Macintosh Web Resources

This section contains Macintosh-oriented sites. For general Web authoring resources, nothing beats the ULTIMATE Macintosh Web site ("Still the BIGGEST, UGLIEST, and MOST USEFUL Macintosh Page on the Web . . ."). MacUpdate and the Info-Mac HyperArchive are large repositories of Mac software. StarNine has an excellent site devoted to tools that work with their very popular WebSTAR Macintosh Web server. NCSA, the birthplace of the Web, has many useful utilities, while MacTech magazine is a great resource for Web developers.

- ✔ ULTIMATE Macintosh: http://www.ultimatemac.com/
- ✔ MacUpdate: http://www.macupdate.com/
- ✔ Info-Mac HyperArchive:
  http://hyperarchive.lcs.mit.edu/HyperArchive.html
- ✔ StarNine Development Services Resource Page: http://dev.
  starnine.com/exws.html
- ✔ NCSA Mac Helpers FTP directory:
  ftp://ftp.ncsa.uiuc.edu/Mosaic/Mac/Helpers/
- ✔ MacTech: http://www.mactech.com/

Macintosh Web Software

We include links to three Mac Web browsers, as well as the excellent BBEdit HTML editor. On the graphics side there are the very versatile Graphic Converter and Mapedit software, which makes creating image maps a breeze.

Cascading Style Sheets

Cascading Style Sheets is a standard for specifying style (that is, fonts, colors, spacing) in Web documents. It makes it very easy to manage a consistent look and feel for a large Web site, and is used extensively in many sophisticated commercial sites. CSS is not that far removed from making simple HTML Web pages, so after you've mastered our book you may want to check out some of these Web resources, or *Cascading Style Sheets For Dummies,* by Damon Dean (Hungry Minds, Inc.).

- ✔ W3C Cascading Stylesheet Web pages: `http://www.w3.org/Style/CSS/`
- ✔ Web Design Group Guide to Cascading Style Sheets: `http://www.htmlhelp.com/reference/css/`
- ✔ CSS School: `http://www.w3schools.com/css/`

Perl

Perl is an immensely powerful and flexible scripting language widely used by system administrators and Web developers. If you want to delve into the creation of more sophisticated Web-based applications, you can take advantage of a huge base of existing programs and tools written in Perl. The key sites for Perl include the Perl Mongers ("The Perl advocacy people") users group Web site. The Comprehensive Perl Archive Network (CPAN) lets you tap the power of a worldwide Perl developer community through thousands of pre-built applications and modules. Essential magazines include the Perl Journal at *Sys Admin* magazine, and the ZDNet Devhead CGI, Perl, and TCL sections. Finally, the Macintosh user will appreciate the first-class Macintosh Perl FAQ.

- ✔ Perl Mongers: `http://www.perl.org/`
- ✔ CPAN — Comprehensive Perl Archive Network: `http://www.cpan.org/`
- ✔ The Perl Journal at Sys Admin magazine: `http://www.sysadminmag.com/tpj/`
- ✔ ZDNet Devhead CGI, Perl, and TCL Pages: `http://www.zdnet.com/devhead/filters/cgiperltcl/`

Java

Java is the sophisticated programming language of choice in creating interactive Web applications. These sites contain a plethora of information about Java, with both developer resources and numerous sample applications:

- The official Sun Java Site: `http://java.sun.com/`
- Earthweb Gamelan Java Site:
  `http://softwaredev.earthweb.com/java`
- Yahoo! Java Resources:
  `http://dir.yahoo.com/Computers_and_Internet/Programming_and_Development/Languages/Java/`
- Java FAQ Archives: `http://www-net.com/java/faq/`

JavaScript

JavaScript (no relation to Java, despite the similar name) is a scripting language built into Web browsers. It lets Web page authors create more dynamic Web pages by using the built-in browser features running on the netsurfers' computer. Just about every sophisticated Web site uses JavaScript in some fashion. The JavaScript FAQ Knowledge Base at irt.org and the IDM JavaScript FAQ will answer all your questions, while the ZDNet Devhead JavaScript Library will give you plenty of examples to work with. Finally, there's always the Yahoo!'s JavaScript resources listing for in-depth explorations of the language.

- JavaScript FAQ Knowledge Base:
  `http://developer.irt.org/script/script.htm`
- IDM JavaScript FAQ: `http://www.intranetjournal.com/faq/js-faq.shtml`
- ZDNet JavaScript Library: `http://www.zdnet.com/devhead/filters/javascript/`
- Yahoo! JavaScript Resources:
  `http://dir.yahoo.com/Computers_and_Internet/Programming_and_Development/Languages/JavaScript/`

XML

XML (Extensible Markup Language) is a method of marking up content using tags that look very similar to the HTML tags you have been learning about in this book. What's nice about XML is that anybody can define a standard set of XML tags in a very structured way so that others can use them. This allows content to be easily interchanged and displayed on all sorts of devices. The official keeper of the XML standard is the World Wide Web Consortium (W3C). Numerous commercial Web sites cover the rapidly growing XML technology beat, the best of which we list here:

- W3C Extensible Markup Language (XML): `http://www.w3.org/XML/`
- XML.org The XML Industry Portal: `http://xml.org/`
- The XML Cover Pages: `http://www.oasis-open.org/cover/`
- IBM XML Zone: `http://www.ibm.com/developerworks/xml/`

ActiveX

ActiveX is Microsoft's answer to Java for Web interactivity. ActiveX enables programmers to extend the Web to do a great deal more, with many different kinds of data than plain old HTML.

- Microsoft ActiveX site: `http://microsoft.com/com/tech/ActiveX.asp`
- CINET ActiveX site: `http://download.cnet.com/downloads/0-10081.html`
- Yahoo! ActiveX Resources: `http://dir.yahoo.com/Computers_and_Internet/Programming_and_Development/Languages/ActiveX/`

Microsoft .NET

Any updated book about Web page creation has to mention Microsoft's .NET initiative. Simply put, .NET will allow applications to communicate and share data over the Internet using XML technology, regardless of operating system or programming language. Think of it as a sophisticated extension of the World Wide Web. While the topic is fairly advanced for beginning Web page creators, it's not too early to start learning about what Microsoft has in mind for the future of the Web. The Microsoft .NET Web site has a very readable explanation and links to numerous developer resources.

✔ Microsoft .NET Web pages:
`http://www.microsoft.com/net/default.asp`

USENET Newsgroups

Whatever your Internet- or Web-related passion, you are sure to find others with the same interests on Usenet. In the Resource.htm file on the accompanying CD-ROM, we include an extensive selection of newsgroups dealing with various aspects of Web page creation. Here you can ask and answer questions, debate, and participate in standard-setting projects. You'll need access to a Usenet NNTP news server from your ISP to take full advantage of these forums. Though in recent years Usenet newsgroups have increasingly succumbed to being overrun by spam, many of the technical groups are still an excellent resource for communicating with the Web developer community. Give them a try.

Appendix E

About the CD-ROM

The CD-ROM on the back cover of this book provides valuable software and resource information to help you get started with your Web publishing endeavors. This appendix tells you what you need to get this software onto your own computer, and, once you have everything loaded, what you can do with this software.

System Requirements

Make sure that your computer meets the minimum system requirements shown in the following list. If your computer doesn't match up to most of these requirements, you may have problems using the software and files on the CD. For the latest and greatest information, please refer to the ReadMe file located at the root of the CD-ROM.

- A PC with a Pentium III 500 MHz or faster processor; or a Macintosh with a 500 MHz Power PC or faster processor.

- Microsoft Windows 9x/2000/Me/XP or later, or NT4 or later; or Mac 7.6.1 or later.

- At least 32MB of total RAM installed on your computer; for best performance, we recommend at least 64MB or more.

- A CD-ROM drive.

- A sound card for PCs; Mac OS computers have built-in sound support.

- A monitor capable of displaying at least 256 colors.

- A modem with a speed of at least 56.6 Kbps.

If you need more information on the basics, check out these books published by Hungry Minds, Inc.: *PCs For Dummies,* by Dan Gookin; *Macs For Dummies,* by David Pogue; *iMacs For Dummies,* by David Pogue; *Windows 95 For Dummies, Windows 98 For Dummies, Windows 2000 Professional For Dummies, Microsoft Windows Me Millennium Edition For Dummies,* all by Andy Rathbone.

Using the CD with Microsoft Windows

To install the items from the CD to your hard drive, follow these steps:

1. **Insert the CD into your computer's CD-ROM drive.**

2. **Click Start➪Run.**

3. **In the dialog box that appears, type** D:\Setup.EXE.

   Replace *D* with the proper drive letter if your CD-ROM drive uses a different letter. (If you don't know the letter, see how your CD-ROM drive is listed under My Computer.)

4. **Click OK.**

   A license agreement window appears.

5. **Read through the license agreement, nod your head, and then click the Accept button if you want to use the CD — after you click Accept, you'll never be bothered by the License Agreement window again.**

   The CD interface Welcome screen appears. The interface is a little program that shows you what's on the CD and coordinates installing the programs and running the demos. The interface basically enables you to click a button or two to make things happen.

6. **Click anywhere on the Welcome screen to enter the interface.**

   Now you are getting to the action. This next screen lists categories for the software on the CD.

7. **To view the items within a category, just click the category's name.**

   A list of programs in the category appears.

8. **For more information about a program, click the program's name.**

   Be sure to read the information that appears. Sometimes a program has it's own system requirements or requires you to do a few tricks on your computer before you can install or run the program, and this screen tells you what you might need to do, if necessary.

9. **If you don't want to install the program, click the Back button to return to the previous screen.**

   You can always return to the previous screen by clicking the Back button. This feature allows you to browse the different categories and products and decide what you want to install.

10. **To install a program, click the appropriate Install button.**

   The CD interface drops to the background while the CD installs the program you chose.

11. **To install other items, repeat Steps 7–10.**

12. **When you've finished installing programs, click the Quit button to close the interface.**

   You can eject the CD now. Carefully place it back in the plastic jacket of the book for safekeeping.

To run some of the programs on the CD, you may need to keep the disc inside your CD-ROM drive. This is a good thing. Otherwise, a very large chunk of the program would be installed to your hard drive, consuming valuable hard drive space and possibly keeping you from installing other software.

Using the CD with Mac OS

To install the items from the CD to your hard drive, follow these steps:

1. **Insert the CD into your computer's CD-ROM drive.**

   In a moment, an icon representing the CD you just inserted appears on your Mac desktop. Chances are, the icon looks like a CD-ROM.

2. **Double-click the CD icon to show the CD's contents.**

3. **Double-click the License Agreement icon.**

   This is the license that you are agreeing to by using the CD. You can close this window once you've looked over the agreement.

4. **Double-click the Read Me First icon.**

   The Read Me First text file contains information about the CD's programs and any last-minute instructions you may need in order to correctly install them.

5. **To install most programs, open the program folder and double-click the icon called "Install" or "Installer."**

   Sometimes the installers are actually self-extracting archives, which just means that the program files have been bundled up into an archive, and this self extractor unbundles the files and places them on your hard drive. This kind of program is often called a .sea. Double click anything with .sea in the title, and it will run just like an installer.

6. **Some programs don't come with installers. For those, just drag the program's folder from the CD window and drop it on your hard drive icon.**

What You'll Find on the CD

The following sections are arranged by category and provide a summary of the software and other goodies you'll find on the CD. If you need help with installing the items provided on the CD, refer back to the installation instructions in the preceding section.

Shareware programs are fully functional, free, trial versions of copyrighted programs. If you like particular programs, register with their authors for a nominal fee and receive licenses, enhanced versions, and technical support. *Freeware programs* are free, copyrighted games, applications, and utilities. You can copy them to as many PCs as you like — for free — but they offer no technical support. *Trial, demo,* or *evaluation* versions of software are usually limited either by time or functionality (such as not letting you save a project after you create it).

A Quick Overview

This book includes a CD-ROM with a variety of PC and Macintosh programs and demos that you will find useful while creating your Web pages. You can use some of these programs for one of the most important tasks in Web authoring: using HTML tags to create the text file that will be seen by users as a Web page.

The programs on the CD are either free, try before you buy, or demo versions. Some of the programs are HTML focused, and others hide the HTML tags and give you a more intuitive interface to work with. Still others enable you to do more advanced things with your Web pages, such as create graphics, create fancy text effects, or check your HTML tags for correctness.

While all the programs on the CD-ROM are free in their current form, some require you to pay a fee to get a fully functional version by registering the program. Other programs are functional and ready to go "as is," with no payment required.

The HTML file "Resource.htm" contained on your CD-ROM has links to numerous online resources, including links to program home pages, which you will find useful as you create your Web pages.

In this appendix, you will find a brief description of the contents of the *Creating Web Pages For Dummies* CD-ROM. Each program listing also includes a pointer to the URL of the program's Web site where you can check for the latest upgrade and support information. Have fun!

Resources

Resource.htm, from Arthur and Bud, your humble authors

For Windows and Mac OS. This is probably the most useful file on your CD-ROM. This HTML file contains links to many great Internet resources of use to the Web page creator. To use this file productively, you'll need an Internet connection and a Web browser installed on your computer. You will find links to all sorts of HTML and image editing tools, to sources of information, and to Usenet newsgroups dealing with the Web. To use this file, simply open it in your browser using the File⇨Open menu.

You can find the Resource.htm file on the CD-ROM in in the *Author* folder Keep this file handy, you'll use it often.

JavaScript Tutorial for the TOTAL non-programmer, from Webteacher Software

For Windows and Mac. We debated about whether to include this excellent set of tutorial Web pages about JavaScript in a book that's mostly about creating HTML. However these days creating Web pages is as much about JavaScript as it is about HTML. Once you get beyond the basics, you probably will want to learn some JavaScript. This is an excellent introduction for anybody with little or no programming experience, and will definitely help you to get a jumpstart on learning JavaScript. Give it a try, it's not as hard as it seems, and when you're ready to learn more try the excellent book *JavaScript For Dummies,* by Emily Vander Veer (Hungry Minds, Inc.).

```
http://www.webteacher.com/javascript/index.html
```

HTML editors

HomeSite, from Macromedia, Inc.

For Windows. Evaluation version. HomeSite is a sophisticated text HTML editor suitable for advanced users. The emphasis is on a streamlined, code-centric approach that aims to deliver total code access and control over the quality and performance of an entire Web site. A good choice for advanced Web coders who need close control over their HTML text.

```
http://www.allaire.com/products/homesite/index.cfm
```

BBEdit Lite, from Bare Bones Software, Inc.

For Mac OS. Freeware version. BBEdit Lite is a Macintosh freeware text editor.

```
http://www.bbedit.com/products/bbedit_lite.html
```

BBEdit Pro, from Bare Bones Software, Inc.

For Mac OS. Demo version. BBEdit Pro has powerful features that make creating HTML for your Web pages easy. The commercial version of this program has many more advanced HTML editing features suitable for power users. We include a demo version of on the CD-ROM. This demo is fully featured but will expire after 24 launches. Incidentally, they have a great motto: "Software That Doesn't Suck." We totally agree.

```
http://www.bbedit.com/products/bbedit.html
```

CoffeeCup HTML Editor, from CoffeeCup Software

For Windows. Trial version. This wonderfully versatile and simple-to-use HTML editor is one of the most popular program downloads on the Internet as we go to press. It's simply packed with features that make creating Web pages a snap. In addition to its impressive editing abilities, the program also comes with numerous add-ons that make life easy for the Web page creator. There are JavaScript code snippets, snazzy text effects, graphics, support for advanced Style Sheet and Dynamic HTML features, and much more. Think of it as the versatile Swiss Army Knife of HTML editors.

```
http://www.coffeecup.com/editor/
```

Dreamweaver, from Macromedia, Inc.

For Windows and Mac. Trial version. Dreamweaver is a serious, award-winning professional Web page authoring program. It has many advanced features, such as the ability to build in Flash graphics on your Web pages, and is a great product to move to after you've mastered the simple Web page design techniques in this book. This is a trial version of this sophisticated and popular program.

```
http://www.macromedia.com/software/dreamweaver/
```

HotDog Professional, from Sausage Software

For Windows. 30-Day Trial. HotDog Professional from Sausage Software is a fast, flexible, and user-friendly HTML editor that has been getting rave reviews on the Net for many years. With its advanced document navigation features and support for advanced Web standards, it's the perfect choice for managing Web sites with large amounts of content.

```
http://www.sausagetools.com/professional/overview.html
```

HotDog PageWiz, from Sausage Software

For Windows. 30-Day Trial. HotDog PageWiz is a great choice if you want to create fast, straightforward Web pages. It comes with ten templates, allowing you to whip up a Web page in four simple steps. Once you have the basics, the integrated editor allows you to tweak your HTML and instantly see what the changes will look like. Great choice for speedy, simple Web page creation.

```
http://www.sausagetools.com/pagewiz/overview.html
```

NoteTab Light, from Fookes Software

For Windows. Freeware version. This nifty little HTML editor has won a raft of awards over the years. It's billed as the ultimate free Notepad replacement and a handy HTML editor. It can handle a heap of files with an easy-to-use tabbed interface. It can also search files, strip HTML tags, and format text quickly. And you certainly can't argue with the price. If you find yourself editing HTML files with Windows Notepad, consider adding this little gem to your desktop.

```
http://www.fookes.com/notetab/index.html
```

NoteTab Pro, from Fookes Software

For Windows. Demo version. We've also included a demo version of NoteTab Pro, which has more features, including a built-in thesaurus and spell checker.

```
http://www.fookes.com/notetab/index.html
```

Graphical tools

CoffeeCup Firestarter, from CoffeeCup Software

For Windows. Trial version. This popular program allows you to create Web animations and graphics in the popular Flash™ format. Flash™ technology is becoming more and more common on the Web because it allows designers to create very sophisticated-looking graphic effects. While professionals toil with complex tools to create Flash™ animations, this great little program allows even a beginner to make neat visual effects for brightening up a Web page.

```
http://www.coffeecup.com/firestarter/
```

Easy Thumbnails, from Fookes Software

For Windows. Freeware version. One of the most useful graphical tools for any Web designer is a program that produces small thumbnail images from big graphic files. A program like Easy Thumbnails is indispensable if you want to create any sort of image catalog on your Web page. It automatically handles many graphic formats; has a simple user interface; rotates images; and adjusts their contrast, brightness, sharpness and quality. No Web page author should be without it.

```
http://www.fookes.com/ezthumbs/index.html
```

GraphicConverter, from Lemke Software

For MacOS. Shareware version. GraphicConverter is a program that converts pictures to various formats. It imports about 145 different formats and outputs about 45 formats. The program also contains features that you can use for image manipulation. If you're using a Mac, GraphicConverter is a very useful utility for manipulating the images you'll use in your Web pages.

```
http://lemkesoft.com/us_gcabout.html
```

Paint Shop Pro, from Jasc Software Inc.

For Windows. Evaluation version. Paint Shop Pro is a powerful and easy-to-use image viewing, editing, and conversion program. It also happens to include many sophisticated drawing and painting tools. This evaluation version will give you an idea of its power. Paint Shop Pro contains features normally found in programs hundreds of dollars more expensive than this. This version includes features that are specifically useful to Web page creators, such as the ability to optimize graphics for the Web and share your photos online.

Animation Shop, from Jasc Software Inc.

For Windows. Evaluation version. Animation Shop is a great standalone utility for anyone interested in creating animations for Web sites. It gives you the ability to easily create buttons, banners, and other cool animations. The simple-to-use wizards guide you through the process of creating your first animations, while more advanced features allow you to control many of the more obscure animation parameters. Paint Shop Pro and Animation Shop are a great value for your money and may be the only paint/graphics programs you'll ever need.

```
http://www.jasc.com/products/psp/
```

Reptile, from Sausage Software

For Windows. Freeware version. Reptile allows you to easily produce any combination of wavy, bubbly, organic, big, small, wide, narrow, rough, or smooth textures. You can then use them as Web page backgrounds or other graphic elements. It generates texture animations and even includes a cool screen saver. Neat and completely free!

```
http://www.sausagetools.com/supertoolz/reptile2.html
```

Ulead GIF Animator, from Ulead Systems

For Windows. Trial version. A fast and powerful GIF animation program that will help you add some motion to your Web pages and graphics. This is a fully functional trial version. As an added bonus, the program can be used to add animation to Flash™ Web sites or to Microsoft PowerPoint presentations. A good, versatile, GIF animation tool.

```
http://www.ulead.com/ga/runme.htm
```

Ulead PhotoImpact, from Ulead Systems

For Windows. Trial version. PhotoImpact is a graphics program specifically designed for working with digital photographs. If you want to prepare photos for the Web, then this is the software package to use. It includes numerous features for tweaking the look and feel of digital photographs, tools for optimizing photos for Web display, special effects filters, and even tools to help you lay out your photo Web pages. Great choice if you have a digital camera.

```
http://www.ulead.com/pi/runme.htm
```

Web page utilities

CoffeeCup Button Factory, from CoffeeCup Software

For Windows. Trial version. You've probably seen all those fancy animated buttons on some Web sites. This software enables you to easily create such buttons either using Java or Flash™ technology. You can use your own images to create the buttons, then add animation, rollover, and sound effects.

```
http://www.coffeecup.com/java/button/
```

CSE HTML Validator Professional, from AI Internet Solutions

For Windows. Demo version. CSE Validator is a powerful, easy-to-use, and user-configurable HTML syntax checker. After you create your Web pages, simply run them through the Validator, and it will tell you if you have any errors in your HTML. The Pro version has more support for advanced features such as XHTML and checking large numbers of files at once.

```
http://www.htmlvalidator.com/
```

CSE HTML Validator Lite, from AI Internet Solutions

For Windows. Lite version. Validator Lite is the perfect choice for the beginner HTML coder. No Web page author should be without a good syntax checker, and either of these programs, Lite or Pro, will do the job admirably.

```
http://www.htmlvalidator.com/lite/
```

J-Perk Web Page Effects, from McWeb Software

For Windows. Shareware version. J-Perk Web Page Effects is a kitchen sink collection of tools, which let you create all sorts of neat special effects on your Web pages. Effects you can create include animations, photo slide shows, text transitions, background effects, news tickers, scrolling credits, pull-down menus, and much more. The list of tools is very impressive, and the software is very easy to use.

```
http://www.mcwebsoftware.com/j-perk/default.asp
```

Mapedit, from Boutell Communications, Inc.

For Windows and Mac OS. Freeware version. Mapedit is an elegant utility for creating image maps for Web pages. An image map is simply a picture that can have clickable image areas linked to other Web pages. You can find out more about Mapedit and image maps by visiting the Mapedit Web site. Fully functional for 30 days.

```
http://www.boutell.com/mapedit/
http://www.boutell.com/mapedit/mac.html
```

Text2Web, from Virdi Software

For Windows. Freeware version. Text2Web is a tool to convert text documents to HTML format. It handles lists and tables, can be run interactively, via the command line, or in batch mode (on many files at once), and has integrated clipboard support if you just want to insert snippets of text into your Web page.

```
http://virdi-software.com/txt2web/desc.shtml
```

Text2Web Pro, from Virdi Software

For Windows. Shareware version. The Text2Web Pro version includes a few more advanced features such as support for meta tags, header/footer code, and text translation. The perfect solution if you have lots of plain text files that you want to convert for your Web site.

```
http://virdi-software.com/txt2webpro/desc.shtml
```

Text Effects, from Blaiz Enterprises

For Windows. Freeware version. Text Effects allows you to create very nice 3D, multicolor, shaded, or rotatable text for that special Web image, greeting card, or logo. It's a nice way to add some excitement to your Web site.

```
http://www.blaiz.net/text_effects.html
```

Text2Html, from CyberMatrix Corporation, Inc.

For Windows. Freeware version. A very basic but quite capable text-to-HTML converter program. It's simple to use and does what it needs to do with a minimum of fuss. If your text conversion needs are simple and straightforward, then this is the program to use.

```
http://www.cyber-matrix.com/txt2htm.htm
```

Other utilities

CuteFTP, from GlobalSCAPE, Inc.

For Windows. Demo version. Long known as one of the most popular program downloads on the Internet, CuteFTP is one of the easiest ways to transfer files between your PC and remote computers. Many Web space hosting providers allow you to install and administer your Web site using the FTP protocol. CuteFTP has many special features that make it very easy to work with such Web hosting systems. It's a feature-packed program, which is also very easy and intuitive to use.

```
http://www.globalscape.com/
```

WinZip, from WinZipComputing, Inc.

For Windows. Shareware version. The Zip format is the de-facto standard for compressing files on the PC. WinZip is the undisputed champion utility for dealing with Zip-compressed files. It's both a standalone program and a set of system extensions that enable you to easily work with Zip archives from within other programs such as Internet Explorer. As an added bonus, WinZip handles numerous other archiving and compression formats commonly found on the Internet, such as gzip, tar, BinHex, UUEncode, MIME, and others. It's an indispensable archiving and compression utility.

```
http://www.winzip.com/
```

WS_FTP Pro, from Ipswitch

For Windows. Evaluation version. If you need a basic transfer program to upload files to your Web site, then the free WS_FTP software will do the job just fine. A good basic utility, with a great price — free!

```
http://www.ipswitch.com/
```

Troubleshooting

We tried our best to compile programs that work on most computers with the minimum system requirements. Alas, your computer may differ, and some programs may not work properly for some reason.

The two likeliest problems are that you don't have enough memory (RAM) for the programs you want to use, or you have other programs running that are affecting the installation or running of a program. If you get an error message such as Not enough memory or Setup cannot continue, try one or more of the following suggestions and then try using the software again:

✔ **Turn off any antivirus software running on your computer.** Installation programs sometimes mimic virus activity and may make your computer incorrectly believe that it's being infected by a virus.

✔ **Close all running programs.** The more programs you have running, the less memory is available to other programs. Installation programs typically update files and programs; so if you keep other programs running, installation may not work properly.

✔ **Have your local computer store add more RAM to your computer.** This is, admittedly, a drastic and somewhat expensive step. However, if you have a Windows 98 PC or a Mac OS computer with a PowerPC chip, adding more memory can really help the speed of your computer and allow more programs to run at the same time. This may include closing the CD interface and running a product's installation program from Windows Explorer.

Reference the ReadMe. Please refer to the ReadMe located at the root of the CD-ROM for the latest product information at the time of publication.

If you still have trouble installing the items from the CD, please call the Hungry Minds, Inc. Customer Service phone number at 800-762-2974 (outside the U.S.: 317-572-3993) or send email to techsupdum@hungryminds.com. Hungry Minds will provide technical support only for installation and other general quality control items; for technical support on the applications themselves, consult the program's vendor or author.

Index

response, measuring, 28
résumés, 115, 116
return visitors, 271
rules, 75, 81

• S •

S tag, 309
SAMP tag, 301
Sanrio Themes, 59
Save As dialog box (Notepad), 119
Save Page As dialog box (Composer), 123
scaling pictures, 186
scanning, 39, 172
school information, 113, 115
SCRIPT tag, 308
Search Engine Watch Web site, 126
search engines
  Alta Vista, 79, 171
  Google, 258, 259
  optimizing files for, 125–129
  spiders, 125, 160
SELECT tag, 303
Select Additional Components dialog
    box (Netscape download), 103–105
Select Program Folder dialog box
    (Netscape download), 105
Select Typical Components dialog box
    (Netscape download), 103
self-descriptions, 113
server-side image maps, 183
server space, 35
servers
  creating own, 219, 246, 282
  defined, 294
  disk space limits, 51
  features to compare, 213–216
  interactive programs on, 244–249
  links within, 152, 154
  options for, 216–219
  overview, 212–213
  streaming software for, 239
  uploading files to, 220–224
Setting Up an Internet Site For Dummies,
    219

Setup Type dialog box (Netscape
    download), 103
SGML, 69, 252, 292
shareware, 292, 328
ShockWave, 238
shrink-wrapped software, 292
simplicity, 16, 17, 196–197
site counters
  for commercial sites, 20
  overview, 244
  sources, 245–246
site management, 292
site services, 214
slow-loading pages, 201
SMALL tag, 304
small text, 203
source code, viewing
  in browsers, 14, 68–69
  in Composer, 122–123, 146–147
spam, avoiding, 160
spamming, 280
SPAN tag, 309
special character tags, 302–303
special effects utilities, 334
speed
  of animated GIFs, 234
  of connections, 173–174, 234, 262
  of servers, 215, 216
spell checkers, 109
spider programs, 125, 160
spontaneous approach, 256–257
spot graphics, 25
SRC option, 151
Standard Generalized Markup Language,
    69, 252, 292
standards, 169, 292
StarNine Development Services
    Resource Page Web site, 319
Start Install dialog box (Netscape
    download), 105
storage limits, 51
streaming multimedia, 230, 238, 239
STRONG tag, 301
structure, designing, 258
Style Sheets, 251

Index 353

Notes

Notes

Notes

Hungry Minds, Inc.
End-User License Agreement

READ THIS. You should carefully read these terms and conditions before opening the software packet(s) included with this book ("Book"). This is a license agreement ("Agreement") between you and Hungry Minds, Inc. ("HMI"). By opening the accompanying software packet(s), you acknowledge that you have read and accept the following terms and conditions. If you do not agree and do not want to be bound by such terms and conditions, promptly return the Book and the unopened software packet(s) to the place you obtained them for a full refund.

1. **License Grant.** HMI grants to you (either an individual or entity) a nonexclusive license to use one copy of the enclosed software program(s) (collectively, the "Software") solely for your own personal or business purposes on a single computer (whether a standard computer or a workstation component of a multi-user network). The Software is in use on a computer when it is loaded into temporary memory (RAM) or installed into permanent memory (hard disk, CD-ROM, or other storage device). HMI reserves all rights not expressly granted herein.

2. **Ownership.** HMI is the owner of all right, title, and interest, including copyright, in and to the compilation of the Software recorded on the disk(s) or CD-ROM ("Software Media"). Copyright to the individual programs recorded on the Software Media is owned by the author or other authorized copyright owner of each program. Ownership of the Software and all proprietary rights relating thereto remain with HMI and its licensers.

3. **Restrictions On Use and Transfer.**

   (a) You may only (i) make one copy of the Software for backup or archival purposes, or (ii) transfer the Software to a single hard disk, provided that you keep the original for backup or archival purposes. You may not (i) rent or lease the Software, (ii) copy or reproduce the Software through a LAN or other network system or through any computer subscriber system or bulletin-board system, or (iii) modify, adapt, or create derivative works based on the Software.

   (b) You may not reverse engineer, decompile, or disassemble the Software. You may transfer the Software and user documentation on a permanent basis, provided that the transferee agrees to accept the terms and conditions of this Agreement and you retain no copies. If the Software is an update or has been updated, any transfer must include the most recent update and all prior versions.

4. **Restrictions on Use of Individual Programs.** You must follow the individual requirements and restrictions detailed for each individual program in Appendix E of this Book. These limitations are also contained in the individual license agreements recorded on the Software Media. These limitations may include a requirement that after using the program for a specified period of time, the user must pay a registration fee or discontinue use. By opening the Software packet(s), you will be agreeing to abide by the licenses and restrictions for these individual programs that are detailed in Appendix E and on the Software Media. None of the material on this Software Media or listed in this Book may ever be redistributed, in original or modified form, for commercial purposes.

5. Limited Warranty.

(a) HMI warrants that the Software and Software Media are free from defects in materials and workmanship under normal use for a period of sixty (60) days from the date of purchase of this Book. If HMI receives notification within the warranty period of defects in materials or workmanship, HMI will replace the defective Software Media.

(b) HMI AND THE AUTHOR OF THE BOOK DISCLAIM ALL OTHER WARRANTIES, EXPRESS OR IMPLIED, INCLUDING WITHOUT LIMITATION IMPLIED WARRANTIES OF MERCHANTABILITY AND FITNESS FOR A PARTICULAR PURPOSE, WITH RESPECT TO THE SOFTWARE, THE PROGRAMS, THE SOURCE CODE CONTAINED THEREIN, AND/OR THE TECHNIQUES DESCRIBED IN THIS BOOK. HMI DOES NOT WARRANT THAT THE FUNCTIONS CONTAINED IN THE SOFTWARE WILL MEET YOUR REQUIRE-MENTS OR THAT THE OPERATION OF THE SOFTWARE WILL BE ERROR FREE.

(c) This limited warranty gives you specific legal rights, and you may have other rights that vary from jurisdiction to jurisdiction.

6. Remedies.

(a) HMI's entire liability and your exclusive remedy for defects in materials and workmanship shall be limited to replacement of the Software Media, which may be returned to HMI with a copy of your receipt at the following address: Software Media Fulfillment Department, Attn.: *Creating Web Pages For Dummies,* 6th Edition, Hungry Minds, Inc., 10475 Crosspoint Blvd., Indianapolis, IN 46256, or call 1-800-762-2974. Please allow four to six weeks for delivery. This Limited Warranty is void if failure of the Software Media has resulted from accident, abuse, or misapplication. Any replacement Software Media will be warranted for the remainder of the original warranty period or thirty (30) days, whichever is longer.

(b) In no event shall HMI or the author be liable for any damages whatsoever (including without limitation damages for loss of business profits, business interruption, loss of business information, or any other pecuniary loss) arising from the use of or inability to use the Book or the Software, even if HMI has been advised of the possibility of such damages.

(c) Because some jurisdictions do not allow the exclusion or limitation of liability for conse-quential or incidental damages, the above limitation or exclusion may not apply to you.

7. U.S. Government Restricted Rights.
Use, duplication, or disclosure of the Software for or on behalf of the United States of America, its agencies and/or instrumentalities (the "U.S. Government") is subject to restrictions as stated in paragraph (c)(1)(ii) of the Rights in Technical Data and Computer Software clause of DFARS 252.227-7013, or subparagraphs (c) (1) and (2) of the Commercial Computer Software - Restricted Rights clause at FAR 52.227-19, and in similar clauses in the NASA FAR supplement, as applicable.

8. General.
This Agreement constitutes the entire understanding of the parties and revokes and supersedes all prior agreements, oral or written, between them and may not be modified or amended except in a writing signed by both parties hereto that specifically refers to this Agreement. This Agreement shall take precedence over any other documents that may be in conflict herewith. If any one or more provisions contained in this Agreement are held by any court or tribunal to be invalid, illegal, or otherwise unenforceable, each and every other provision shall remain in full force and effect.

Installation Instructions

The CD-ROM for *Creating Web Pages For Dummies,* 6th Edition offers valuable information that you won't want to miss. To install the items from the CD to your hard drive, refer to Appendix E in this book.